UNMASKING
PATRIARCHY

UNMASKING PATRIARCHY

Gender Is
the Cover Story—
Not the Culprit

PATTY BEAR

BARNSTORMERS PRESS

Published in 2026 by
Barnstormers Press

Hardcover ISBN: 979-8-9994659-2-4
Paperback ISBN: 979-8-9994659-3-1
E-ISBN: 979-8-9994659-4-8
Library of Congress Control Number: 2026901542

Interior design by Stacey Aaronson

Printed in the United States of America

*For you—the one who dares to look beneath the
surface and confront the truth.
May this book offer the tools to see clearly,
heal deeply, and reclaim your power.*

TABLE OF CONTENTS

PART I

RECOGNIZING THE NAVIGATIONAL ERROR

CHAPTER 9: "SHE'S CRAZY"—TRAUMATIC COGNITIVE DISSONANCE AND THE MANIPULATION OF REALITY • 169

PART II

THE SYSTEMS THAT GROW WHEN WE REFUSE TO

CHAPTER 10: EXTRACTION SYSTEMS—DESIGNED TO FEED THE CENTER • 195

CHAPTER 11: WORDS AS WEAPONS—THE HIJACKING OF COMMUNICATION • 203

PART III

THE RETURN TO SELF—
AWAKENING FROM THE SCRIPT

UNMASKING PATRIARCHY

AUTHOR'S NOTE

In the world of aviation, disasters rarely happen because of a single catastrophic failure. They happen when small things stack up. When one person is afraid to speak. When another won't listen. When someone in the cockpit clings to power instead of seeking clarity.

For years, this kind of leadership—authoritarian, hierarchical, emotionally immature—was the norm in aviation. It was the captain's word or nothing. Crew members were discouraged from questioning decisions, even when they saw danger. This silencing of dissent cost lives. Again and again.

The Tenerife disaster. United 173. Avianca 052.

Tragedies that never should have happened.

Then something began to change.

In the 1980s and '90s, commercial aviation began to shift from ego-based leadership to collaborative, emotionally mature decision-making. Crew Resource Management (CRM) was born—not as a buzzword, but as a survival skill. Pilots were retrained to listen, to collaborate, to self-regulate under stress. Hierarchy remained—but domination was replaced with mutual respect and shared responsibility.

The result? Aviation has become one of the safest industries in the world.

Not because people stopped making mistakes.

But because the system stopped protecting egos—and started protecting lives.

This book is about that kind of shift. Not just in aviation, but in everything.

It's about what becomes possible when domination is no longer the gold standard for leadership. When clarity replaces control. When emotional maturity becomes the foundation for cultural evolution.

I write about aviation and patriarchy not as an outside observer, but as someone who has lived both from the inside out—first as a child, then as a woman navigating some of the most male-dominated cultures on earth.

I was born into an Old Order Mennonite community—an insular, intensely patriarchal world where men were unquestioned authorities and women were commanded to be silent, submissive, and obedient. Girls were raised to serve; boys were raised to rule. Entitlement and domination were treated as natural expressions of male authority, and violence was both hidden and rationalized as a byproduct of "the natural order." I grew up watching the distance between what the church claimed and how it behaved.

And I grew up watching my violent father be portrayed as a folk hero on the front pages of major newspapers as he argued for his "manhood entitlements" and presented himself as a victimized husband and father—a story I later wrote about in my memoir. Those contradictions were the first cracks in the spell of indoctrination—and the beginning of my lifelong work of connecting dots that were never expected to be connected.

From that world, I entered another virtually all-male arena: the United States Air Force Academy. I was part of the early classes that included a small percentage of women after the legal prohibitions were lifted. We were admitted, but hostility framed everyday life as we navigated what was already an arduous undertaking. Women were so scarce that simply existing in uniform felt like standing fully exposed—an easy target. Every day was a test—not once, but again and again.

After graduation, I went to military pilot training and joined the small number of women military aviators. I later advanced to become an aircraft commander and served in the first Gulf War.

After the military, I entered the airlines—again flying in environments shaped by rigid hierarchy, unquestioned authority, and persistent hostility toward women. On my first flight as a new-hire airline pilot, the captain refused to shake my hand or speak to me except to call for checklists. Another captain refused to call me by name, referring to me only as "Number Two."

Patriarchal cultures block women from entry, and then—when the door finally cracks open—they insist that if we prove ourselves, we will be accepted, that it's about competence rather than gender. But the truth is different: you must keep proving yourself for decades, and even then, you are treated as the exception that "proves" the rule that women are unfit, unqualified, or only present because of quotas.

I retired as a Boeing 777 captain after thirty years as an airline pilot. Those years gave me a front-row seat to the system itself—to see its patterns, to understand them, and to recognize them in other environments and relationships. It also taught me not to take the hostility personally, because it wasn't personal, it was structural.

And I was there when aviation began to shift—from authoritarian, ego-driven command structures to more collaborative, emotionally mature leadership. I saw how much safer and more humane systems become when domination gives way to shared responsibility. And I saw how profoundly pilots—most of them men—benefited when the culture stopped rewarding the loudest, most obnoxious personalities and started rewarding the clearest mind.

Flying around the world widened the frame even more—Asia, the Middle East, North America, South America, Europe. The accents and uniforms changed, but the behavioral patterns didn't. Patriarchy—whether religious, cultural, political, or interpersonal—behaved as though it had attended the same school. The same entitlements. The same vanishing of women's personhood. The same silencing of voices. The same masks of charm overlaid on the same patterns of coercion, domination, and emotional immaturity.

My purpose in writing this book is to synthesize the many fragments of patriarchal dysfunction into one clear picture—so the reader can see what is otherwise obscured.

Patriarchal systems rely on fragmentation: violence in one category, coercive control in another, workplace discrimination over here, religious silencing over there, historic erasure somewhere else, prohibitions on leadership in yet another area. When behaviors are compartmentalized, the system behind them becomes harder to name. My upbringing, my training, my career, and my lifelong effort to understand behavior and systems gave me a unique vantage point to see what connects them all.

I lived patriarchy in childhood.

I navigated it in adulthood.

I saw it reproduced across cultures and continents.

And I studied it for years—reading the experts in each of these compartmentalized fields and integrating that information into my lived understanding.

I also saw what becomes possible as high-stakes systems begin to grow out of authoritarianism.

This book is long for a reason: clarity is cumulative. Deconditioning is a process of pattern recognition—of seeing one piece, then another, until the entire structure comes into view. Once you see the pattern, you cannot unsee it. Until then, it is confusing.

But this is how people outgrow dominance hierarchies, even when the hierarchy itself refuses to evolve.

My hope is that this book accelerates that process for you.

Not by giving you slogans, but by giving you sight.

Not by telling you what to think, but by helping you recognize what you already sense.

If you are reading this, something in your life or your world already doesn't add up. Maybe it's your marriage. Maybe it's the double standard at work. Maybe it's the way women's accomplishments are erased, how violence is excused, or how men are allowed emotional immaturity that women must endlessly compensate for. Or maybe you've begun to see your own patterns of enabling that system.

Whatever brought you here, I want you to know:

You are not imagining it.

You are not too sensitive.

You are not alone.

And none of this is accidental.

Patriarchy is organized. It is intentional. It hides behind masks because it fears exposure. It cannot survive a critical mass of people who see it clearly and refuse to treat it as benign.

Emotional maturity—clarity, accountability, self-leadership—is the antidote.

I have seen cultures change. I have lived through indoctrination and walked myself out. I have seen what happens when abusive authority is unmasked, and when collaboration replaces coercion. I wrote this book because clarity is contagious—and because once you step out of illusion, the world changes shape around you.

My hope is that this book becomes a companion in your own threshold crossing—a flight plan for navigating the world as it is, and building the world as it could be.

A Navigation Guide for Reclaiming Your Agency and Charting Your Own Course

WHY THIS TOPIC MATTERS NOW

Something old is tightening its grip because something new is trying to be born. Patriarchal systems are showing their true face—louder, sharper, and more desperate than before. Around the world we are watching a resurgence of authoritarianism, fragility masquerading as strength, and certainty masquerading as expertise.

It is well known that the most dangerous moment in an abusive relationship is when the woman is leaving or has just left. That is the moment when control escalates, when violence peaks, when the abuser becomes most desperate. That is where we are now. Patriarchy is an abusive system and increasing numbers of women have slipped its grasp—financially, psychologically, spiritually, intellectually. They are increasingly skeptical of religious doctrines crafted by men, for men, and enforced on women. They are reevaluating marriage, motherhood, labor, and leadership. The old order feels the loss of control—and it is lashing back.

Around the world, patriarchal systems are reasserting themselves—through legislation, through religion, through culture, and through relationships—while simultaneously eroding the maturity required to sustain a healthy society. What we are witnessing is not random. It is a coordinated return to dominance, hierarchy, and emotional immaturity. Patriarchal systems are loudest when they feel threatened and most vicious when they gain total control.

The greatest danger today is the naïve hope that the promises of patriarchal manipulators can be believed; the comforting illusion that freedoms and rights earned in one generation cannot be taken from the next. They can. They are. And the insistence that "it won't happen to people like us" is precisely what makes it possible.

This topic matters now because clarity is the one force authoritarian systems cannot survive. Clarity is revolutionary. Clarity is a refusal. Clarity is the end of the spell. When we see the pattern clearly—when we name it and understand it—we stop feeding it with our confusion, our doubt, and our misplaced hope. Clarity, transparency, and questioning are not small acts. They are the quiet architecture of liberation. They are how we outgrow a system that depends on our blindness to survive. They are our superpowers—and the tools that will shape whatever future comes next.

CHARTING A COURSE

This is not a book about men. It is a book about emotional maturity—and the systems that grow in its absence. It is about what happens when immaturity gains cultural power. When ego fragility is codified into tradition, religion, and law. When the refusal to take responsibility becomes a style of leadership. When the most emotionally underdeveloped or dysfunctional people in a family or culture—or a country—rise to the top.

And it is about what becomes possible when we see these patterns clearly.

Emotional maturity changes more than relationships. It changes what we can perceive. It sharpens our ability to think, discern, and trust our own internal instruments. It lets us recognize manipulation, coercion, and erasure—not as isolated incidents, but as predictable patterns in systems designed to weaponize our confusion.

This isn't just a psychological story. It's a systemic one.

When we understand the emotional architecture of a system, we stop feeding what harms us.

We stop contorting ourselves to fit its demands.

We stop mistaking domination for order, or silence for peace.

This book offers a way of seeing—one that pulls back the curtain on patriarchal behavior and reveals the psychological roots beneath it. Not to condemn individuals, but to illuminate the structure. To name what has been normalized so long it became invisible architecture. To reclaim the clarity that patriarchy depends on us not having.

Let's call things by their true names.

Let's begin.

Note: This book does not ask for performance—it invites perception. But if you find, by the end, that your clarity wants a place to land, you'll find a small collection of invitations in the Afterword. These are not action steps in the traditional sense. They are subtle refusals. Gentle ways of living what you now see.

PART I

RECOGNIZING THE NAVIGATIONAL ERROR

This section exposes the developmental and emotional roots of patriarchy. It reveals how fragile egos, unfinished maturity, entitled dependency, and childish logic become the blueprints for systems of domination.

At the center of this architecture are three archetypes: the Eternal Child, who longs for freedom without responsibility; the Godfather/ Strongman, who demands obedience and calls it order; and the Fairy Godmother/Eternal Mother, who is expected to animate a cold system with warmth and magic and to carry the emotional and practical labor that patriarchy needs to function day to day. Together, these roles create the crazy-making cognitive dissonance that keeps patriarchy intact and destabilizes anyone who notices— pushing them back into self-doubt and compliance.

BLUF:
Bottom Line Up Front

1

Context and
the History of Patriarchy

BLUF: PATRIARCHY IS NOT A NATURAL OR INEVITABLE DESIGN—IT IS A DETOUR, A TRAUMA-BORN SYSTEM THAT EMERGED FROM RUPTURE, NOT PROGRESS. WHAT BEGAN AS A SURVIVAL STRATEGY BECAME A CULTURAL SCRIPT— REPLACING RELATIONAL BALANCE WITH HIERARCHY, EMOTIONAL SUPPRESSION, AND CONTROL. ROOTED IN INSECURE ATTACHMENT AND DEVELOPMENTAL ARREST, PATRIARCHY MAPS IMMATURITY ONTO POWER AND PASSES IT DOWN AS TRUTH. TO CHART A NEW COURSE, WE MUST FIRST UNDERSTAND THE TERRAIN WE'VE INHERITED.

DEBUNKING THE MYTHS OF PATRIARCHY

BLUF: *Patriarchy is not natural, inevitable, or ancient. It is a recent, imposed system justified by faulty narratives about biology and history.*

Patriarchists—those who uphold and justify patriarchal systems—often make several claims to defend its existence. First, they argue that patriarchy is "natural," rooted in biology, and that men are inherently driven to dominate while women are instinctively submissive.[1] Second, they claim that patriarchy has existed since the beginning of human civilization, as if it were the inevitable social order. Third, they insist that the only alternative to patriarchy is a matriarchy—defined as a mirror image where women dominate men.

Each of these claims is historically and anthropologically inaccurate.

While some degree of biological difference between the sexes exists, the idea that men are biologically hardwired to rule over women is a distortion of both evolutionary science and human history. Dominance hierarchies are not universal across species, and many primates—our closest relatives—exhibit cooperative, matrilineal, or egalitarian social structures.[2] Human societies, too, have not always been patriarchal. Scholars estimate that patriarchy is a relatively recent social construct, emerging between 6,000 and 10,000 years ago—a small fraction of human history.

Furthermore, evidence from matrilineal and matriarchal societies challenges the idea that female submission is "natural." If patriarchy were an innate human condition, it would not require such enormous social, legal, religious, and cultural investments to police.[3] The systematic suppression of women—through indoctrination, coercion, force, violence, and restrictive laws—reveals that patriarchy is not self-sustaining. It is an imposed structure, not an organic inevitability.

THE MYTH OF MATRIARCHAL DOMINATION

The claim that women seek to replace patriarchy with a dominance-based matriarchy is another distortion. This assumption reveals more about patriarchal psychology than historical reality. In psychological terms, this is projection—attributing one's own tendencies (in this case, a hierarchical need for control) onto others.[4]

In fact, some matriarchal and matrilineal societies do exist today and have existed historically, but they do not mirror patriarchy in structure or function. Unlike patriarchal systems, which are built on dominance, coercion, and rigid control, these societies often emphasize egalitarian decision-making, collective leadership, and balance between genders. These historical and contemporary examples reveal that social structures can be arranged in ways that do not require one gender to dominate the other.[5]

SECTION I: THE RISE OF PATRIARCHY — TRAUMA, POWER, AND SOCIAL UPHEAVAL

BLUF: Scholars suggest patriarchy emerged not from progress but from rupture—driven by environmental instability, fear, and shifts in power.

Understanding why patriarchy emerged requires an examination of historical, psychological, and social patterns. Scholars such as Gerda Lerner, Riane Eisler, and Heide Goettner-Abendroth have explored the transition from early egalitarian or matrilineal societies to male-dominated systems.

Various theories attempt to explain this shift, including:

The Advent of Agriculture

The transition from nomadic hunter-gatherer societies to agrarian societies created inheritance-based wealth systems, where controlling women's reproduction became a way to control lineage and property.

The Rise of Warfare

Some argue that patriarchal structures solidified as warrior cultures took hold, elevating physical dominance and conquest while subjugating women.

Religious Codification

Many early patriarchal systems entrenched male dominance through religious doctrine, reinforcing hierarchy as divine order.

Economic and Labor Divisions

As societies expanded, specialized labor roles emerged, and over time, men claimed positions of power while restricting women's autonomy.

REGRESSION MASQUERADING AS PROGRESS

Goettner-Abendroth challenges the modern assumption that patriarchy was an evolutionary advance. Rather than a step forward, she sees it as a historical hijacking—a regression into fear-based domination masked as civilization.

She offers a compelling lens: that patriarchy was not an inevitable outcome of human evolution, but a rupture—a profound spiritual and cosmological shift that disrupted older, life-honoring traditions.

In her view and others, early matrilineal societies were not about female domination, but about balance, mutuality, and reverence for the rhythms of life—earth, fertility, death, and renewal. Leadership was often rooted in maternal values: nurturance, continuity, and collective well-being.

With the rise of patriarchy came a cosmological inversion. Life was no longer understood through the lens of cyclical time or embeddedness in nature—but through hierarchy, linearity, and abstraction. Feminine wisdom and earth-based deities gave way to sky gods who demanded obedience and hierarchy. Wisdom traditions tied to the body and the land were replaced by systems of control, disembodiment, and moral rigidity.

This inversion did not merely rearrange power. It hijacked the meaning of life itself—rewriting who mattered, what mattered, and how value was defined. Patriarchy claimed the mantle of progress while systematically erasing emotional wisdom, mutual governance, and relational intelligence.

SECTION II: PATRIARCHY AS A TRAUMA SYSTEM

> *BLUF: Historical trauma, invasion, and disrupted caregiving created the emotional conditions for domination systems to take root.*

This cosmological inversion was not only spiritual—it was psychological. The rise of domination systems was not just a matter of warfare or theology. It reflected a deeper rupture in our emotional architecture. What followed was not emotional development—but emotional dissociation. Not security—but control.

This framing helps us see patriarchy not as the result of natural evolution, but as the scaling of emotional dysfunction—codified into law, religion, and culture.

While no early scholar explicitly coined the phrase "patriarchy is a trauma system," this framing is strongly supported by the research and implications of several major thinkers—before it was named directly by clinicians like Christine Forner.

Riane Eisler (*The Chalice and the Blade*) describes a cultural shift from partnership models to dominator systems—driven by fear, environmental collapse, and invasion.

Marija Gimbutas (*The Civilization of the Goddess*) presents archaeological evidence of peaceful, goddess-honoring Neolithic societies, later disrupted by violent Indo-European incursions.

Lloyd deMause (*Foundations of Psychohistory*) argues that domination, war, and hierarchy are the external consequences of widespread, unresolved childhood trauma.

Alice Miller (*For Your Own Good*) connects adult cruelty and authoritarianism to normalized childhood abuse disguised as discipline.

These scholars converge on a single insight: that patriarchy is not born of progress—but of pain. From this perspective, patriarchy did not represent a logical or inevitable step in human evolution, as many traditional histories suggest. It emerged from relational trauma—from the collective impact of unpredictable environments, early loss, emotional absence, and disrupted caregiving.

These conditions distort emotional development and relational safety at the individual level—and when scaled across generations, they produce systems of control, domination, and fear.

We can see this clearly in the behavioral profile of patriarchy:

❖ A need for dominance and submission

❖ Entitlement to power, sex, resources, or control

❖ Resistance to accountability or collaboration

❖ Devaluation of emotional expression and care

❖ Punishment of vulnerability and deviation

These are not the hallmarks of secure human development.
They are the scars and strategies of unresolved trauma.

ADDING THE CLINICAL LENS: CHRISTINE FORNER

While Eisler, Gimbutas, and Miller laid essential groundwork, Christine Forner—a trauma therapist, researcher, and specialist in dissociation—takes the next step.

She directly names patriarchy as a self-perpetuating trauma system: a global architecture of emotional avoidance, collective neglect, and relational rupture that harms everyone within it.[6]

In her work on trauma and misogyny, Forner argues that we may be living in a trauma loop so widespread that neither men nor women—neither boys nor girls—can truly thrive.

She describes patriarchy as a structure not built on care, but on psychological fragmentation—maintained through fear, disconnection, and the avoidance of vulnerability.

This clinical framing reinforces what earlier scholars intuited: that patriarchy is not a neutral system—it is a dissociated one. It punishes care. It rewards cruelty. It selects for immaturity—and scales it into power. And it does so not out of strength, but out of the inherited terror of vulnerability.

From this vantage point, patriarchy isn't simply an ideology. It is a collective trauma defense masquerading as tradition—a global normalization of emotional avoidance passed off as moral order. Patriarchy didn't just reorganize power. It reorganized the human nervous system. What we call civilization may, in fact, be the long echo of unhealed grief.

SECTION III: FROM SURVIVAL STRATEGY TO ARRESTED DEVELOPMENT

> *BLUF: Attachment science shows that trauma, neglect, chaos, or role reversal in childhood can lead to developmental gaps, insecure attachment patterns, and relational dysfunction and overt and covert domination patterns.*

Attachment science helps clarify this picture. When a child's emotional needs go unmet—through abuse, neglect, inconsistency, or emotional role reversal—they adapt to survive. These adaptations become what psychologists call attachment styles. They are not personality flaws—they are relational survival strategies.

However, if these patterns are never examined or updated in adulthood, they become arrested development: a refusal—or inability—to grow into true emotional maturity. This immaturity hides beneath cultural norms, institutions, and ideologies. But at its core, it reflects a deep fear of self-responsibility and the vulnerability required to relate to others with honesty, empathy, and integrity.

Let's briefly examine the four primary attachment styles and the behaviors they generate—especially as they relate to power, emotional labor, and domination.

Secure Attachment

"I trust myself and others. I can ask for what I need and honor others' needs too."

BEHAVIORS:

Seeks mutuality and open communication
Comfortable with both intimacy and boundaries
Responds to conflict without retreat or escalation
Practices accountability and repair

DOMINANCE LEVEL:

None. Secure individuals do not dominate—they relate.

Anxious-Preoccupied Attachment

"I need closeness to feel safe, and I fear rejection or abandonment."

BEHAVIORS:

Over-functioning and emotional caretaking
People-pleasing and approval-seeking

Hypervigilance to others' moods
Escalation when needs go unmet (e.g., criticism, chasing)

COVERT DOMINATION BEHAVIORS:

Emotional pressure to maintain closeness
Attempts to earn love through self-abandonment
Use of guilt or flooding when afraid

Dismissive-Avoidant Attachment

"I don't need anyone. Closeness is dangerous."

BEHAVIORS:

Withholding affection or withdrawing in conflict
Pride in self-sufficiency and detachment

Minimizing others' needs and emotions
Passive relational sabotage or neglect

COVERT & OVERT DOMINATION BEHAVIORS:

Emotional withholding as control
Shaming others for emotional expression
Aloofness used to maintain power
Relational laziness masked as stoicism

Fearful-Avoidant (Disorganized) Attachment

"I want connection, but I fear it. I don't trust anyone—including myself."

BEHAVIORS:

Push-pull dynamics (cling, then withdraw)
Emotional chaos and volatility
Jealousy, distrust, sabotage
Trauma-based lashing out

OVERT DOMINATION BEHAVIORS:

Explosive anger or emotional punishment
Control through unpredictability
Threats of abandonment
Passive-aggressive retaliation

CAN ATTACHMENT STYLES CHANGE?

Yes. While attachment styles form early as a survival strategy, they are not permanent.[7]

Emotional maturity can be earned—through self-reflection, reparenting, boundary work, grief integration, and the development of secure internal anchors. These shifts don't happen all at once, but they *do* happen—especially when we begin to name patterns, set limits, and stop outsourcing our safety to people who cannot offer it.

While this book is not a guide to healing attachment wounds, the Afterword offers a few suggestions for where to begin healing.

One of the most powerful outcomes of this work is a growing sense of internal steadiness—and with it, the ability to navigate emotionally immature dynamics without collapsing, over-functioning, or becoming entrapped.

Secure attachment is not just for the lucky. It is a skill that can be practiced—and a compass that can be reclaimed. However, when insecure attachment is left unresolved—especially in those with power—it doesn't just lead to emotional distance or clinging. It can escalate into control, coercion, and outright violence and cruelty.

People who fear abandonment may lash out to force closeness. People who fear intimacy may dehumanize to avoid vulnerability. And in disorganized states, fear and longing fuse into explosive volatility.

What begins as a strategy for emotional survival can become an offensive tactic—a weapon used to control, punish, dominate, and humiliate.

This is how patriarchy turns emotional immaturity into policy, punishment, abuse, and power.

SECTION IV: PATRIARCHY AS A SCALED SYSTEM OF INSECURE ATTACHMENT

> *BLUF: Patriarchy is not merely a dominance hierarchy or male-centered system—it's a relational blueprint rooted in insecure attachment, with behavior patterns and unexamined beliefs passed down through the generations.*

If we view patriarchy not simply as a belief system but as a relational blueprint, it begins to look eerily like insecure attachment dynamics on a mass scale. It doesn't just permit emotional immaturity—it requires it to sustain itself.

Here's how each insecure attachment style manifests in the architecture of patriarchy:

Anxious-Preoccupied Attachment

CORE PATTERN:

Clinging, over-functioning, hypervigilant to emotional cues

PATRIARCHAL EXPRESSION:

Many women and marginalized individuals are conditioned to *earn love* and *prove worth* through self-sacrifice and caretaking.

They are cast in the role of emotional attuners, forever tending to the unmet needs of more powerful others, hoping for safety or recognition.

The system rewards compliance and punishes autonomy—reinforcing fear of abandonment.

Dismissive-Avoidant Attachment

CORE PATTERN:

Detachment, control through distance, denial of needs

PATRIARCHAL EXPRESSION:

Often seen in men conditioned by patriarchy: emotionally walled off, rewarded for stoicism and dominance.

Vulnerability is pathologized; emotional labor is outsourced.

Intimacy is replaced by dominance or duty.

When proximity is demanded, they may react with contempt, shutdown, or aggression—punishing emotional requests as weakness or intrusion.

This form of avoidance becomes emotionally violent: a cold war of control, silence, or withdrawal.

Fearful-Avoidant (Disorganized) Attachment

CORE PATTERN:

Push-pull dynamics, deep mistrust, craving connection while fearing it

PATRIARCHAL EXPRESSION:

Found in systems shaped by trauma and betrayal: the same figure who promises protection also inflicts harm.

Power becomes fused with fear, producing chaotic or volatile behavior. Authority is idealized, feared, and obeyed—but also resented.

This style can swing into explosive cruelty, punishment, or relational sabotage, especially when closeness threatens perceived control.

Secure Attachment (Not the Norm in Patriarchy)

CORE PATTERN:

Mutuality, emotional regulation, capacity for repair

WHY IT'S DANGEROUS TO THE SYSTEM:

Securely attached people recognize red flags and walk away.

They are less susceptible to emotional manipulation, less likely to surrender their agency, and more willing to disrupt dysfunctional dynamics.

In a control-based system, this is a threat—not a goal.

Patriarchy is not just a dominance hierarchy or a system that centers men. It is a relational blueprint—one that systematically disrupts secure attachment, not just between individuals, but across entire cultures.

In this system, insecure attachment isn't a private struggle—it's scaled. It's woven into policies, hierarchies, and institutions that enforce control through fear, punishment, and emotional coercion. It rewards suppression, punishes vulnerability, and reframes insecurity as strength, leadership, or faith.

Viewing patriarchy through the lens of insecure attachment reframes what we often call "tradition" or "toxic masculinity." These aren't individual flaws—they're inherited behavior patterns, passed down as normal.

In the next chapter, we'll name the traits of emotional immaturity—not as moral failings, but as developmental delays. These traits don't just live in individuals—they're institutionalized until they become the blueprint for power itself.

What begins as a survival strategy becomes doctrine when scaled. And every unresolved attachment wound—when left unexamined—eventually demands a scapegoat.

But understanding how patriarchy emerged is only part of the story.

To dismantle it, we must understand how it is sustained—not just through laws and institutions, but through roles we're trained to perform.

Patriarchy doesn't survive through tyrants alone. It's upheld by ordinary people playing roles they never consciously chose—roles shaped by culture, trauma, and survival. These roles keep us performing, competing, or collapsing within a system built to preserve hierarchy. But once we see the system not just as a structure—but as a script—we can begin to question the roles we've been assigned.

2

Emotional Immaturity and the System That Never Grew Up

BLUF: EMOTIONAL ADULTHOOD IS THE QUIET REVOLUTION THAT DISMANTLES PATRIARCHY. THIS CHAPTER DEFINES PATRIARCHY AND OUTLINES THE CORE TRAITS OF EMOTIONALLY IMMATURE INDIVIDUALS—EGOCENTRISM, DENIAL, EMOTIONAL AVOIDANCE, AND COERCIVE RELATIONAL PATTERNS. THESE TRAITS ARE NOT JUST PERSONAL AND NOT LIMITED TO A SINGLE GENDER—THEY ARE STRUCTURAL. THEY BUILD A WORLD WHERE FRAGILITY RULES, ACCOUNTABILITY IS SHUNNED, AND RIGID ROLES REPLACE REAL RELATIONSHIP.

Understanding how patriarchy began is only part of the story. To unravel it, we must understand how it persists—not just through policy and tradition, but through emotional immaturity woven into everyday roles and relationships.

Patriarchy endures through scripts we are handed early in life—scripts shaped by culture, trauma, expectation, and survival. Some are taught to enforce the system's rules. Others are praised for embodying its ideals. Still others are burdened with its shame. These roles—especially the Standard Bearer and the Scapegoat—function as emotional technologies of control, quietly reinforcing the system without open force.

To challenge patriarchy at its root, we must look beneath these roles to the developmental patterns that give rise to them.

Because at its core, patriarchy is not just a political or cultural structure—it's a system built on arrested emotional development.

When growth is interrupted, reality becomes distorted. And the behavioral patterns found in patriarchal societies—rigid dominance hierarchies, exploitation of women, suppression of dissent, black-and-white thinking, and an obsession with control—mirror the traits of emotionally immature individuals.

SECTION I: WHAT IS PATRIARCHY? A MULTI-LENS DEFINITION

> *BLUF: Defines patriarchy structurally, historically, behaviorally, and relationally, and shows how it distorts reality and erases women.*

Patriarchy is a complex, centuries-old system of social organization that centralizes male authority and dominance, both in public institutions and private relationships. It can be understood through several overlapping lenses:

- **Structurally,** patriarchy organizes society around hierarchical power, with men positioned as decision-makers, protectors, and providers, while women and other marginalized groups are positioned as dependents, caretakers, or subordinates.

- **Historically,** it has shaped everything from legal codes and religious doctrine to inheritance laws and cultural myths. Patriarchy is not the natural order—it is a constructed system that evolved to consolidate and preserve control, especially over women's labor, reproduction, sexuality, and autonomy.

❖ **Behaviorally,** patriarchy upholds dominance and control as virtues while discouraging emotional depth, empathy, vulnerability, and collaboration. It promotes rigid gender roles and punishes deviation from them, fostering environments where power is maintained through coercion, fear, and entitlement.

❖ **Relationally,** patriarchy creates asymmetrical interpersonal dynamics. In families, marriages, workplaces, and religious communities, it conditions people to accept unequal partnerships —where one person holds emotional, financial, or moral authority, and the other is expected to comply. These dynamics are presented as "natural," but they suppress intimacy, autonomy, and mutual growth.

Ultimately, patriarchy functions by distorting reality. It casts control as leadership, dependence as love, and fear as morality. It relies on myths that justify inequality, and it subtly—or overtly—rewards those who comply while punishing those who question it.

And most devastatingly:

Patriarchy renders women largely invisible—erased from history, silenced in sacred texts, excluded from positions of power, and blamed for humanity's downfall (as in the myth of Eve). It systematically devalues the feminine while exploiting it, using both reverence and ridicule to keep women in a state of subordination.

It is not merely a social system. It is a worldview—one that must be unmasked before it can be dismantled.

SECTION II: WHAT IS EMOTIONAL IMMATURITY?

BLUF: Outlines the five foundational traits of emotionally immature people (EIPs), along with a visual-style summary of their cognitive, emotional, defensive, and interpersonal traits.

Emotional immaturity is a developmental arrest—a failure to fully mature in how one experiences emotions, relates to others, and engages with reality.[8] While it exists on a spectrum, emotionally immature people (EIPs) consistently exhibit five foundational characteristics, regardless of their personality style or level of social functioning.

1. Egocentrism

EIPs are self-preoccupied and emotionally self-referential, much like young children. They view relationships through the lens of how others affect them, with little curiosity about another's inner experience. Their empathy is limited or absent. Even when socially polished or intelligent, they rarely "get" other people on a deeper emotional level. Everyone else is either useful or threatening.[9]

2. Affective Realism and Rejection of Reality

EIPs define reality by how they feel in the moment ("If I feel it, it must be true")[10]. This emotional reasoning distorts their ability to see things clearly or hold multiple truths at once. When faced with facts that challenge their worldview or self-image, they deny, dismiss, or twist those facts into something that reinforces their feelings. Complex ideas are reduced to simplistic sound bites, and emotional logic replaces rational thought.

3. Resistance to Self-Reflection

Emotionally immature people lack interest in self-awareness. They avoid examining their role in conflict, resist feedback, and rarely experience true self-doubt. When challenged, they double down, becoming defensive, evasive, or self-righteous. They don't grow because they don't believe there's anything to learn about themselves.

4. Emotional Avoidance and Intimacy Fear

EIPs may be emotionally reactive, but their feelings are typically shallow, rigid, and overwhelming. They:

- Struggle to tolerate strong emotions in themselves or others.
- Avoid emotional intimacy—especially when it requires vulnerability.
- Shut down conversations with anger, withdrawal, or guilt-tripping.
- Rely on others for emotional regulation but resent being seen as needy.

They crave closeness but sabotage it. The moment someone tries to connect on a deeper level, EIPs often provoke conflict, dismiss kindness, or emotionally disappear.

5. Rigid Roles and Relational Dysfunction

EIPs view human beings as roles (parent, spouse, child, boss) rather than as complex individuals. Their worldview is binary—people are either above them or beneath them, submissive or dominant. They are often:

- Intimidated by others' independence.
- Reactive to differences in opinion.
- Emotionally coercive—using shame, guilt, fear, or self-pity to manipulate outcomes.
- Incapable of healthy mutuality or repair.

CORE PATTERNS OF EMOTIONAL IMMATURITY

Cognitive Patterns

Black-and-white thinking

Rejection of complexity

Literal interpretations and concrete logic

Overreliance on rules or roles

Embrace of "ends justify the means" reasoning

Emotional Patterns

Shallow emotional range and poor emotional modulation
Aversion to personal growth
Irritability, anxiety, or explosive anger
Victim mentality and hypersensitivity to criticism

Defensive Behaviors

Denial, blame-shifting, projection
Low stress tolerance, meltdowns, stonewalling
Refusal to take responsibility
Aggression and/or passive aggression

Interpersonal Dynamics

Poor listening
Low empathy and/or inability to relate to others
Difficulty respecting others' boundaries
Need for control through roles, power, or manipulation
Inability to repair or reflect after conflict

SECTION III: WHEN THE CHILD RULES THE WORLD

> *BLUF: Illustrates the danger of unintegrated emotional development being given social and institutional power, framing patriarchy as developmental arrest at scale.*

Imagine a small child placed in charge of a family. He demands constant attention and praise. He interrupts every conversation to re-center himself. He expects meals, toys, and comfort on demand but has no interest in who provides them or at what cost. He cannot tolerate frustration or boundaries. When someone says no, he screams, cries, lashes out, or retreats into sulking silence. When things go wrong, he blames everyone else: *She made me do it!* When his sibling builds a tall tower of blocks, he storms over and knocks it down. Sharing is unthinkable. Taking turns is intolerable. Accountability is terrifying.

Now imagine that child growing older—but never growing up.

Instead, he gains physical power, political authority, and cultural control. His self-centered worldview calcifies into law. His tantrums become wars. His refusal to accept limits becomes environmental collapse. His impulsivity is cloaked in doctrines of "decisiveness," his bullying recast as "leadership." His inability to reflect or empathize becomes national policy. He continues to lie to avoid consequences, lashes out when criticized, and rewrites history to always make himself the hero. He demands to be exalted— and punishes those who won't play along.

This is not just a metaphor. This is the emotional blueprint of patriarchy.

It is not a mature structure that simply went astray. It is the psychological equivalent of handing the keys to civilization over to someone stuck in the pre-operational stage of childhood development.[11] A mind that cannot integrate nuance, cannot sit with discomfort, cannot share power, and cannot say, *I was wrong.*

Patriarchy is not the wise elder—it is the unchecked child.

Its institutions were built to center its fragility, to silence opposition, and to demand caretaking without reciprocity. It infantilizes its followers while maintaining the illusion of supreme control. But like any emotionally immature person, it fears real intimacy, collaboration, and change—because those require the maturity it refuses to cultivate.

To see this clearly is to break the spell. It is the beginning of emotional adulthood—not just for individuals, but for humanity.

SECTION IV: NOT ALL MEN, AND NOT JUST MEN

> *BLUF: Clarifies that patriarchy affects both genders, functioning as an emotional and ideological system rather than simply a gender-based conflict.*

In emotionally immature systems—whether narcissistic family structures, cults, or large-scale ideologies like patriarchy, white supremacy, or religious extremism—the entire group is affected. Emotional immaturity dominates and indoctrinates everyone inside. It is passed down through relationships, parenting, institutions, and social rewards. It becomes inheritance.

Women, as the primary scapegoats of patriarchy, have historically been among the first to see through its illusions. Not because women are inherently more mature—but because they are the ones most harmed by the system's demands. When the pain of staying becomes greater than the fear of leaving, the scapegoat becomes the first to walk away. That act of refusal is emotional maturity in action.

But this doesn't mean only women see it—or that all women leave. Many remain emotionally immature within the system, policing other women or resisting change. Likewise, some men outgrow the system and begin the process of individuation. Patriarchy doesn't just harm women—it stunts men's growth, too. It keeps them emotionally and often socially dependent and isolated in rigid roles. But it also gives them power—enough power to keep many from questioning the trade-off.

Patriarchy is not really about gender.[12] Gender essentialism is simply the mask it wears.

Just as white supremacy is not really about race—and fundamentalism is not truly about God—patriarchy is not truly about protecting men (and certainly not about protecting women). Behind all of them is the same core dysfunction: grandiosity, entitlement, and a refusal to engage with reality as it is.

In short, any supremacy system avoids reality and responsibility because what they are avoiding is being in relationship with anyone not them, or not like them.

At the end of the book is an appendix titled "The Everyday Cost of Emotional Immaturity" to outline how emotional immaturity shows up in practical, tangible ways across different domains of life.[13]

For now, what matters most is this: emotional immaturity is not a minor quirk or private pattern. It is a structural force. It builds systems. And those systems shape lives.

3

The Fragile Ego of Patriarchy— A Core Navigational Vulnerability

BLUF: EXPLORES HOW EMOTIONALLY IMMATURE SYSTEMS PRODUCE FRAGILE EGOS THAT MISTAKE REACTIVITY FOR STRENGTH AND INSTITUTIONALIZE IMMATURITY AS LAW.

Everything is either growing or dying. When growth stops—when a river stops flowing—it becomes stagnant and toxic. People are the same way. When growth stops, they become stagnant and toxic—toxic to themselves and toxic to others. This chapter explores how emotionally immature systems fail to provide reality-based boundaries, leading to egos that are either brittle or inflated. Healthy ego strength grows through boundary-setting, attuned feedback, and the ability to tolerate frustration.[14] Without these developmental supports, a child is trapped in a narcissistic or tyrannical bubble that often gets normalized—and even rewarded—in patriarchal systems. We'll explore how ego fragility is not simply personal weakness, but a systemic vulnerability. It becomes institutionalized. It is protected, elevated, and confused with strength. And it becomes the navigational blueprint of domination systems.

SECTION I: WHAT IS EGO STRENGTH?

BLUF: Defines ego strength as the resilient, flexible capacity to remain grounded, tolerate correction, and engage with reality—contrasted with the reactivity of fragile egos.

Ego strength is one of the most misunderstood capacities in human development. It's not dominance. It's not control. It's not a hardened sense of self that never bends. Ego strength is the inner resilience to remain grounded when challenged. It's the ability to hold one's shape without collapsing into shame—or lashing out in rage.

At its core, ego strength is what allows us to stay connected to reality, even when reality is uncomfortable. It is the capacity to experience frustration, contradiction, and correction without losing our sense of self. This kind of psychological flexibility is not flashy. It rarely draws attention. But it is one of the most essential markers of emotional maturity.

A person with healthy ego strength can:

- Tolerate feedback without spiraling into self-loathing or defensiveness.

- Receive correction without needing to punish the messenger.

- Integrate new information without experiencing ego injury.

- Hold a cohesive sense of identity across different relationships and situations.

- Navigate conflict and difference without collapsing or retaliating.

The ego, in psychological terms, is the part of the psyche that helps us evaluate reality, regulate impulses, and integrate our life experiences. It is not inherently good or bad—it is necessary. The question is not whether someone has an ego, but whether their ego is strong enough to hold the complexities of life.

A strong ego does not mean an inflated ego. In fact, the stronger the ego, the less it needs to prove itself. A healthy ego doesn't require constant validation or control because it knows who it is. It doesn't have to dominate a conversation or silence opposition to feel secure. It can coexist with difference. It can hear "no" and survive. It can be wrong and grow.

By contrast, a fragile ego is not simply insecure—it is reactive, rigid, and emotionally dependent. It cannot tolerate challenge without interpreting it as threat. It outsources regulation, avoids feedback, rewrites reality to stay intact, and punishes contradiction. It confuses control with connection and certainty with truth. Under pressure, it doesn't bend—it breaks or dominates.

This is where ego fragility becomes dangerous. When the ego cannot regulate itself, it outsources regulation to everyone around it. It requires others to tiptoe around its feelings, avoid its triggers, and manage its image. In fragile egos, any form of disagreement becomes betrayal. Any form of accountability becomes an attack.

This is not maturity—it is emotional dependency masquerading as power. And when fragile egos are elevated to positions of leadership, they build systems that mirror their own instability: systems allergic to feedback, hostile to change, and violent toward truth.

True ego strength, by contrast, becomes the internal architecture that allows us to engage with the world honestly and collaboratively. It is what makes personal growth possible. It is what allows for leadership without control, conviction without cruelty, and presence without performance.

Without ego strength, there is no growth. There is only defense.

SECTION II: THE DEVELOPMENTAL ARC OF THE EGO

BLUF: Outlines six developmental theorists whose work reveals how ego strength is built (or impaired) through early childhood experiences.

Ego strength is not a trait we're born with—it is something that must be built over time. Like a bridge, it requires support, stress-testing, and gradual expansion. It begins in childhood through everyday experiences: being told "no," receiving attuned correction, being soothed during frustration, and having our feelings acknowledged even when our behaviors are redirected.

When these foundational experiences are missing or distorted, the ego doesn't vanish—it simply forms around the distortions. It becomes brittle, inflated, or dependent. Understanding how this happens requires looking at the developmental map: the ordinary yet profound sequence of psychological tasks children must navigate to grow up.

Here are six key theorists who help us trace the construction—or collapse—of ego strength.

1. ERIK ERIKSON – PSYCHOSOCIAL STAGES OF DEVELOPMENT

Erikson identified eight stages of psychosocial development, two of which are especially formative for ego strength:[15]

Stage 2: Autonomy vs. Shame and Doubt (ages 1-3)

At this stage, children begin testing their independence—exploring, saying no, making choices. If caregivers support this budding autonomy while offering safe, consistent boundaries, the child learns self-trust. But if caregivers shame the child's efforts or overly control their actions, the child may internalize doubt and inhibition instead.

Stage 3: Initiative vs. Guilt (ages 3-5)

Here, children begin initiating actions, testing limits, and learning how to navigate the social world. Healthy ego development allows them to try, fail, repair, and try again. Over-correction or neglect at this stage can lead to chronic guilt or inflated defensiveness.

KEY INSIGHT:

When children are either excessively controlled or never corrected, ego development is disrupted. They either become hyper-compliant and anxious—or entitled and impulsive, both of which signal fragile ego structures.

2. DONALD WINNICOTT – TRUE SELF AND FALSE SELF

Winnicott observed that children develop a sense of "true self" when their feelings and expressions are met with empathy, containment, and realistic boundaries. But when a child must perform for approval—suppressing their authenticity to please or appease—they begin to construct a "false self."[16]

This false self isn't necessarily fake—it's adaptive. It allows the child to maintain connection and avoid rejection. But over time, it disconnects them from their own inner compass.

KEY INSIGHT:

A fragile ego is often a survival strategy. It forms not around truth, but around what was safest to be. It becomes a performance—seeking applause, not wholeness.

3. MARGARET MAHLER – SEPARATION AND INDIVIDUATION

Mahler emphasized the importance of the separation-individuation process: the gradual movement a child makes from symbiosis with the caregiver to autonomous selfhood. When this phase is disrupted—by overprotectiveness, engulfment, or emotional abandonment—the child may either cling excessively to others or push them away in fear.

KEY INSIGHT:

A strong ego grows through safe separation.[17] A fragile ego either fuses with others or defends against intimacy, lacking the internal security to navigate relational boundaries.

4. HEINZ KOHUT – SELF-PSYCHOLOGY AND NARCISSISTIC INJURY

Kohut's work on narcissism reframed it as a developmental injury. Children need to be mirrored—to have their joy, sorrow, and triumphs reflected by caring adults. When this need is unmet or shamed, the ego fails to solidify cohesively. The result is a fragile sense of self that overreacts to criticism and seeks constant external validation.[18]

KEY INSIGHT:

The adult who cannot tolerate "no" is often protecting a wounded child who never felt fully seen or affirmed. Narcissistic reactivity is not about power—it's about unresolved pain.

5. WILFRED BION – CONTAINMENT AND THOUGHT DEVELOPMENT

Bion offered a powerful metaphor: the caregiver as a container. When a parent can "hold" a child's distress without panic or shutdown, the child learns to hold it too. Emotional regulation develops through co-regulation: a parent's calm becomes the child's anchor. When this containment is missing, the child becomes overwhelmed and reactive.[19]

KEY INSIGHT:

Fragile egos aren't just emotionally volatile—they never learned how to process emotion safely. Without containment, feelings become threats rather than information.

6. DANIEL SIEGEL – INTERPERSONAL NEUROBIOLOGY

Modern neuroscience confirms what these earlier theorists intuited: the brain develops in relationship. Siegel emphasizes how children "borrow" their caregivers' nervous systems to learn regulation, boundary navigation, and empathy.[20] This scaffolding creates the neural architecture for later emotional resilience and integration.

KEY INSIGHT:

Emotional maturity is not willpower—it's wiring. Children who receive attuned support learn to self-regulate. Those who don't are left trying to build emotional houses on unstable ground.

DEVELOPMENTAL TRAUMA AND COMPLEX PTSD

When childhood is marked by emotional inconsistency, neglect, enmeshment, or abuse, the ego cannot develop through healthy frustration and repair. Instead, it forms around survival. The result is often a high-functioning exterior with deep internal fragmentation—what some call "performative maturity" masking emotional dysregulation.

KEY INSIGHT:

These individuals learn to survive, not to integrate. Perfectionism, defensiveness, collapse, or rage aren't personality flaws—they are protective adaptations in the absence of developmental safety.[21]

HOW THE EGO GROWS (OR DOESN'T)

Children need:

- To hear "no" and survive it.
- To be corrected and still feel loved.
- To wait their turn.
- To try, fail, and try again—with support.

Frustration tolerance isn't just about patience—it's the seed of curiosity, inventiveness, and collaboration. It's what allows us to pursue long-term goals, sit with discomfort, and see others as real. Without it, the ego cannot grow. It either hardens into entitlement or collapses into helplessness. And both outcomes lead to the same thing: a fragile adult ego that depends on others to regulate reality.

SECTION III: THE MAKING OF A FRAGILE EGO

BLUF: Explores how overcontrol and overindulgence both disrupt ego development, leading to unstable personalities that rely on others to regulate reality.

A strong ego can tolerate limits, boundaries, disappointment, and correction. A fragile ego cannot.

Instead of growing stronger through experience, it builds an alternate reality—one where it is always right, always central, always justified. In this reality, feedback becomes betrayal, boundaries become rejection, and difference becomes danger. But this isn't simply a character flaw. Its roots are developmental.

Children are not born knowing how to regulate themselves. They borrow regulation from their caregivers—through boundaries, correction, soothing, and consistent feedback.[22] This process, repeated over time, builds an internal compass: a sense of "I can handle this" in the face of challenge.

But when a child is either:

- **Overindulged** (never told no, never given structure), or
- **Overcontrolled** (never allowed to explore, make mistakes, or assert will),

. . . the ego cannot mature.[23] It becomes fragile—either inflated and entitled, or brittle and fearful. Both are emotionally dependent and reality-avoidant. Both are compensations for missing developmental scaffolding.

SPOILING VS. AUTHORITARIANISM—TWO SIDES OF THE SAME WOUND

At first glance, these two parenting styles seem opposite. One is permissive; the other, controlling. But both result in the same outcome: an ego that cannot function without external props.

Spoiling offers no containment. The child believes they are the center of the universe, and their feelings and wants should dictate reality. Frustration is intolerable. Boundaries feel offensive. The ego inflates without structure.

Authoritarianism offers no room for exploration. The child becomes brittle—either hyper-compliant or defiantly oppositional. There's no space to test ideas, assert needs, or develop emotional agility. The ego hardens under pressure but remains hollow underneath.

In both cases, the child doesn't learn to self-regulate—they learn to perform or collapse. They become dependent on the external environment to maintain their sense of worth and identity.

THE FRAGILE EGO IN ACTION

A fragile ego is not simply sensitive—it is unstable. It requires constant reinforcement and validation to stay intact. Without this, it begins to unravel emotionally or behaviorally. Here's how it tends to show up:

Feedback feels like an attack. Even gentle correction evokes defensiveness or shame.

Boundaries feel like rejection. The fragile ego reads "no" as abandonment.

Difference feels like danger. Any dissent is perceived as threat to self-worth.

Because it cannot metabolize discomfort, the fragile ego rewrites reality instead. It recasts villains and heroes. It erases inconvenient facts. It silences contradiction. This isn't always conscious—but it is deeply strategic. The ego must preserve the illusion of centrality to survive.

And when reality pushes back—when the world refuses to conform—a fragile ego doesn't adapt. It revolts. Or collapses. Or manipulates its way back to the illusion of control.

SECTION IV: CONTAINMENT, REBELLION, AND THE MAKING OF MANUFACTURED CONSENT[24]

> *BLUF: Examines how survival adaptations like charm, guilt-tripping, and flattery develop in childhood and later become manipulative adult strategies.*

Children are born with instincts for survival, not self-regulation. When faced with discomfort, disconnection, or distress, they reach for whatever strategies will restore a sense of safety—crying, performing, shutting down, defying. These are not flaws. They are adaptive responses used by undeveloped nervous systems to preserve connection.

With healthy containment and relational safety, these early survival strategies evolve. A toddler's meltdown becomes a five-year-old's negotiation. A seven-year-old's "no!" becomes a teenager's boundary. This is how ego strength grows—through friction, containment, and repair.

But in emotionally immature systems—especially those shaped by authoritarianism, neglect, or inconsistency—this evolution doesn't occur. Instead, children adapt to the environment by suppressing their needs, performing compliance, or manipulating outcomes. These strategies help them survive. But when they become habitual, they eventually replace growth with performance.

REBELLION AS A RITE OF PASSAGE

Rebellion is not a sign of disrespect—it is a developmental necessity. It is the child's first "no," the first act of separation that says: *I am not you.* It allows for differentiation, exploration, and the testing of personal limits.

A child who never rebels may have lost touch with their sense of self. A child who only rebels may be stuck in reaction. Both reflect ego structures that haven't fully matured. True growth lies in integration: the ability to say no without destroying connection—and to hear no without collapsing or retaliating.

When rebellion is punished or shamed, the child becomes compliant—

but loses self-trust. When rebellion is romanticized or ignored, the child may inflate—rejecting all correction as control. Both distort the ego. Both disrupt healthy navigation of boundaries, identity, and mutuality.

CONTAINMENT IS NOT CONTROL—IT'S GROWTH

Containment is the emotional holding environment a child needs to feel safe while learning about boundaries, frustration, and reality. It is not domination—it is presence. It says: You can feel big feelings and still be loved. You can test limits and still belong.

Without containment, rebellion becomes either suppressed or weaponized. A child learns to perform safety rather than feel it. They develop what Winnicott called the "false self"—a version of themselves that stays agreeable or invisible to maintain connection. Over time, this becomes a relational template: Don't be real. Be good. Don't speak up. Stay safe.

This doesn't just impair growth—it creates the conditions for emotional manipulation to take root.

MANUFACTURED CONSENT: SURVIVAL DISGUISED AS AGREEMENT

When children don't feel safe being real, they begin to perform agreement to preserve belonging. This isn't conscious deception—it's survival. But over time, survival becomes a script. And the child forgets it's a performance at all.

These strategies may look like:

- Nodding to avoid punishment.
- Smiling when scared.
- Taking the blame to preserve peace.
- Suppressing needs to avoid rupture.

In childhood, these tactics protect the relationship. But when carried into adulthood, they become powerful tools of coercion and control:

- Guilt-tripping
- Stonewalling
- Charm used as leverage
- Passive-aggressive withdrawal
- Strategic praise to gain favor
- Emotional collapse as manipulation

These are not signs of bad character. They are unexamined adaptations. But left unchecked, they become the psychological infrastructure of relational coercion.

THE CONSEQUENCE OF BYPASSING GROWTH

In emotionally mature systems, children gradually shift from survival to collaboration. They learn to influence without overpowering. They learn to hear "no" and recover. They discover that their needs matter—and so do others'.

But in patriarchal or narcissistic systems, these ego-fragile strategies are not just overlooked—they are rewarded. Charm is seen as competence. Withdrawal is interpreted as strength. Emotional manipulation is mistaken for leadership. What began as survival becomes a blueprint:

- Wearing someone down becomes relentless badgering.
- Crying to gain attention becomes emotional blackmail.
- Shutting down becomes stonewalling and control.
- Pushing boundaries becomes calculated transgression.

And without reflection, these become the default. Not just in relationships—but in families, institutions, and entire cultural systems.

SECTION V: THE FRAGILE EGO AS A CORE

NAVIGATIONAL ERROR

> *BLUF: Explains how fragile egos distort truth, resist accountability, and restructure entire systems to preserve control and avoid growth.*

A fragile ego is not just a personality flaw. It is a miscalibrated compass. It distorts the way we orient to feedback, power, relationship, and responsibility. Instead of helping us navigate reality, it builds a world in which the ego remains at the center—regardless of the truth.

It cannot hold tension, so it demands harmony through control. It cannot metabolize correction, so it reinterprets accountability as cruelty. It cannot differentiate self from others, so it centers its own comfort as universal truth.

This isn't strength. It's disorientation—emotional immaturity dressed up as authority.

A fragile ego is reactive, not responsive. It confuses internal discomfort with external threat. It needs others to regulate its feelings, reflect only what it already believes, and protect it from contradiction. In this state, the ego becomes the source of a thousand tiny distortions. And when those distortions go unchallenged, they metastasize into collective dysfunction.

Without ego strength, the psyche has no ballast. No true north.

And when "no" feels like annihilation, domination becomes the only substitute for maturity.

This is the real danger:

Instead of developing flexibility, the fragile ego builds rigidity.

Instead of strengthening through friction, it avoids growth entirely.

It seeks applause, not reflection. Control, not collaboration.

It becomes a closed circuit of self-confirmation—where truth is filtered, people are reduced, and dissent is pathologized. And when fragile egos are handed power, their disorientation doesn't stay private.

They remake the systems around them in their own image.

What should be institutions of spiritual community become engines of propaganda. What should be leadership becomes performance. What should be connection becomes manipulation. What should be accountability becomes exile.

This is how private immaturity becomes public policy. And how the internal failures of a fragile ego become the navigational errors of a culture.

THE PSYCHOLOGY OF CONSENT BYPASSING

What makes this even more dangerous is that fragile egos don't operate in isolation. They form early—and they adapt quickly. Children develop a stunning range of strategies to bypass resistance and get their needs met, even in the absence of true relational safety. These strategies, though normal in childhood, become toxic when they're never outgrown.

And so, the child who once sweet-talked their way to a cookie becomes the adult who love-bombs their partner into compliance.

The child who pouted until they got what they wanted becomes the manager who stonewalls dissent.

The child who wore a parent down with endless pleading becomes the politician who reshapes public opinion through repetition and outrage.

When these tactics are left unexamined, they become part of the psychological infrastructure of coercion.

LIST OF WAYS CHILDREN MANUFACTURE CONSENT

1. Persistence and Repetition

- "Please? Please? Just this once?"

- Asking repeatedly until the parent gives in out of exhaustion.

- A strategy of wearing down resistance through sheer volume or stamina.

- Harmless at first—but if effective, it teaches that boundaries aren't fixed and "no" means "maybe."

Grown-up version: relentless negotiating, pushing past boundaries, "badgering" to get their way.

2. Emotional Appeal

❖ Sad face. Big eyes. Meltdown. Silent sulk.

❖ Leveraging sadness, guilt, or emotional discomfort to elicit a "yes."

❖ Taps into a caregiver's empathy or conflict-avoidance.

Grown-up version: guilt-tripping, stonewalling, crying as a manipulation tool, feigned helplessness.

3. Charm and Flattery

❖ "You're the best mommy in the whole world . . . can I have it now?"

❖ Using affection, sweetness, or praise to butter up the parent first.

❖ Emotional currency as a trade: "I'll be good/loving if you give me what I want."

Grown-up version: love-bombing, manipulative charm, strategic kindness to soften a no.

4. Bargaining

❖ "If I clean my room, can I have ice cream?"

❖ "I'll be really good if . . ."

❖ Introducing a transaction or compromise—even when none was requested.

Grown-up version: quid pro quo relationships, performative "good behavior" to secure advantage.

5. Reframing the Request

❖ "It's not really candy—it's fruit gummies!"

❖ Minimizing or disguising the real nature of the ask.

❖ Linguistic sleight-of-hand to avoid triggering the expected no.

Grown-up version: doublespeak, euphemisms, manipulation of facts or language to gain consent.

6. Triangulation

* "Dad said I could."
* "Grandma lets me."
* Bringing in another authority to override the current one.

Grown-up version: pitting people against each other, using third-party validation to manipulate outcomes.

7. Delay and Ambush

* Asking in the middle of chaos.
* Asking when the parent is distracted, tired, or already overwhelmed.
* Finding opportune moments when resistance is lowest.

Grown-up version: timing conversations for maximum advantage—catching someone off guard, leveraging emotional fatigue.

8. Entitlement and Escalation

* "But I want it!"
* "Why not? That's not fair!"
* Responding to "no" with anger or accusation.
* Makes the parent feel they've caused harm or injustice.

Grown-up version: outrage as a tactic, moral high-grounding to silence dissent.

9. Silence and Withdrawal

* Shutting down. Going quiet. Pouting.
* Creating discomfort or tension as a form of protest.
* The "punishment" of disconnection to extract a "yes."

Grown-up version: cold shoulder, passive-aggressive punishment, emotional withholding.

10. Testing the Boundaries

- ❖ "What if I only take a little?"

- ❖ Doing the thing anyway—and watching the reaction.

- ❖ Pushing against limits just enough to see if enforcement is real.

Grown-up version: boundary-pushing, plausible deniability, strategic transgressions.

These are developmentally normal behaviors. In childhood, they're part of the experimentation process—children are testing agency, boundary strength, and their social environment.

But when they are:

Never met with healthy containment, or
Reinforced as effective, or
Carried into adulthood unconsciously,

. . . they become extraction tools—strategies for bypassing consent rather than building collaboration.

Children do manufacture consent, and when this developmental strategy is not grown out of (or when it is rewarded and refined into adulthood), it becomes part of the psychological architecture of coercion and manipulation. This is not just how manipulation is learned. It's how domination becomes justified—first in the family, then in the world.

SECTION VI: CONSEQUENCES IN ADULT LIFE

> *BLUF: Details how fragile egos impact leadership, relationships, accountability, and cultural decision-making at scale.*

Once these early fragilities solidify into personality patterns, they begin to shape every domain of adult life—from relationships and leadership to systems and culture. A fragile ego is not a private burden. It becomes a public hazard.

Because fragile egos cannot tolerate feedback, limits, or contradiction, they reject the very conditions necessary for growth. They defend against discomfort instead of learning from it. They prioritize emotional safety over truth, pride over repair, and image over reality.

These deficits are not harmless. They ripple outward—distorting decision-making, derailing collaboration, and compromising every system they touch.[25]

THE MARSHMALLOW STUDY AND THE FRAGILE EGO

In the 1970s, psychologist Walter Mischel conducted the now-famous Marshmallow Study.[26] Children were offered a choice: eat one marshmallow now, or wait a few minutes and receive two. The results revealed a compelling link: those who could delay gratification often went on to demonstrate stronger emotional regulation, academic success, and long-term resilience.

Despite later critiques, the study's central insight holds: frustration tolerance shapes our long-term capacity for resilience and growth. Fragile egos lack this capacity. They struggle with even minor obstacles. Discomfort is unbearable. Delay feels like deprivation. Correction feels like attack. In this state, maturity halts. Problem-solving collapses. And entitlement escalates.

The inability to hear "no" in childhood—if not outgrown—becomes one of the most dangerous traits in adulthood.

HOW FRAGILE EGOS SHOW UP IN ADULT LIFE

This inability to wait, adapt, or accept limits doesn't just show up in experiments—it becomes a defining feature of how fragile egos operate in real life.

1. INABILITY TO TOLERATE FRUSTRATION

What should be a moment for learning becomes a crisis. Fragile egos lack perseverance. When things go wrong, they don't adapt—they explode, collapse, or deflect. Reactivity replaces reflection. Obstacles are not problems to solve—they are insults to the ego.

2. AVOIDANCE OF ACCOUNTABILITY

Accountability requires admitting fault and making repair. Fragile egos can do neither. Every challenge is interpreted as a threat. To protect pride, they deny, deflect, or blame. Mistakes become someone else's fault. Growth is impossible.

3. MANIPULATIVE BEHAVIORS

Because fragile egos cannot tolerate direct confrontation, they resort to indirect control: guilt-tripping, charm offensives, passive-aggression, emotional withholding. These behaviors aren't random—they're learned strategies to maintain control without risking vulnerability.

4. POOR LEADERSHIP

Leadership requires collaboration, curiosity, and the ability to integrate diverse perspectives. Fragile leaders can't do this. They don't listen—they command. They don't course-correct—they punish dissent. Loyalty matters more than wisdom. Control replaces vision.

5. DISTORTED DECISION-MAKING

A fragile ego cannot admit when it's wrong. Decisions become about preserving pride, not solving problems. Complexity is avoided. Nuance is flattened. Data is ignored. Outcomes are sabotaged by the need to appear infallible.

6. EMOTIONAL VOLATILITY

Simple disagreements trigger disproportionate emotional reactions—rage, shutdown, coldness, or retaliation. The room becomes about managing the fragile person's mood. Others learn to tiptoe, comply, or self-abandon to avoid explosion.

7. RELATIONSHIP DYSFUNCTION

Fragile egos can't engage in mutual repair. They struggle with empathy in conflict. They interpret boundaries as rejection and requests as criticism. Over time, this erodes intimacy. Romantic breakdowns, family estrangement, and collective burnout often follow.

8. ISOLATION OR ENMESHMENT

Without ego strength, people tend to either push others away—or fuse with them in unhealthy ways. Some become emotionally isolated, unable to tolerate difference. Others demand total loyalty and conformity. In both cases, true interdependence is impossible.

SYSTEMIC CONSEQUENCES

When fragile egos rise to power, they shape the systems around them. These systems:

- Demand conformity.
- Erase dissent.
- Prioritize image over substance.
- Reward sycophants and scapegoat truth-tellers.

These are not systems built for growth. They are systems built for ego protection. They cannot solve problems because they cannot admit problems exist. Fragility becomes policy. Insecurity becomes law.[27]

THE PATTERN REPEATS

Fragile egos not only break systems—they raise the next generation. Parenting becomes another domain where emotional immaturity plays out:

- Children are either overcontrolled or under-contained.
- Boundaries are inconsistent or weaponized.
- Autonomy is punished or romanticized.

The result? New generations of fragile egos, repeating the cycle—this time with more resources, more platforms, and more power.

SECTION VII: THE INSTITUTIONALIZATION OF FRAGILITY

> *BLUF: Shows how emotionally immature individuals rise into leadership and build systems that protect their fragility through policy, culture, and coercion.*

Fragile egos do not stay small. When left unexamined, they scale. They rise into positions of authority—not because they are wise or grounded—but because they are relentless in seeking validation, control, and emotional insulation. And once in power, they reshape the systems around them to reflect their inner instability.

They don't create rules for justice—they create them to avoid discomfort.[28] They don't seek truth—they seek reinforcement. They don't lead—they perform.

The result is a world where emotional immaturity is embedded into law, culture, religion, and leadership—where fragility is not healed, but codified.

WHAT SYSTEMS BUILT ON FRAGILE EGOS LOOK LIKE

These systems are not built to serve truth or human flourishing. They are built to protect the emotionally unwell by turning their fragility into policy.

- **Authoritarian regimes:** where questioning is punished, and obedience is rewarded.

- **Religious orthodoxy:** where complexity is heresy and conformity is called holiness.

- **Nationalism and militarism:** where force is equated with virtue and dissent with betrayal.

- **Patriarchy:** where male fragility is masked as divine order, and women are controlled to maintain illusion.

- **Corporate hierarchies:** where performance is prized above people, and truth-telling is penalized as insubordination.

These are not systems of strength. They are systems of containment—designed to defend a disoriented ego at scale.

WHEN FRAGILITY BECOMES POLICY

Once fragile egos dominate institutions, the same patterns emerge repeatedly:

- **Challenge = Treason**—Feedback becomes betrayal.

- **Correction = Attack**—Accountability is framed as persecution.

- **Dissent = Erasure**—Those who disagree are shamed, exiled, or discredited.

- **Visibility = Threat**—Especially when it comes from the marginalized, the perceptive, or the unafraid.

In these systems:

- Sycophants are rewarded.

- Integrity is punished.

- Propaganda replaces transparency.

- Emotional volatility replaces leadership.

These are not systems that adapt. They are systems that entrench.

CLARITY AS REBELLION

These systems fear one thing: clarity. Because clarity is a mirror. And fragile egos cannot bear to be seen.

Clarity breaks the spell of distortion. It interrupts the false consensus. It reveals that the emperor has no clothes—not because he is evil, but because he was never taught to wear the garments of truth. To see clearly in a world built on fragile egos is not just brave—it is revolutionary.

WHEN FRAGILITY MASQUERADES AS STRENGTH

We imagine harm as something loud—abuse, domination, cruelty. But often, the deepest harm wears a smile. It hides behind power suits and sacred texts. It disguises itself in the language of order and the rituals of reverence.

But beneath the mask is a fragile ego:

- Unwilling to grow.

- Incapable of repair.

- Terrified of contradiction.

- Desperate for control.

This is the root structure of patriarchy—not divine authority, but emotional immaturity, dressed in robes and rules.

We are not ruled by strength. We are ruled by a fear of being wrong. By a terror of shame. By a collective refusal to grow up.

In the next chapter, we'll explore how this fragility doesn't just shape behavior—but thinking itself. Patriarchal systems don't just defend ego— they distort reality to protect it. From magical thinking to circular logic, from emotional reasoning to projection, we'll examine the cognitive distortions that uphold systems of control and call them truth.

Because patriarchy does not run on wisdom. It runs on the mind of the unparented child—dressed in moral certainty, theological authority, and institutional respectability.

And once we recognize that, we stop mistaking emotional immaturity for divine command.

4

The Childish Logic of Patriarchy

BLUF: APPLIES CHILDHOOD DEVELOPMENTAL THEORY TO REVEAL HOW PATRIARCHAL LOGIC MIRRORS IMMATURE COGNITIVE PATTERNS AND DISTORTS REALITY INTO A SYSTEM OF GENDERED DOMINANCE.

SECTION I: THE NATURAL STAGES OF CHILDHOOD DEVELOPMENT

> BLUF: Introduces Piaget's framework of early childhood development to illustrate which traits are appropriate in children but not intended to be carried into adulthood.

Understanding emotional maturity begins with understanding the normal trajectory of childhood development. Children are not born with the capacity to process complexity, take responsibility, or see the world from multiple perspectives. These are learned capacities—emergent qualities that develop through challenge, experience, and support. But when early developmental stages are never fully navigated and outgrown, they become frozen.

Emotional immaturity, especially as it manifests in patriarchal systems, is not just a personal failing—it is a developmental arrest. To grasp the depth of its distortion, we must first understand what normal development looks like.

EARLY CHILDHOOD: THE PREOPERATIONAL STAGE (AGES ~2–7)

Jean Piaget described this phase as marked by egocentrism, animism, and rigid, black-and-white thinking.[29] In this stage:

- **Egocentrism:** Children believe their experience is universal. They cannot yet grasp that others have different thoughts, feelings, or perspectives. "If I want something, everyone must want it."

- **Animism:** Inanimate objects are imagined having thoughts and feelings. "The chair tripped me."

- **Magical Thinking:** Cause and effect are replaced with wishful or story-based logic. "If I'm good, the sky won't rain on my birthday."

- **Rigid, Polarized Thinking:** Everything is either good or bad, right or wrong. There is little ability to hold nuance or paradox. "If I make a mistake, I'm a bad person."

Children in this stage also demonstrate:

- **Impulsivity:** Immediate gratification trumps delayed consequences.

- **Rule Absolutism:** Rules are seen as fixed and moral rather than contextual or flexible.

These traits are developmentally appropriate in children—but when they persist into adulthood, especially in systems of power, they become dangerous distortions.[30]

MIDDLE CHILDHOOD: THE CONCRETE OPERATIONAL STAGE (AGES ~7–11)

In this stage, children begin to grasp logic and cause-and-effect thinking. However, their thinking still lacks abstraction:

- **Improved Perspective-Taking:** Children start to understand that others have different points of view.

- **Moral Complexity Begins:** "It was wrong, but maybe it was an accident."

- **Logical Thinking:** Cause and effect become clearer, but thinking remains concrete and bound to the present.

- **Emerging Empathy:** The beginnings of relational thinking appear, though still self-referential.

Children here begin to internalize rules and social expectations—but often still need external validation and approval.

ADOLESCENCE: FORMAL OPERATIONAL STAGE (AGES ~12–18)

Here we see the emergence of:

- **Abstract Reasoning:** The ability to think about ideas, systems, beliefs, and hypothetical futures.

- **Idealism and Rebellion:** Adolescents begin to challenge authority and imagine better systems—though often through black-and-white lenses.

- **Identity Formation:** "Who am I?" "What do I believe?"

- **Emotional Volatility:** The brain is still developing impulse control and emotional regulation.

While emotional intelligence and executive functioning are still forming, this stage represents the launch pad for adult self-leadership—if it is supported by nurturing, boundaries, and models of emotional maturity.

SECTION II: WHAT HAPPENS WHEN DEVELOPMENT GETS STUCK?

> *BLUF: When childhood development remains incomplete, both emotional and psychological immaturity carry into adulthood—and scale into patriarchal norms, institutions, and ideologies.*

When people—or entire cultures—remain locked in earlier developmental stages, we see the persistent traits of emotional immaturity: difficulty with self-regulation, fear of emotional states, and manipulative strategies to get needs met. But these traits don't exist in isolation. Over time, when emotional immaturity becomes entrenched, it often solidifies into psychological immaturity—a deeper distortion in how people think, cope, and interpret reality.

Emotional immaturity becomes psychological immaturity when it hardens into worldview.[31]

What begins as poor regulation, magical thinking, or fear of shame can crystallize—if left unchecked—into fixed cognitive distortions, rigid identity structures, and a stubborn resistance to reality itself. This is when immaturity stops being a passing phase and becomes a personality pattern. It is no longer just an emotional reaction—it becomes a psychological architecture.

While emotional immaturity centers on reactions to internal states (like shame, fear, or anger), psychological immaturity governs how we reason—how we interpret those emotions, justify behaviors, and make sense of others and the world. Together, they create an arrested worldview—one that resists accountability, rejects complexity, and externalizes responsibility.

Here's how both forms of immaturity show up in adult behavior and patriarchal systems.

EGOCENTRISM IN ADULTHOOD

→ Power-hungry leaders who believe they are the center of every story and cannot take feedback.

Emotional immaturity: fragile ego.
Psychological immaturity: belief that disagreement equals threat.

ANIMISM IN ADULTHOOD

→ Systems that treat institutions, ideologies, and reputations as more "real" than actual people.

Emotional immaturity: fear of losing identity.
Psychological immaturity: magical thinking and mythic projection.

BLACK-AND-WHITE THINKING

→ Rigid moralism, tribalism, and punitive ideologies.

Emotional immaturity: fear of ambiguity.
Psychological immaturity: distorted logic and inability to hold nuance.

EXTERNALIZED RESPONSIBILITY

→ "She made me do it" or "It's not my fault."

Emotional immaturity: shame avoidance.
Psychological immaturity: projection, denial, and entitlement.

IMPULSIVITY AND LACK OF FORESIGHT

→ Short-term thinking and reactionary leadership.

Emotional immaturity: poor self-regulation.
Psychological immaturity: low capacity for sequencing or long-range thinking.

EMOTIONAL MANIPULATION AND CHARM

→ Adults who use tantrums, guilt, seduction, or silence to control.

Emotional immaturity: need for soothing or dominance.
Psychological immaturity: strategic deflection, deception, or role-play.

Patriarchy, as a system, reflects these traits writ large. It enshrines the preoperational mindset into law, religion, education, and relationships. It is a culture led not by rational adults, but by the psychological equivalents of children who never finished growing up.

And it's not accidental—it's familiar. In emotionally immature systems, both individuals and institutions replicate these dynamics repeatedly because they "work" in the short term. They relieve anxiety, avoid vulnerability, and reinforce hierarchy. But they do so at great cost.

When we understand the stages of normal childhood development, we stop being surprised by the dysfunctions of patriarchal systems and start recognizing them for what they are: arrested development masquerading as tradition.

The next step is to recognize how this immaturity plays out in our logic and reasoning—how childish thinking distorts adult conversations, policies, and identities.

SECTION III: CHILDISH REASONING THE LOGIC THAT KEEPS US SMALL

> *BLUF: Patriarchal systems normalize immature logic patterns—such as animism, projection, circular reasoning, and magical thinking—and reward them as authority, morality, or cosmic order.*

Patriarchy is not simply a structure of power—it is a worldview built on a cognitive style that mirrors the first stages of childhood development.[32] Its logic is not the reflective reasoning of adulthood, but the circular, rigid, impulsive, and magical thinking of a child trying to make sense of a complex world.

The emotional immaturity that permeates patriarchal systems doesn't just shape how people behave—it shapes what entire cultures come to believe is "natural," "moral," or "divinely ordained." Story becomes reality. Tradition becomes doctrine. Law becomes myth in legal form.

One of the earliest—and most consequential—forms of immature thinking carried into adulthood is animism: the tendency to project human-like traits, motives, or moral meaning onto objects or beings.

In childhood, animism is developmentally appropriate. In patriarchy, it becomes a defensive strategy for adult immaturity—a way to invent reality and then enforce it as truth. It becomes a narrative weapon.

Before we explore the other cognitive distortions patriarchy relies on—projection, magical thinking, emotional reasoning, circular logic—we begin with animism because it forms the earliest blueprint for patriarchy's myth making. It is one of the foundational ways patriarchy turns women into objects, objects into symbols, and symbols into destiny.

Symbols can be hijacked—emptied out, reassigned, and refilled with new meaning. A symbol will not protest its new assignment, not even when it is desecrated or used to harm others.

The swastika was once a sacred symbol of blessing—until it was stripped, inverted, and weaponized. Symbols do not defend themselves. But people might.

First you strip a woman of personhood.

Then you animate the shell with whatever traits serve you.

The shell becomes a symbol.

And the symbol becomes the story the culture believes.

Once we see patriarchy through the lens of arrested development, the logic that holds it together becomes obvious.[33] After animism, we will trace the other distortions that build upon it and watch how they fuse into a story about "male" and "female," "masculinity" and "femininity," "leader" and "supporter," "divine order" and "natural law"—a story so old, so repeated, so mythologized, it no longer feels like a story at all.

Animism is where the story begins—but it is not where it ends. Once a culture assigns mythical qualities to women, the rest of the distortions fall into place like a script already written.

SECTION IV: ANIMISM — THE FIRST STORY PATRIARCHY TELLS

> *BLUF: Examines how patriarchal culture uses animism to mythologize, dehumanize, and control women, nature, and institutions by projecting fantasy traits onto them.*

Animism—the tendency to attribute human-like qualities, emotions, or intentions to non-human entities—is a normal phase of childhood development. A child speaks to a teddy bear as if it understands, gets angry at a "mean" chair that bumped them, scolds a doll for being "bad," or imagines the moon is following them home. In early life, this reflects imagination, not delusion. It is one of the ways the psyche learns to make meaning in a world too big and too complex to grasp directly.

In childhood, animism serves multiple developmental functions:

* **Sense-making & predictability** – attributing intention ("the wind is bitter") helps the world feel coherent rather than random.

* **Relation & companionship** – dolls and stuffed animals function as *transitional objects* (Winnicott): safe stand-ins for connection when caregivers are absent. Imagining that the night-light "protects me" helps the child feel less powerless in a world full of unknowns.

* **Emotional regulation & projection** – a child can "give" anger, sorrow, or fear to a toy, making intense emotions external and manageable rather than overwhelming.

* **Practice in empathy & morality** – animating a doll or bear gives the child a way to rehearse care, apology, fairness, turn-taking, and repair.

* **Agency & mastery** – arranging dolls into stories, fighting imaginary foes, or making an action figure perform impossible feats gives the child a sense of control and competence.

❖ **Story & language development** – animism strengthens symbolic thinking, narrative structure, and early meaning-making.

In other words: animism is not a flaw. It is a bridge. A child uses it to meet the world halfway—to feel accompanied, to experiment with emotion safely, to learn what it means to be in relationship. But when animism persists into adulthood—especially when institutionalized into religion, law, media, or cultural myth—it stops being a relational bridge and becomes its opposite: a domination script.

Children animate objects to be *in* relationship.

Patriarchy animates women to *avoid* relationship.

Where the child animates to connect, patriarchy animates to control.

1. *The Personification of Nature as Feminine (and Its Subjugation)*

HOW IT SHOWS UP:

Nature is often feminized ("Mother Earth," "She is fertile and giving") yet treated as something to be conquered, controlled, and exploited.

Patriarchal ideologies romanticize nature as nurturing but simultaneously justify its domination.[34]

EXAMPLES:

"The land must be tamed and made productive."

"Mother Nature is abundant and terrible."

WHY IT MATTERS:

This animistic framing supports a hierarchical mindset where "rational" (masculine) forces are meant to control the "irrational" (feminine/natural).

2. Sacred Masculine and Feminine Archetypes (Gendered Animism in Religion & Mythology)

HOW IT SHOWS UP:

Many patriarchal religious and mythological systems animate gendered cosmic forces: masculinity = order, logic, dominance; femininity = chaos, submission, nature.

Male gods rule and create, while female deities are emotional, nurturing, or punished.

EXAMPLES:

"The Sky God rules over the Earth Goddess."
"Eve caused the fall."

WHY IT MATTERS:

These animistic projections reinforce patriarchal dominance as natural and divinely sanctioned.[35]

3. Animating Institutions to Reinforce Control

HOW IT SHOWS UP:

Institutions like marriage, family, and religion are treated as living entities with moral authority.

People are expected to sacrifice their well-being to protect these "entities."

EXAMPLES:

"Marriage is sacred, and divorce damages it."
"The family name must be protected."

WHY IT MATTERS:

This protects systems from critique while silencing the people inside them.

4. *Demonizing Women Through Animistic Metaphors*

HOW IT SHOWS UP:

Women are animalized or demonized in ways that justify their control, punishment, or fear.

EXAMPLES:

"She's a witch, a siren, a temptress."
"She's a snake, a viper, a black widow."

WHY IT MATTERS:

These portrayals reduce women to projections of threat, stripping them of personhood.[36]

5. *Infantilizing Women Through Doll-Like Animism*

HOW IT SHOWS UP:

Women are framed as fragile, beautiful, obedient, and in need of male protection.

EXAMPLES:

"She's a delicate flower."
"She's my little angel."

WHY IT MATTERS:

This denies women adult agency and reinforces emotional immaturity in gender roles.[37]

6. *Patriarchal Language as Animism*

HOW IT SHOWS UP:

Abstract values like "honor," "purity," and "tradition" are treated as sentient beings we must obey.

EXAMPLES:

"You've disgraced the family honor."
"Real men are alpha males (like wolves)."
"Feminism is destroying the natural order."

WHY IT MATTERS:

These ideas are used to guilt, shame, or punish deviation from patriarchal roles.[38]

WHY NAMING ANIMISM MATTERS

When a culture animates women into something more than human—or more often, something less than human—it creates a narrative that then justifies the behavior that follows. Animism becomes both the story *and* the logic for the story—a circular loop that protects itself from scrutiny. When women are framed as storms, angels, witches, dolls, or temptresses, they are no longer seen as full human beings. They become characters in someone else's ego-centric script, in the same way a teddy bear becomes a projection screen for the child who owns it.

Because this strategy is often subtle, romanticized, or mythologized, it is easy to mistake it for truth—and just as easy to dismiss it as "only a story" when questioned. That plausible deniability is part of its power. Animism, left unnamed, becomes a cognitive distortion that feels natural, harmless, even poetic.

But animism is only the beginning. It is one of several cognitive distortions—alongside projection, magical thinking, circular reasoning, and emotional reasoning—that together form the childish worldview of patriarchy. In the next section, we will trace these distortions one by one to show how they harden into a fixed story about who men are, who women are, and what each is "for."

SECTION V: BEYOND ANIMISM — OTHER COGNITIVE DISTORTIONS IN PATRIARCHAL THINKING

> *BLUF: Outlines a full set of immature cognitive patterns used in patriarchal logic, including magical thinking, projection, circular reasoning, and emotional reasoning.*

Patriarchal logic often mirrors the reasoning of young children: emotionally reactive, self-centered, contradictory, and illogical. Below are key distortions commonly seen in patriarchal systems.

1. *Magical Thinking*

"If I say it's true, it must be true."

Magical thinking in childhood includes ideas like believing one can fly if they wear a cape or that thinking about something hard enough makes it real. In patriarchy, this distortion shows up as the belief that declaring something makes it true.

EXAMPLES:

"Women are naturally nurturing, so they should stay home."
"Men are the protectors by design."
"Patriarchy isn't real because I don't see it."
"If I repeat this lie often enough, it becomes truth."
"I create my own reality" becomes: *"If I pretend hard enough, consequences disappear."*

WHY IT MATTERS:

This distortion avoids accountability and reality testing.[39] It treats declarations as facts, collapsing the distinction between belief and evidence.

2. Circular Reasoning (Because I Said So)

"I'm right because I'm the authority, and I'm the authority because I'm right."

This reasoning is familiar to any parent of a toddler—but patriarchy codifies it. It declares men the ultimate authorities and justifies this by referencing male-authored systems, including the concept of a male God.

EXAMPLES:

"Men are meant to lead—just look at history." (Written by men.)

"God said so." (God is defined, by men, as male.)

"The Bible says women should submit." (Interpreted and enforced by patriarchal tradition.)

WHY IT MATTERS:

This logic traps people in self-referential systems that refuse evidence or alternate views. It's a hall of mirrors built for ego.[40]

3. Projection: "She Made Me Do It"

"I did a bad thing, but it's your fault."

Projection is when children—and immature adults—displace their own feelings or behaviors onto others. In patriarchy, this means women are blamed for the harm done to them or accused of having beliefs and behaviors that belong to others.

EXAMPLES:

"She dressed that way—what did she expect?"

"If she had respected him, he wouldn't have gotten violent."

"Feminists just want to dominate men." (when in fact patriarchy is the one doing the dominating)

WHY IT MATTERS:

Projection keeps perpetrators feeling innocent while their victims carry the shame.[41]

4. Emotional Reasoning: "If I Feel It, It Must Be True"

"If I feel criticized, you're attacking me."

This distortion assumes that feelings are facts, a hallmark of early childhood.

EXAMPLES:

"You made me feel bad, so you're being abusive."

"If I'm angry, it means you did something wrong."

"You're questioning my behavior, so you're attacking me."

WHY IT MATTERS:

Emotional reasoning blocks growth because emotional discomfort is treated as evidence of injustice.

5. I Want It, So I Should Have It

"My desire is justification enough."

This mindset views all wants as valid claims—common in toddlers but corrosive in adult power systems.

EXAMPLES:

"I want her, so I get her."

"If I feel attracted to you, you owe me attention."

"If I want control, I deserve control."

WHY IT MATTERS:

Patriarchy often disguises entitlement as tradition or natural order.[42]

6. Motivated Misinterpretation

"I'll twist what you said to mean what I need it to mean."

Patriarchal thinking often reinterprets others' motives to fit its narrative.

EXAMPLES:

"Feminism is just man-hating."

"You're only angry because you're emotional."

"You said no, but you didn't mean it."

WHY IT MATTERS:

This tactic invalidates others' voices and uses misrepresentation as a form of control.[43]

7. I Should Always Win

"If I'm not winning, the rules must be wrong."

Children often insist on winning and change the rules when they don't. Patriarchy institutionalizes this tendency.

EXAMPLES:

Double standards: "I get to interrupt; you're being rude." "I get to be angry, but if you get angry, you're being hysterical."

Moving the goalposts: "Now that women are in the workforce, they need to be perfect mothers too."

Punishing competence: "If a woman excels, she must be cheating or arrogant."

Any loss is an injustice.

WHY IT MATTERS:

Fairness becomes impossible when one side is always allowed to redefine it.

8. Legalism and Literalism: The Letter vs. the Spirit

"I followed the rule, so you can't be mad—even if I harmed you."

This kind of thinking obsesses over technicalities to avoid responsibility.

EXAMPLES:

"It wasn't illegal, so I didn't do anything wrong."

"I never said exactly that."

"There's no law against being a jerk."

WHY IT MATTERS:

This mindset avoids moral development by hiding behind surface compliance.

9. Contradiction Without Awareness

"I get to believe two things at once—even if they cancel each other out."

Patriarchy often holds two opposing beliefs at the same time—and punishes others for noticing. This isn't simple hypocrisy. It's a power move. When rules contradict, those in power can always win by shifting the goalposts.

EXAMPLES:

"Women are deemed too emotional to lead in public—but in private, they're expected to serve as the family executive, managing the emotional, logistical, and relational lives of everyone around them."

"We honor motherhood—but oppose paid leave, childcare, and support for this role."

"She's incompetent and fragile—but somehow still a threat to male power."

WHY IT MATTERS:

Contradiction creates confusion. Confusion creates compliance. When truth can shift on command, clarity becomes rebellion.[44]

10. Appeal to (Male) Authority

"If a man said it, it must be true."

EXAMPLES

The assumption that truth = masculinity = superiority.

Authority figures (especially men) are not to be questioned, regardless of evidence.

The belief that male perspectives are objective and universal, while women's perspectives are subjective and merely personal.

WHY IT MATTERS:

This distortion invalidates women's voices by design.[45] It cements male perspectives as the default lens of truth, morality, and logic—rendering women's insights, wisdom, and lived experiences irrelevant, emotional, or unreliable. It trains entire societies to doubt women automatically and rely on male interpretation, even when the facts contradict it.

HISTORICAL AND RELIGIOUS EXAMPLES:

In many legal systems, women's testimonies were considered half the value of a man's, or excluded entirely (e.g., Islamic jurisprudence, early Roman law).

Eve's role in Christian theology became a justification for centuries of male authority in churches and families: she was according to mythology "first to sin," therefore women were deemed more gullible and in need of control.

In ancient Greece, Aristotle declared that women were "deformed males," biologically and intellectually inferior—an idea that shaped Western thought for centuries.

Even in modern settings, women experts are interrupted, dismissed, or have their ideas overlooked until repeated by a man.

PATTERN:

This isn't just about individual bias—it's a systemic mechanism that delegitimizes female authority at every level, from scholarship and science to politics, art, and religion.

These fallacies mirror a child's reasoning style: relying on authority figures and repetition rather than evidence or reflection. Patriarchy disguises its immaturity in rituals, roles, and divine language—but underneath the costume is a fearful, reactive mindset desperate to control what it cannot understand.

SECTION VI: GENDER ESSENTIALISM — PATRIARCHY'S FAIRY-TALE BIOLOGY

> *BLUF: Gender essentialism is childhood logic frozen into culture—an invented story about male and female "essence" treated as scientific fact, divine order, and destiny.*

Gender essentialism claims that men and women have immutable, inner "natures" that dictate who they are and what they're for.[45]

In patriarchy, the masculine ideal is imagined as strong, certain, leader-like, stoic, courageous, powerful, knowledgeable, dominant, disciplined, objective, unemotional, straightforward, protective, providing, intimidating, self-assured, and unconcerned with others' opinions.

The feminine is imagined as small, soft, delicate, beautiful, pure, tempting, self-sacrificing, accommodating, nurturing, kind, cautious, moody, needy, yielding, naïve, emotional, pleasing, manipulative, passive, jealous, weak-willed, vain, materialistic, irrational, and two-faced.

The masculine is written as personhood with agency.

The feminine is written as personality without agency.

One is a subject. The other is a prop.

In patriarchy's fairy-tale biology, these gender traits are decreed as divine design—unquestionable, unchangeable, scientific fact and fate.

But in reality, gender essentialism is a mishmash of immature thinking formed into a story that provides simplistic understanding for a culture of arrested development.

HOW CHILDISH LOGIC HARDENS INTO 'SCIENCE' AND 'NATURE'

Essentialism is the product of many distortions acting together:

- **Animism:** Treats "man" and "woman" as enchanted containers with built-in traits; projects fantasy and shadow qualities onto whole groups of individuals and then declares that projection "reality." Declares one group natural leaders and another natural followers.

- **Egocentrism (Main-Character Logic):** Assumes the male perspective is universal and primary; women exist to relate to and support the protagonist.

  - **Entitlement / "I want it, so I should have it":** Desire presented as right.

  - **I Should Always Win / No Turn-Taking:** Creates a heads-I-win, tails-you-lose game.

- **Magical Thinking:** "If we declare it 'natural,' it becomes true." Repetition replaces evidence and collective belief becomes proof. This isn't a single person's delusion—it's a group spell sustained by repetition.

- **Circular Reasoning:** "Men lead because leadership is male." The claim proves the claim.

- **Projection:** Attributes traits assigned to the masculine as "superior", while assigning "inferior" and/or unwanted traits to the feminine.

- **Emotional Reasoning:** "If it feels true, it must be true." Facts that contradict gender essentialism's narrative—for example, evidence of women's strength or men's indecision—must be discarded in favor of what *feels* true.

- ❖ **Polarized / Binary Thinking:** Either-or categories (leader/supporter, rational/emotional) erase spectrum and nuance.

- ❖ **Rule Absolutism:** "That's just how it is." Convention masquerades as morality.

- ❖ **Motivated Misinterpretation:** Twists facts to fit the desired script ("Women are fickle—they don't really know what they want"). "My story is *the* story."

- ❖ **Contradiction Without Awareness:** Slides in and out of the script as convenient ("All men want one thing" / "Not all men"). Everything masculine is positive—until men behave badly and then gender essentialism shrugs: "Boys will be boys."

Once the story hardens into gender essentialism, patriarchy no longer needs force to maintain itself—it only needs belief.

WHY THIS MATTERS

1 - The Moral Dimension

After the pre-operational stage of childhood (ages ~2–7) comes the "age of reason," when children begin developing conscience, perspective, and empathy.

When earlier stages are not outgrown but concretized into gender essentialism, moral development stalls.

The failure to relate to others as equal in humanity becomes moral immaturity—the inability to grant women the same fairness, agency, and autonomy men want for themselves.

When maturity isn't merely neglected but refused, immaturity devolves into moral corruption, and—at its worst—moral depravity: the willingness to harm others with indifference because they've been reduced to objects, slaves, and/or entertainment.

*2 - **The Practical Dimension***

Gender essentialism is a stew built on egocentrism that permanently centers one half of humanity and permanently demotes the other. It animates "masculine" and "feminine" traits, declares them divine decree, and translates that decree into assigned roles in patriarchy's script. And those assigned roles come with a job description.

THE MAIN-CHARACTER ASSIGNMENT

In patriarchy's gender essentialist world, men are the protagonists—agents, deciders, inheritors. Women are the supporting cast—nurturers, reflectors, rewards, threats, servants, and scapegoats to carry moral responsibility.

Women must relate to the main character to serve, soothe, and sustain his story—expected to perform the role and carry out the duties with a smile. Because the feminine role is not only to serve but to perform pleasure in serving and to act out "the natural order" so that it looks real.

Of course, gender essentialism traps men in an acting role too. It shrinks their full humanity, confining personhood to a narrow script of invulnerability, dominance, and suppression of care. A one-dimensional character that limits their range of individuality too. Yet because that script centers and advantages them, it is less often questioned—even as it costs intimacy, nuance, and freedom.

Gender essentialism gives men the illusion of individuation and independence while assigning women a life of care, service, and self-erasure.

Essentialism doesn't discover truth—it manufactures it.

It starts with a belief ("men are, women are" and "men lead, women follow"), forces people into matching roles, and then points to those roles as proof that the belief was true all along. That isn't science. It's a loop—enforced by ritual, repetition, and threat.

In practice, it turns social roles into destiny and preference into law.

In the next chapter, *Patriarchy's Entitled Dependency*, we'll trace what happens when the work of developing independence and interdependence—learning to meet one's needs responsibly—is outsourced according to gender.

When one half of humanity is trained to be served and the other half to serve, dependency ceases to look like immaturity. It begins to look like order.

5

Patriarchy's Entitled Dependency

BLUF: THIS CHAPTER EXPLORES HOW PATRIARCHY INTERRUPTS THE NATURAL ARC OF HUMAN MATURITY— OUTSOURCING RESPONSIBILITY, DISTORTING INTERDEPENDENCE INTO DEPENDENCY, AND REWARDING THE ILLUSION OF INDEPENDENCE SUSTAINED BY OTHERS' INVISIBLE LABOR.

SECTION I: THE MATURITY ARC

> *BLUF: Healthy adulthood is a widening arc—from self-care to stewardship—across multiple domains of life; when any part of this maturity is off-loaded onto others, dependency is disguised as strength and the entire system starts to hollow out.*

Maturity is not a single trait but a network of capacities that unfold together. Each domain strengthens the others and rests on a foundation of core competencies; when any foundational competencies are underdeveloped, the whole system wobbles. These eight domains map the terrain of full human maturity—the capacities needed to care for self, others, and the world.

Each domain is a dimension of life in which we evolve from dependence → self-care → contribution → stewardship. Together, they form a full-spectrum picture of human development.

THE DOMAINS OF THE MATURITY ARC

1. Physical Maturity—Survival and Sustenance

Core focus: Keeping oneself (and later others) physically alive and safe.

Early dependency: Caregivers feed, clothe, shelter, and protect.

Developing capacity: Learning hygiene, nutrition, cooking, health care, home maintenance, financial stability.

Mature expression: Providing stability and safety for others; creating systems of care that sustain life.

Patriarchal distortion: Delegating physical labor and logistics to others; equating provision with dominance.

2. Emotional Maturity—Regulation and Relational Presence

Core focus: Recognizing, expressing, and regulating emotions responsibly.

Early dependency: Caregivers soothe and name emotions.

Developing capacity: Self-soothing, empathy, emotional language, frustration tolerance.

Mature expression: Emotional honesty, attunement to others without self-erasure, repair of harm.

Patriarchal distortion: Expecting others to regulate one's emotions; expecting others to repair what we broke, emotional outsourcing disguised as strength.

3. Psychological Maturity—Self-Knowledge and Integration

Core focus: Developing identity, reflection, and inner coherence.

Early dependency: External validation shapes early self-concept.

Developing capacity: Self-reflection, discernment, adaptability, executive functioning, reality testing.

Mature expression: Self-leadership, accountability, synthesis, wisdom.

Patriarchal distortion: Egocentrism, projection, circular logic, blame; refusal of introspection, intellectualization without empathy.

4. Moral Maturity—Responsibility and Reciprocity

Core focus: Expanding one's circle of ethical concern, assuming responsibility for harm

Early dependency: Rule-following out of fear or reward.

Developing capacity: Understanding fairness, justice, consequence.

Mature expression: Acting from internalized principles; standing for the common good.

Patriarchal distortion: Self-serving morality, rebellion without responsibility; authoritarianism disguised as order.

5. Relational Maturity—Companionship and Collaboration

Core focus: Building reciprocal relationships and communities.

Early dependency: Caregivers meet all social needs.

Developing capacity: Friendship, cooperation, shared goals, conflict resolution.

Mature expression: Interdependence—balancing individuality and belonging.

Patriarchal distortion: Using others as extensions of the self; confusing dominance, caretaking, or compliance with love.

This is where friendships, marriage, kinship, and community belong—not as survival mechanisms, but as the evolutionary flowering of connection itself: to love, to be known, to build together.

6. Creative / Meaning-Making Maturity—Imagination and Symbolic Life

Core focus: Bringing beauty, ritual, and coherence to existence.

Early dependency: Absorbing family rituals, myths, and culture.

Developing capacity: Storytelling, symbolic thinking, aesthetic sense, humor, play.

Mature expression: Creating and sustaining rituals, traditions, art, and holidays—the "magic and sparkle" that weave memory and belonging. Sometimes called cultural maturity or symbolic stewardship.

Patriarchal distortion: Cynicism, reductionism, or trivialization of meaning; outsourcing creativity and ritual to commercial culture.

7. Spiritual Maturity—Perspective and Transcendence

Core focus: Awareness of interconnectedness and purpose beyond ego.

Early dependency: Adopted beliefs, magical thinking, borrowed authority.

Developing capacity: Questioning inherited meaning systems, experiencing wonder, developing personal ethics.

Mature expression: Humility, reverence, service, seeing the sacred in ordinary life.

Patriarchal distortion: Dogmatism, spiritual narcissism, or complete detachment from meaning.

8. Ecological / Planetary Maturity—Stewardship of the Whole

Core focus: Recognizing interdependence with the natural world.

Early dependency: Adults manage the physical environment, leaving children free from awareness of managing overwhelming limits.

Developing capacity: Gratitude, conservation, respect for limits.

Mature expression: Stewardship of earth and systems that sustain all life.

Patriarchal distortion: Extractivism; treating the planet, Nature, and women (as a subset of Nature) as a warehouse of gratification.

Each of these domains mature through feedback, challenge, and responsibility. Together they describe what adulthood is meant to become: not merely the mastery of one's own life, but the capacity to sustain life itself. When any domain arrests—when physical labor, emotional regulation, or moral accountability are off-loaded onto others—dependency is disguised as dominance, and the system begins to hollow from within.

Having mapped what comprehensive maturity looks like, we can now trace how it normally develops—and where patriarchy interrupts that trajectory.

THE MATURITY ARC IN MOTION—HOW AGENCY DEVELOPS

Human development is not a straight line but a widening arc of agency. From learning to tie a shoe to learning to care for others, each stage expands both capacity and conscience. Every new skill asks the same quiet question in a larger arena: *Can I be trusted with more?* The following stages trace that movement—from dependence to stewardship, from needing care to becoming a source of it.[46]

Stage 1: Self-Care and Immediate Agency

Maturity begins with the smallest acts of self-management: tying a shoe, brushing teeth, cooperating with regular sleep routines.

In these early experiments with autonomy, a child learns to plan, sequence, and correct—discovering that effort brings order and order brings comfort.

The emotional reward is immediate: *I did it myself.* Each success links intention with outcome, planting the first seed of organized action. These lessons in self-care are also lessons in dignity—where self-maintenance becomes self-respect.

Stage 2: Contribution to the Family System

As a child grows, agency extends outward. Chores and small routines—feeding a pet, setting the table, putting toys away—introduce the principle of reciprocity.

Behavior must now align with the rhythm of others.

The child experiences belonging through usefulness: *my work matters to the group.*

Here the concept of responsibility begins to root, teaching that shared environments require shared upkeep.

Stage 3: Complex Tasks and Anticipation

With new skills come larger responsibilities: planning a meal, managing an allowance, babysitting a sibling occasionally.

These tasks call for foresight, prioritization, and evaluation—capacities that stretch both attention and empathy.

The emotional reward shifts from praise to internal satisfaction: *I can handle complexity; others trust me.*

Agency now matures into reliability, and confidence becomes character.

Stage 4: Caring Without Direct Reward

At the next level, maturity deepens through non-transactional care—acts offered without immediate return.

Community service, mentoring, or tending an elder teach patience, empathy, and sustained effort for someone else's welfare.

This is where responsibility turns ethical when the work itself becomes meaningful. The reward is no longer applause but the quiet integrity of contribution.

Here agency expands from self-maintenance to stewardship in development—the capacity to act for the sake of something beyond the self.

Stage 5: Stewardship Integrated Adulthood

At full expression, the arc of agency becomes the architecture of adulthood.

We balance personal goals with care for family, community, and planet—evaluating, revising, and improvising across life's domains. Here, executive function becomes character and agency becomes stewardship: the ability to self-govern in alignment with values rather than rewards.

The emotional reward is coherence—the deep satisfaction of living as someone dependable, trustworthy, and whole.

In healthy individual development, maturity widens in concentric circles: self-care becomes shared care, and shared care ripens into stewardship. When this process is interrupted—or rewarded only in self-serving forms—agency narrows into entitlement and the development of maturity halts.

In healthy cultural development, those same stages of growth build upon one another, broadening capacity, accountability, and care across the collective. Patriarchy interrupts the arc midway and builds dysfunction into the system itself. It rewards early independence for boys in the public sphere, and early over-responsibility for girls in the private/emotional sphere, while discouraging the later work of interdependence and stewardship between these realms.

Patriarchy trains the self to act but not to reflect—to acquire but not to sustain. The result is a partial adulthood: for men, one that performs maturity in the arenas of visibility and reward while quietly outsourcing the labor of responsibility to others; and for women, one that performs labor and responsibility while that visibility and reward are outsourced away from them. The economy of this design ensures that the most essential labor—the sustaining, organizing, thankless work of life—stays invisible and unrewarded.

In such a system, agency narrows into entitlement, and the work of becoming whole is left unfinished.

SECTION II: WHERE PATRIARCHY BREAKS THE ARC

> *BLUF: Patriarchy freezes development midway: it cultivates men's competence only where it yields status, offloads the rest of adulthood's labor onto others, and turns the private sphere into a sanctuary for male immaturity propped up by invisible executive functioning.*

THE POINT OF RUPTURE

In healthy development, agency expands outward. The child's proud *"Look what I can do!"* widens from skills that serve the self to abilities that sustain others. Initiative ripens into self-leadership, then into collaboration—creating what can't be achieved alone—and finally into stewardship, where agency is guided by care.

Each stage builds on the last, teaching the individual to link effort with consequence and responsibility with freedom.

Patriarchy halts this sequence midway, especially for its main character. It valorizes early independence—the pride of *"I can do it myself"*—and freezes development there. The self-referential satisfaction that should propel further growth stalls in a culture that mistakes ego for evolution. The remaining developmental labor—emotional, moral, relational, and physical—is assigned to others.

This is the developmental rupture on which patriarchy is built: ego without apprenticeship, power without responsibility, agency without limits, leadership without stewardship, and image without substance.

Patriarchy raises men inside an ego-centric incentive field: develop competence where it benefits *me*—pay, status, image, admiration, access, or sexual reward—and externalize or ignore the work that sustains others unless it burnishes *my* image. The result is a reward-driven compartmentalization of maturity. Responsibility narrows into performance. Growth stops at the mirror.

THE PRIVATE SPHERE AS SANCTUARY FOR IMMATURITY

Patriarchy doesn't only stunt development—it divides it.

Men are trained to perform competence in public and to enjoy incompetence in private. They learn mastery in visible arenas that provide rewards and cultivate inconsistency and avoidance in invisible ones. In public, they show initiative, foresight, and problem-solving. At home, they often perform confusion, helplessness, or fatigue—behaviors that would never be tolerated in their workplaces.

The same man who manages budgets, teams, or battlefields may claim he "doesn't know where anything is" in his own kitchen. He may need to be repeatedly told what to do, how to do it, and when—and then expect praise for token participation. Behaviors he would discipline or fire an employee for are reframed as endearing in himself. This selective incapacity is not neurological; it is cultural. It preserves comfort and superiority while offloading the invisible labor of daily life onto others.

The pattern extends far beyond chores.

Many men expect unconditional positive regard: affection that ignores mistreatment, admiration that ignores incompetence, and respect as household leaders despite limited participation or understanding of domestic life. Patriarchy trains men to expect *childcare for the adult self*—for someone else to anticipate their needs, regulate their moods, repair their relationships, and nurture their self-esteem.

"Dad's in a bad mood" becomes an atmospheric command: everyone else must self-regulate so he doesn't have to.

He is conditioned to seek intimacy without relating, comfort without accountability, and rest without reciprocity. The home becomes the nursery of the public man—the place where the exhaustion of adulthood is left at the front door, and where dependence is reframed as deservingness.

This regression is rewarded because it ensures that women's energy focuses on sustaining male comfort and status. Thus, the maturity arc is not merely interrupted—it is divided at the threshold of the home.

But someone must do the work that is refused. Once the arc breaks, responsibility doesn't vanish—it migrates.

THE THANKLESS WORK PARADOX

Most of what keeps humans alive and societies humane is rhythmic, ordinary, and unrewarded: cooking, cleaning, laundry, scheduling appointments, checking homework, nurturing friendships, pregnancy and birth, elder care, kin-keeping, and the orchestration of rituals and holiday traditions that lend life richness and continuity. These labors are not optional. They are the scaffolding of civilization.

They are also the force multipliers that make men's public performance possible—even when women also work in the paid labor force. Behind the scenes, she sustains the systems that allow him to go to work unburdened, and to come home unburdened again by pretending that this invisible labor is simple, natural, and beneath his attention.

By coding care and domestic order as low-status and effortless, patriarchy can dismiss, discount, and discredit them.

He may deign to do this work, but only when it gains temporary favor or visible reward.

This forms a visibility–reward loop:

1. Work that is visible and individually rewarded (boardroom, battlefield, paycheck, podium) attracts male effort investment.

2. Work that is invisible and collectively beneficial (home, care, relational repair) is assigned to women and declared "natural."

3. Because women carry it, men need not develop competence in those domains; because men don't develop it, the work is further devalued.

4. The loop protects egocentrism while masking dependency on others' constant executive labor.

A society cannot function on ego alone—or even on a paycheck alone.

Men's single-minded focus only "works" because women typically supply the unpaid operating system of life: logistical executive function (calendars, sequencing, priorities), relational regulation (attunement, repair), care (meals, meds, forms), safety (anticipatory scanning), teaching (manners, goals, development), and ritual (family culture, holiday "magic").

Patriarchy, unable to admit this reliance, makes the labor invisible—and discounts the laborers.

EXECUTIVE FUNCTION: THE ADULT OPERATING SYSTEM

The executive function that women perform so seamlessly it looks effortless is the brain's architecture for planning, logic, and adaptive self-governance. It translates intention into coordinated, sustained action: initiating, expecting outcomes, revising plans, integrating others' needs, and adjusting to feedback for the sake of collective well-being.

In healthy development, executive function matures through responsibility that widens from self to others to the world. It grows through frustration tolerance, feedback, reality testing, and the discipline of thankless work—the kind that makes life sustainable.

Patriarchy interrupts this process and channels men's higher functioning into the narrow domains that yield visible reward. Planning, foresight, and revision mature only where they advance the self; the rest—caregiving, maintenance, meaning-making—is outsourced and made invisible.

This is why many men can show high-functioning logic and people skills in the workplace and in leadership positions yet claim confusion in domestic and relational life. The same people who expect standard operating procedures, attention to detail, and accountability at work dismiss similar order at home as controlling or excessive. The refusal to master the systems that sustain life is not incompetence—it is ideology.

Their executive function was never trained through non-transactional responsibility—the work done for love, fairness, necessity, or those dependent upon them.

If there's no external reward, why do it?

Defining domestic and relational labor as low status—and therefore beneath the main character's effort—is part of patriarchy's self-interested orientation. It sustains the illusion that in serving himself, he serves everyone else—patriarchy's own trickle-down economy, where men keep the power and women are expected to be grateful for the drops of runoff.

The result is a developmental asymmetry: men perfect executive function in arenas that feed ego and status, while women carry it in the arenas that sustain existence.

Executive function grows through responsibility; responsibility expands through empathy; empathy deepens through unseen work.

Patriarchy interrupts that sequence by making unseen work someone else's job.

WHY THIS MATTERS

Patriarchy grants adult power to those who cultivate public competence in narrow, reward-linked domains while neglecting the wider spectrum of life.

It protects only what it knows: transactionalism, impulsivity, extraction, externalized blame, and short-term gratification.

It devalues what it refuses to learn: the quiet disciplines that sustain continuity, care, and community.

It forces others to compensate for its immaturity and then defines that compensation as "love."

Its leadership is crisis-driven instead of planned, entitled instead of responsible, extractive instead of reciprocal, repetitive instead of adaptive, reactive instead of reflective, obsessed with control instead of wisdom.

Entitled dependency is not an accident of patriarchy; it is its engine.

SECTION III: AVOIDING THE ANXIETY OF INDEPENDENCE — UNDER FUNCTIONING AND SUBSTITUTE STRATEGIES

> *BLUF: Because true independence is anxiety-provoking, many people under function instead—avoiding responsibility and using collapse, charm, blame, or coercion to extract care—patterns that, when normalized at scale, become patriarchy's operating system.*

Modern man still flees from freedom. He escapes from the burden of decision, from the weight of responsibility, from the anxiety of choice.
—Erich Fromm, a summary of his work *Escape from Freedom*[47]

THE INNER RECOIL

Freedom feels exhilarating—until it asks something of us. To step into independence is to accept accountability for the outcomes of our choices. Fromm called this the central tension of modern life: we long for autonomy but fear its weight. True freedom means there is no one else to blame, no parent to rescue us, no authority to hide behind. It demands self-governance, foresight, and courage in the face of uncertainty.

Patriarchy transforms this existential tension into a cultural design. It sells freedom as fantasy: not responsibility, but permission. For men, the promise is a life without constraint—the child's dream of doing whatever one wants, whenever one wants. For women, the promise is security: you will never be alone if you provide endless care. The "balance" between these roles looks like equality but functions as avoidance. Each gender is offered protection from growth—one from accountability, the other from autonomy.

The trade, however, is not equal. Patriarchal conditioning rewards men for staying unchanged while forcing women to adapt. Men are praised for and brag about their consistency—*"I'm the same man I've always been"*—while women's natural evolution through relationship, pregnancy, caregiving, and self-reflection is labeled instability or immaturity. Her body changes; his does not. Her responsibilities multiply; his may not shift at all. Even in households where both partners work, she is expected to stretch into new capacities while he is celebrated for staying the same.

In patriarchy's trickle-down economy, she must grow to sustain his illusion of mastery. Her development—emotional, psychological, logistical—becomes the scaffolding beneath his comfort. He can appear larger precisely because she is carrying the unseen weight of adaptation and a more abundant life.

WHEN MATURITY IS REFUSED

All growth involves friction: two steps forward, one step back. Temporary regressions are normal. Refusal, however, is different. It's a pattern of underfunctioning—a flatline in development where the energy of growth is redirected into resistance. Instead of learning from consequence, the immature person externalizes it. Someone else is blamed, someone else is expected to fix it, someone else is enlisted to carry the load.

Under functioning is not always loud. It often masquerades as confusion, exhaustion, or charm. Its aim is simple: to remain comfortable while others do the work of maturity.

When a person chronically refuses to assume adult responsibility, it looks like:

PATTERNS OF AVOIDANCE

- Minimal or token effort
- Procrastination or lateness
- Pretending ignorance or incompetence
- Helplessness and collapse
- Avoidance of problem-solving or follow-through
- Unresponsiveness

PATTERNS OF DEFLECTION

- Blaming others for one's failures
- Playing the victim of one's own consequences
- Focusing on others' reactions to unfairness or mistreatment rather than on the unfairness and mistreatment itself.
- Seeing feedback as punishment rather than guidance
- Rewriting the past in nostalgic terms
- "Future-faking"—grand plans that replace real progress

DISTORTIONS OF EFFORT

- ❖ Exaggerating minor contributions while minimizing others' work
- ❖ Devaluing maintenance or care as "easy" or "unimportant"
- ❖ Wanting to have it both ways—claiming authority but rejecting accountability
- ❖ Treating responsibility as optional and gratitude as owed

EMOTIONAL REGRESSION

- ❖ Volatility, sulking, or self-pity when challenged
- ❖ Entitlement to comfort at others' expense
- ❖ Disordered sense of time and consequence: every discomfort feels like injustice

When accountability feels like danger, immaturity disguises avoidance as confusion or hostile defensiveness. The person who "doesn't know how" or "forgets" repeatedly is not lacking capacity—they are avoiding exposure to the anxiety of independence.

CARE STRATEGIES – HOW WE GET OUR NEEDS MET WHEN WE REFUSE MATURITY

Refusing to grow doesn't erase our needs—it simply ensures that someone else must meet them. Immature dependency is less about helplessness than about *strategy*: finding ways to elicit care without directly asking, demanding it outright, or showing care for others.

A mature person can articulate a need and tolerate a no. An immature person must secure yes without risking rejection. The result is a repertoire of tactics designed to extract care, validation, or labor from others without ever appearing to depend.

PASSIVE STRATEGIES

- ❖ Whining, complaining, sighing, hinting, or grunting instead of speaking directly
- ❖ Procrastination, forgetfulness, or lateness as cues for rescue
- ❖ Collapse or exaggerated fatigue to elicit sympathy
- ❖ Playing helpless or confused to provoke instruction or intervention

COVERT STRATEGIES

- ❖ Charm, flattery, or token effort exchanged for praise
- ❖ Manipulation through guilt or emotional pressure
- ❖ "Accidental" mistakes that compel others to fix the fallout
- ❖ Pretending not to hear or understand when responsibility is named

AGGRESSIVE STRATEGIES

- ❖ Defiance, intimidation, or coercion
- ❖ Emotional volatility or threats of withdrawal
- ❖ Blame, ridicule, or verbal assault when challenged
- ❖ Controlling through dominance rather than cooperation

REGRESSIVE STRATEGIES

- ❖ Sabotaging others so they feel they owe repair
- ❖ Using self-pity or despair to re-center attention
- ❖ Demanding unconditional positive regard while giving little in return

Collapse is particularly deceptive. It appears as vulnerability but functions as control. The person who falls apart at the smallest challenge recruits caretakers who step in to stabilize the environment. Over time, collapse becomes a care-eliciting behavior—a way to ensure someone else carries the anxiety of freedom.

None of these patterns are moral failings. They are adaptive responses to the terror of self-governance. Each one substitutes emotional leverage for self-leadership, extracting from others what maturity would otherwise provide from within.

THE SYSTEMIC REFLECTION

When scaled into culture, these private behaviors become patriarchy's architecture. Under-functioning is reframed as charm, dominance, victimhood, or genius. Extraction is often renamed leadership. The labor of those who compensate is renamed love.

Patriarchy doesn't punish immaturity—it protects and rewards it. It organizes entire systems around the avoidance of growth, ensuring that dependency stays invisible and entitlement is still dignified. What begins as individual evasion becomes cultural design.

SECTION IV: PATRIARCHY'S INTENTIONAL DEPENDENCIES — THE PARADOX OF ENTITLED DEPENDENCY

> *BLUF: Patriarchy manufactures dependence while denying it: those in power secretly rely on the very people they call "dependent," turning unacknowledged reliance into a childlike entitlement that demands care without ever owning the need for it—setting the stage for the Eternal Child as a starring role.*

Gender essentialism tells a simple story: men independent, women dependent; men providers, women provided for; men leaders, women followers.

But who is being *provided for* with unconditional care?

Who is being *protected* with unconditional forgiveness?

And who is actually *leading* without being credited for it?

Beneath patriarchy's tale of masculine self-sufficiency lies a quieter reality: the system that boasts of autonomy is built upon the invisible labor and vision of others. The image of the self-sufficient man rests on a vast, hidden scaffolding of care. Someone cooked the meals, cleaned the clothes, remembered the birthdays, soothed the feelings, and maintained the household so that he could imagine himself free.

The culture that calls itself independent depends upon unacknowledged interdependence—and forbids those who provide it from naming their contribution.

THE INVERSION OF DEPENDENCE

Every extractive system hides this same reversal. The one called *dependent* is usually the one doing the sustaining.

The plantation owner claimed that the enslaved person could not survive without him. He provided food and shelter, he said, and cared for those he owned. Yet it was the enslaved who cultivated the food, built the house, and kept the entire operation alive. The so-called provider was utterly dependent on the labor of those he claimed to protect. And tellingly, he kept the enslaved from fleeing—the very people he claimed could not live without him.

Patriarchy repeats this pattern. The man who claims to "provide" depends on the unpaid, uncredited labor of others for his very stability. Like the master, he insists that his dominance is benevolence—while ensuring that those beneath him cannot leave.

Across time and geography, patriarchy has systematically blocked women's access to the very tools of independence it claims to stand for. Slaves were once prohibited from reading; women have been barred from basic education and higher education and the professions that would allow financial autonomy and cultural status. Each restriction was framed as protection or piety—*too dangerous, too demanding, too unbecoming for women.* But the intent was the same as the plantation master's: to ensure dependency while disguising it as care.

Benevolence and hostility are contradictory. The hostility with which patriarchal culture has resisted women's advancement reveals the lie behind its "chivalry." The same hand that gallantly holds the door also bars the doors it doesn't want women to enter.

THE MANUFACTURED DEPENDENCY

Patriarchy's traditional structure divides the responsibilities of adulthood into gendered halves. Men are assigned the visible, status-bearing roles of "protector" and "provider," while women are assigned the ongoing, invisible maintenance of life.

- ❖ Men are assigned to bring home the money—and to gate keep access to those same workplaces, professions, and pay scales.

- ❖ Men "protect" society—yet they start most of the wars and commit most acts of violence, framing their own aggression as service.

- ❖ Men claim authority over households—yet rely on women to manage every logistical and emotional detail that makes daily life possible.

In this system, dependency isn't accidental; it's deliberately manufactured."

A man's independence rests on a woman's compulsory labor. A woman's dependence is enforced by tradition, law, and economic design. Both are trapped, but not equally: his dependency is *entitled* and rewarded; hers is manipulated and exploited.

Like the slave master, patriarchy insists that those it dominates are naturally dependent while constructing the very conditions that make independence impossible. The master cannot admit that he *needs* the enslaved to survive so they can provide for him, because that admission would expose his own immaturity—his inability to sustain himself without domination.

THE PARADOX OF ENTITLED DEPENDENCY

This is patriarchy's central psychological twist: the dominator depends on the dominated while insisting it is the other way around. It is the logic of the child in the crown—the one who demands care while calling himself sovereign.

Entitled dependency is need without ownership of need. It is the expectation of care without the capacity or willingness to reciprocate it. It is the refusal to acknowledge interdependence while feeding upon it.

Psychologically, it stands for the point where development should have turned outward toward responsibility but instead loops back inward toward extraction. Like the toddler who cries, "I can do it myself!" while someone else cuts the meat, patriarchy clings to an illusion of independence that requires constant caretaking.

A civilization built on entitled dependency performs maturity while secretly avoiding it. Independence becomes theater. Dependency becomes destiny. The labor of those who sustain the illusion is made invisible so that the myth can continue.

This is where the story turns from system to psyche, from structure to archetype.

For behind the mask of mastery stands the figure we have seen all along: the one fleeing the anxiety of independence:

The Eternal Child.

6

The Eternal Boy—
When Adulthood Is Refused

BLUF: IN THESE NEXT THREE CHAPTERS, WE'LL BE
DESCRIBING ARCHETYPAL PATTERNS—NOT MEN AND WOMEN
AS MONOLITHS, BUT THE GENDERED ROLES PATRIARCHY
ASSIGNS, THE SCRIPTS IT HANDS EACH OF US TO PERFORM
IN ITS THEATER OF LIFE. IN THIS CHAPTER, WE EXPLORE THE
ARCHETYPE OF THE ETERNAL CHILD.

SECTION I: THE FIRST HERO'S JOURNEY — ADOLESCENCE TO ADULTHOOD

> *BLUF: Adulthood is not chronological; it is a developmental threshold that requires the death of the child self and the deliberate work of individuation—work most modern cultures no longer guide.*

THE FIRST HERO'S JOURNEY—ADOLESCENCE TO ADULTHOOD

Every culture once understood this: before you can take your place in the world, something in you must die, and something new must grow in its place. The child self cannot lead the adult life.

Across time and geography, the passage from adolescence into adulthood was marked by formal initiations and a rite of passage. A separation from the familiar, a crossing into the unknown, and a return as someone with new capacities, new responsibilities, and a new status in the community.

A few formal rites of passage still exist: bootcamp, medical residency, the priesthood, but not for most of the population. Nevertheless, these same initiations and rites of passage are woven into the stories you read and the movies you watch. They are the structure behind the stories. The journey of transformation, the rite of passage that the main character embarks on. Joseph Campbell, the great mythologist, wrote about the stages of this passage of transformation as the timeless universal story structure and named it The Hero's Journey.[48]

Campbell drew heavily on Carl Jung's work on transformation and his identification of Individuation as a lifelong task when he mapped the stages of the Hero's Journey. What earlier cultures recognized as initiation and rite of passage became an understanding of how we internally develop character and a self-definition and the character arc in stories and movies is how we also understand the consequences of not growing and not building character.

What begins in early childhood as the simple task of separating self from other eventually becomes something far more demanding: the work of becoming a person who can stand in the world without a parent holding your hand.

Individuation is not a luxury it is a developmental imperative.

It is the work of becoming a well-defined full adult. Of constructing wholeness.

And our developmental tasks do not end once we reach legal adulthood. They continue throughout the lifespan, each stage asking something harder, deeper, and more honest of us. That is the nature of individuation: it is not a single leap, but a lifelong series of threshold crossings, each one inviting us to shed a version of ourselves we've outgrown.

The child inherits a world; the adult shapes it.

The child seeks protection; the adult offers it.

The child depends on structure; the adult builds it.

Individuation is the slow, often uncomfortable, always liberating process of disentangling who we truly are from who we were taught to be and defining ourselves. Discovering not just our talents and capacities, but our character. It is a spiral journey toward our higher, more expansive, more capable selves. A realizing of the potential we carried at birth.

EARLY SEPARATION: HOW THE CHILD MIND MAPS THE WORLD

One of the earliest precursors of later individuation begins in early childhood. As cognition comes online, the child makes sense of a complex world by dividing it into simple, binary categories: good/bad, safe/scary, big/small, self/other. If I am this, then I am not that. If I am a girl, then I am not a boy.

And then gender essentialism enters—not yet as ideology, but as scaffolding for a new brain struggling to sort experience into meaning. The kernel of the development of greater understanding and meaning, essentialism like binary thinking, allows us to flatten complexity so the young mind can begin to understand more.

What are little boys made of? Snips and snails and puppy-dogs' tails.
What are little girls made of? Sugar and spice and everything nice.

That's gender essentialism: girls are, boys are. It's simple. Comforting. Wrong—but developmentally useful.

And then reality intrudes.

The child meets a boy who is gentle, or a girl who is ferocious. The rigid categories don't fit anymore, and something in the psyche stretches. What was once a necessary container becomes a prison. That tension between experience and assumption is what forces the next developmental expansion.

This is the quiet rehearsal for a much larger leap later in life.

THE SECOND SEPARATION: ADULTHOOD AS A THRESHOLD

The passage from late adolescence into adulthood is not always incremental. It is often a rupture of consciousness. A separation that again demands the psyche stretch. Letting go of one thing to reach for another.

In nature, it's the bird pushed from the nest—not as punishment, but because flight cannot be learned inside the familiar. Human cultures have always known this, which is why rites of passage were not celebrations of age, but structured encounters with the unknown.

Every initiation—whether tribal, religious, military, or monastic—followed the same arc:

1. Separation from the known world

2. Liminal ordeal and testing

3. Return with new status, new identity, new responsibilities

You left as an adolescent.

You returned as someone you could rely on and thus the community could also rely on.

You returned with a new identity: adult. And a new status as a full member of the community.

Modern society has mostly abandoned formal initiation, but the psychological need has not disappeared. The wiring remains. The myth remains. The Hero's Journey remains.

And the most important truth inside the Hero's Journey is this:

You must choose it.

The ordeal can be assigned.

But the tasks must be accepted, and the trials must be met alone, and the navigation and tests can only be completed by you. Adulthood cannot be bestowed.

The path of Individuation that continues in adulthood cannot be outsourced.

You must walk into the unknown on purpose—or stay a child in a grown body.

SECTION II: THE ARCS OF TRANSFORMATION — GROWTH, STAGNATION, AND CORRUPTION

> *BLUF: A life can evolve, stall, or corrupt: when the call to grow is refused, stagnation hardens into entitlement—and eventually becomes a breeding ground for manipulation and harm.*

In every story worth telling, the main character is not defined by their starting point, but by the change they undergo.

A protagonist is the one who *must* grow—the main character who is summoned, challenged, undone, reshaped, and returned as someone larger than the self who began the journey.

A supporting character exists to stabilize, assist, or catalyze that arc—but not to undergo it.

Patriarchal cultures adopted this same structure and assigned the roles in advance:

❖ Men were named the protagonists—the ones expected to face trials, leave home, confront danger, and (in theory) become worthy of leadership.

❖ Women were assigned the supporting roles—the ones who prepare, provision, tend, soothe, nourish, and reflect and absorb the costs of the hero's transformation.

So, the visible, public, celebrated rites of passage—the ones sung into myth, etched into legend, and reenacted in epics—centered boys becoming men.

And the quiet, hidden, embodied rites—the ones rooted in blood, labor, stamina, and relational burden—fell to girls becoming women.

In mythology, men risk their lives to battle dragons; in reality, women risk their lives to deliver children.

Only one was recorded as an initiation.

But outside patriarchy's storyboards, women are not side characters.

They grow, shed skins, bury identities, confront danger, endure pain, and rise—with or without narrative permission. Their initiations have simply been private, unsanctioned, and often involuntary:

❖ Sexual violation

❖ Forced marriage

❖ Forced childbirth

❖ Domestic servitude and violence

❖ Betrayal, abandonment, scapegoating

❖ Surviving what no one will name

These are not "supporting roles."

They are unsung transformational arcs.

But because this chapter is tracing patriarchy's refusal of growth—the Eternal Boy—the uninitiated man, the failed protagonist—our focus here will stay with the *male-coded arc*: the myth of the boy who never becomes a man, and the cultural systems that reward his refusal.

A later chapter will return to the women—to those who now choose the main-character arc for themselves, not as "supporting players," but as full agents of transformation.

THE POSITIVE ARC: THE PATH OF GROWTH

The positive arc is this classic story of transformation:

❖ A call is heard

❖ A familiar comfort must be left

❖ Trials are faced

❖ An old identity dies

❖ Internal and external skills are forged and tested

❖ A fuller self emerges

This is the adolescent who becomes an adult not by marking birthdays, but by evolving—by sacrificing the protections and the comforting beliefs of childhood in exchange for the capacities of adulthood.

This is the arc that builds character, responsibility, discernment, and self-governance. And once an adult learns that growth is not a one-time passage but a way of life, the Hero's Journey becomes cyclical. Each stage of life calls us to shed another skin.

Individuation is not "becoming who your culture wants you to be, it is repeatedly *becoming more of who you are as an individual. And doing so by outgrowing your old self and growing into a new self that is more capable, more defined, more whole.*

THE NEGATIVE ARCS: WHEN THE CALL IS REFUSED

But free will works both ways.

A person can refuse the call. They can avoid risk, cling to comfort, bypass effort, or outsource responsibility. They can defend the child self instead of outgrowing it.

There are two main ways a life goes stagnant:

1. *The Stalled Arc*

The person hangs on to comfort: simple understandings, familiar lies, old habits.

They perform adulthood but do not inhabit it.

They inherit identity; they do not generate it.

They claim loyalty, duty, and stability as an identity rather than character.

They say, "It's just who I am."

They don't meet challenges, they avoid challenge.

The don't engage curiosity, they engage defenses to the new.

They don't take the tests because they haven't studied for them.

They drop out of growth.

You can refuse the call, but you can't opt out of the consequences. They just get delayed and they accumulate. And one day life tests you with a challenge you didn't see coming and that you're not remotely prepared for because you avoided the work and that failure becomes part of your fall. And if you've avoided doing the work for long enough the gap between what you should have developed and what you did is exposed. That exposure becomes part of a larger fall and affects the people around you. And if growth has been avoided long enough it can have permanent consequences in our lives.

When stagnation festers long enough it results in a significant failure of some kind and can curdle further into corruption.

2. The Corrupt Arc

Here the refusal to grow doesn't just stagnate—it acquires an aggressive nature.

The person discovers that manipulation, charm, control, force, or grievance can get them what growth would have required them to earn. They learn they can take from others what they want. They can lie, steal, cheat, deceive, and they can get away with it.

They are not naive. They know better. They choose the lie, they choose corruption. And they like it!

Breaking Bad—The Corrupt Arc

In the television series *Breaking Bad*, Walter White doesn't break down—he breaks out of the moral universe.

At first, he tells himself his criminality is for his family.

And then we see the grievances from decades prior that fuel his behavior—*I wasn't respected, I was overlooked, I deserved more*—simply meets opportunity and expands.

He knows right from wrong.

He chooses wrong anyway—because it's faster, easier, and profitable and fun as he finally admits, "I liked it."[49]

And the tragedy isn't just his own life it's how many people he pulls into his corruption. Because the corrupt character rarely wants to take his journey alone. He pulls others into his web of corruption and destruction and pulls them down with him. Corruption doesn't just metastasize in him it spreads out to everyone around him so that no one else is innocent either.

Patriarchy with its refusal to grow, to change, is built on these two negative arcs. The people who won't define themselves and instead allow themselves to be defined by others. The people too unmotivated to meet the challenges of character building. And the corrupt actors who convince them to be more like him. To take the shortcuts just this once. To justify the means with the end. To tell the lies. To exploit others. To have little remorse. To tolerate the dysfunctional because it's easier, less effort, more fun. Refusing growth doesn't keep innocence, it solidifies entitlement.

Patriarchy is built on this arc. It does not punish the refusal to grow—it rewards and institutionalizes it.

But someone must be the adult. If everyone is a child, the world falls apart. And yet, those who take the effortless way out don't want to be told what to do. They want to tell others what to do. So, they claim the status of the adult role in public and don the costume of the elder and wear it over their undeveloped self.

They know adulthood is the aim—but that's demanding work. Far easier to perform it than to embody it. That's pseudo-individuation: a theater of maturity.

To understand how this passage is completed—or refused—we turn to Jung's idea of individuation. And once we put that lens on, the pattern clarifies: the archetype beneath both failures is the *Eternal Child*—refusal of initiation disguised as identity, an allergy to limits, pressure, and responsibility.

SECTION III: THE ETERNAL CHILD — THE PSYCHOLOGICAL PATTERN OF REFUSED ADULTHOOD

BLUF: The Eternal Child is not innocent; it is a refusal of individuation marked by fear of limits, allergy to responsibility, and a reliance on others to absorb the consequences of one's undeveloped self.

Carl Jung—the founder of analytical psychology—warned that when the work of individuation is refused, the psyche becomes trapped in a kind of state of permanent adolescence.[50]

He called this condition the *Puer Aeternus*—the Eternal Boy—and described it this way:

"The Puer typically leads a provisional life, due to the fear of being caught in a situation from which it might not be possible to escape . . . Plans for the future slip away in fantasies of what will be, what could be, while no decisive action is taken to change. He covets independence and freedom, chafes at boundaries and limits, and tends to find any restriction intolerable."

Marie-Louise von Franz, Jung's longtime collaborator and one of the foremost interpreters of his work, later expanded on the concept in *The Problem of the Puer Aeternus.*

A Swiss analyst and scholar, von Franz was known for translating Jung's theories into practical psychological language and for exploring how myth and archetype reveal recurring patterns of the human psyche. Her insights about the *Puer*—especially his fantasy life, avoidance of limits, and dependence on the mother—remain foundational in-depth psychology:

"There is a strange attitude and feeling that one is not yet in real life. For the time being one is doing this or that, but whether it is a woman or a job, it is not yet what is really wanted, and there is always the fantasy that sometime in the future the real thing will come about. If this attitude is prolonged, it means a constant inner refusal to commit oneself to the moment... The one thing dreaded throughout by such a type of man is to be bound to anything whatever."[51]

FIVE TRAITS OF THE ETERNAL CHILD

Fear of Commitment

Avoids binding choices and keeps options open—a deep-seated fear of responsibility that leads to avoiding adult roles and obligations. He fears anything that might "trap" him—a job, a place, a decision, a partner—and lives in the fantasy that the *real* life, the *real* relationship, the *real* purpose will begin later. It's a form of emotional insurance against accountability.

The "Provisional Life"

Lives in a state of *what if,* never fully committing to work, place, or relationship because each decision could foreclose other possibilities. The allure of potential replaces the weight of presence.

Allergy to Limits / Hunger for Freedom

Boundaries feel like threats. Work, patience, and discipline feel like imprisonment. He equates maturity with loss and calls constraint "control." His freedom is not autonomy—it is avoidance dressed as independence.

Avoidance of Reality—Inflation and Idealism

Escapes into fantasy and grand ideals as temporary refuge. Vision substitutes for effort. The inner stance is *too special to be bound.* The Puer is intoxicated by possibility and allergic to process; he mistakes *feeling inspired* for *being transformed.*

The Mother Complex

Von Franz described "a young man who has an outstanding mother complex . . . characteristics of adolescence with too great a dependence on the mother." He expects to be cushioned from consequence and rescued when his provisional life collapses. He idealizes the one who protects him and blames her for his dependence—oscillating between rebellion and regression.

Together, Jung and von Franz give us a remarkably precise portrait of the *Eternal Child*: a psyche that refuses gravity, responsibility, and consequence.

He lives in pursuit of excitement and escape. He confuses intensity with aliveness and rebellion with individuality.

He resists duty, limits, and commitment because they feel like confinement. He longs for freedom but fears responsibility.

He worships potential but avoids process. He wants to be admired but not to produce works that can be admired.

Someone else must manage the consequences.

In Jung's view, this was not innocence—it was pathology. He saw the refusal to mature as a kind of inner tyranny: the ego's demand to stay adored and unchallenged.

Where the integrated adult seeks reality, the *Eternal Child* seeks exemption—wanting the fruits of maturity without the labor of growth.

He may be charming, persuasive, and sometimes even brilliant, but beneath the charisma lies the terror of limits, accountability, and time itself.

Caroline Myss, in her book *Sacred Contracts*, an encyclopedia of archetypes, describes the *Puer Eternis* as:

"manifests as an inability to grow up and embrace the responsible life of an adult. Like Peter Pan, he resists ending a cycle of life in which he is free to live outside the boundaries of conventional adulthood. ...A consistent inability to be relied on and the inability to accept the aging process . . . is sometimes floundering and ungrounded between stages of life, because he has not laid a foundation for a functioning adulthood," [52]

The *Eternal Child* believes that rules are for others. He sees feedback as insult, partnership as a threat, and limitation as humiliation. He cannot evolve—only defend the illusion of being already complete.

When this pattern takes hold in an individual, relationships collapse under the weight of unmet responsibility.

When it takes hold in a culture, it builds systems that reward emotional immaturity and punish adulthood.

The *Puer Aeturnus* never intends to become dangerous—he only intends never to grow up.

SECTION IV: THE CHILD SELF AND THE GIFT — WHAT THE ETERNAL CHILD REFUSES TO DEVELOP

> *BLUF: Every child carries a Gift, but only adulthood can forge it; the Eternal Child wants the identity without the initiation—admiration without effort, potential without process.*

The Child Self—even in adulthood—is not a flaw to be discarded or shamed. It carries the seeds of imagination, hope, wonder, curiosity, delight, individuality, greatness—and comes bearing a unique Gift.

Every child arrives carrying a mystery.

They are not a blank slate, not an empty vessel waiting to be written on. They have a gifted self—the seed of their uniqueness, individuality, and potential. A coded essence already pulsing with instructions for the life it longs to become. Inside the child is the first whisper of the oak inside the acorn, the dancer inside the toddler, the healer inside the infant whose face already carries an old soul's gaze, the inventor inside the tinkerer, the scientist inside the one who catalogues insects, the storyteller inside the kid who rearranges reality with words.

The Child Self does not yet know how to become what it is, but it feels the glimmers of recognition—and the pressure and promise—of that future self.

This is why children play the future before they can live it.

Why they dress up in costumes, imagine impossible roles, rehearse greatness in bedrooms and backyards.

A child pretending to be a teacher is not "just pretending"—she is making first contact with the gifted self who will one day be asked to teach something.

A child who turns a stick into a sword is already negotiating the courage his gift will one day require.

A child who crowns herself queen and directs others with imperious certainty is not "being dramatic"—she is already practicing for a future that will ask her to step up and lead.

Play is rehearsal for the self trying to be born.

The first callings of later life are the Child Self's faint recognition of the Gift within—the unique essence each human being brings into the world. It is the first pulse of specialness that is not ego, but true identity. The quiet intuition:

There is something I am meant to do. There is something only I can bring. There is a particular value I carry that is needed by others.

That knowing is not a delusion of grandeur. It is the presence of a calling before the language exists to name it.

And because the child can sense both the grandeur and the gap—the mighty oak inside the acorn, but no idea yet how to become a tree—there is both wonder and pressure, excitement, and fear.

THE ROLE OF INDIVIDUATION—FORGING THE GIFT

If the Child Self is the gifted acorn, then individuation is the inner process that breaks the shell, sends roots down into the ground, and stretches upward toward the sky—making the gifts of the full-grown oak visible.

Individuation is not a personality makeover or a self-improvement journey. It is a lifelong apprenticeship to developing and delivering the Gift we were born carrying. It is the slow, relentless, reality-bound process that takes what was once fantasy and forges it into form.

It does not happen in comfort. It happens in heat, pressure, and solitude. It is often confusing, maddening, and frustrating. Shaped by obstacles, demanded by crises, refined by failures, clarified by loneliness, strengthened by resistance. It calls every part of us forward—our intelligence, intuition, instincts, courage, imagination, endurance, creativity, and problem-solving capacities.

We become gifted adults not despite the challenges we face, but *because of them.*

The Gift is not handed to us; it is forged.

Forged because talent alone isn't enough.

Forged because the Gift must break free from the safety of fantasy and stand upright in reality.

Forged when we are asked to try again. And again. To rethink, remodel, refine.

Forged when the world says a cold "no" and some fierce inner impudence answers, *"Watch me. I will find a way."*

Forged when we must grow bigger on the inside than the obstacle in front of us.

The Child Self carries the mysterious Gift, but it is the larger self that methodically, relentlessly sculpts and shares it.

This is why every true story of mastery, artistry, leadership, invention, or meaningful contribution follows the same rhythm:

1. **A spark**—the Child Self has a glimpse

2. **A summons**—an invitation, opportunity, or inner knowing

3. **A road of trials**—reality pushes back

4. **A refinement**—skill, character, and integrity are forged in the fire

5. **A return**—the Gift is finally offered to the world

The child imagines the calling.

The adult must become the vessel that can carry it.

THE REFUSAL OF THE FORGE — THE ETERNAL CHILD AND THE UNDEVELOPED GIFT

If the Child Self carries the Gift in seed form, the Eternal Child is the one who refuses the soil, the weather, the seasons, the stretching, the root-breaking, the storming—the very forces that would have grown him into the oak he imagines himself already to be.

The Eternal Child does not lack capability.

He lacks willingness.

He wants the identity without the initiation.

The feeling of greatness without the friction of growth.

The admiration owed to achievement—without the achievement.

He wants to be seen as special while avoiding everything that produces exceptionality: effort, repetition, correction, pressure, practice, failure, endurance, refinement.

He likes doing something once and calling it mastery.

He likes praise for "what he could be," and resents the reflection of what he actually is.

He wants token effort to count as equal contribution, and token achievement to count as legacy.

When reality pushes back, he does not rise—he seethes. When life offers feedback, he does not integrate—he collapses, explodes, or flees. When consequences arrive, he does not adjust—he blames, shames, distracts, or attacks. He wants freedom from responsibility, while clinging to the dependencies that shield him from consequence. And because he will not do the work needed to grow, he reframes the work as an insult.

- ❖ Pressure becomes "control."
- ❖ Expectation becomes "nagging."
- ❖ Feedback becomes "disrespect."
- ❖ Accountability becomes "persecution."
- ❖ Consequences become "unfair."

He reinterprets every invitation to grow as an attack on his specialness.

And so, the Gift remains permanent potential, trapped in the amber of fantasy. Never shaped. Never tested. Never shared. A life lived rehearsing—and demanding—significance rather than earning it.

He enjoys risk, so long as it doesn't require commitment. He loves novelty but not change—because real change confronts the smaller self and demands the birth of a larger one.

He is not unable to develop—he is unwilling to grow.

This is why the Eternal Child must mythologize himself and his behaviors. Because nothing in lived reality confirms the identity he wants, it must be imagined, performed, and reflected instead. If you won't become your bigger self, you must convince others you already are. And when a person refuses to grow, they must build a story in which stagnation is a virtue.

And here is patriarchy's great inversion:

It takes this refusal to grow up and calls it strength, authority, consistency—even manhood.

The system does not shame immaturity.

It does not correct the refusal to engage reality.

It indulges it. It elevates the fantasy and mythologizes it.

SECTION V: PATRIARCHY'S REWARD SYSTEM — HOW REFUSAL TO CHANGE BECOMES POWER

BLUF: Patriarchy protects emotional immaturity by mythologizing the unchanging man, recasting women's maturity as control and men's refusal to grow as authenticity, constancy, or strength.

MYTHOLOGIZING THE UNCHANGING MAN

One of patriarchy's quieter distortions is the idea that *real men do not change.* Not after marriage. Not after children. Not after life-altering events that would require any mature human being to grow.

This resistance is often presented as a point of pride:

❖ "I'm the same man I've always been."

❖ "You knew who I was when you married me."

❖ "I haven't changed in twenty years."

❖ "That's just how I am."

As if remaining unchanged were a marker of integrity rather than evidence of developmental arrest.

Patriarchy treats this refusal to evolve as though it were some kind of stoic heroism—a badge of masculine honor, as if holding the same mindset at forty-five years old that you had at twenty required courage, strength, or principle.

But refusing to change does not require strength.

It requires nothing.

It is the path of least resistance—a mixture of laziness, entitlement, and self-centeredness framed as "authenticity."

In any other developmental model, not adapting would be recognized as a failure to grow. But here, the burden is flipped: the person refusing to evolve is called "consistent," while the person asking for maturity is called "controlling."

Marriage needs new forms of relating.

Fatherhood requires new forms of responsibility and presence.

Shared life requires new forms of collaboration.

These are not extreme demands.

They are the ordinary expectations of adulthood.

But for the Eternal Child, change is experienced as intrusion, and the suggestion of adaptation is interpreted as domination. So, the woman who expects evolution is framed as demanding, while the man who refuses growth casts himself as loyal to who he "really is."

It is a highly convenient definition of identity: if nothing in him ever must change, then everything that needs to change belongs to her.

And once again, the result is the same: his comfort is still the constant; her adaptation becomes the compensation.

FUNCTIONAL WOMEN, DYSFUNCTIONAL FRAME — HOW MATURITY GETS RECAST AS CONTROL

One of the most disturbingly disorienting features of patriarchal relationships is the way women's functional, adult behavior is reframed as a problem while men's refusal to grow is treated as normal, harmless, or even admirable.

A woman plans, anticipates needs, adapts, makes decisions, or asks for shared responsibility—and her behavior is labeled "controlling," "overreacting," or "never satisfied."

A man refuses to adapt, refuses to learn, refuses to assume responsibility—and his behavior is framed as authenticity, rugged independence, or "just the way he is."

In other words:

She is pathologized for functioning.

He is celebrated for avoiding function.

She becomes the problem for noticing the problem.

He becomes the victim of her noticing.

This is patriarchy's emotional shell game: maturity rebranded as control, irresponsibility reframed as freedom.

The adult woman becomes the overfunctioning mother; the Eternal Child becomes the misunderstood man. And in that inversion, the culture repeats its oldest spell: she must grow to survive him, and he must never grow to keep her bound.

We have in this chapter traced the map of the rite of passage from adolescence to adulthood and what this leap in consciousness demands of us: the capacity to lead ourselves—to assume responsibility for our own needs, impulses, limits, and consequences. The rite of passage is an acceptance of responsibility for our own growth and our own navigation in the world.

But the Eternal Child refuses the handover of responsibility.

Instead of becoming the grown self who governs his own life, he fantasizes about becoming the one who governs others. He imagines himself the ultimate adult, the ultimate authority, the Godfather—all-powerful, all-knowing, infallible—not through the slow grind of acquiring wisdom, developing skill, investing labor, or enduring repeated initiations, but through costume, posturing, and projection. He wants the authority of the grown man without ever having to become one.

And here patriarchy offers him a shortcut to challenging work.

He doesn't have to develop true bigness in himself. He only must use his cleverness to make others smaller. He mocks, demeans, denigrates, degrades, humiliates. Instead of building himself, he diminishes others.

Rather than growing up and taking responsibility for himself, the Eternal Child is invited to imagine that he is already the natural leader—and that the true "children" who need direction, containment, and obedience are women, subordinates, and anyone outside his favored group.

In this reversal, he does not have to outgrow his dependency. He simply delegates it and denies it. In his fantasy world, others must feel dependent on him—but must also not burden him. Someone else must serve, stabilize, soothe, defer, and absorb the costs of his unfinished development.

The boy who won't lead himself becomes the man who insists on leading everyone else. This is the birth of the Strongman: not a mature leader, but the fantasy of leadership—a child strutting in a crown, armed and enthroned, mistaking an inflated ego for authority.

And his fantasy does not stay private. He takes it public.

Historian Ruth Ben-Ghiat, in her book *Strongmen*,[53] identifies this authoritarian archetype as a central figure of modern power structures—men who consolidate control not through reasoned leadership, but through fear, myth-making, propaganda, and emotional manipulation. They appear invincible only because their image is carefully engineered; beneath the spectacle lies a structure held together by insecurity, coercion, and illusion.

The Strongman draws others into his fantasy—men and women alike—persuading some that they are lesser and seducing others with the promise of being more. Many follow because they long for a life without limits, without accountability, without the burdens of adulthood. They want to live inside his exemption from reality, close enough to his illusion that they might be spared the work of becoming whole.

And so the search begins—not for maturity, but for the man who can make immaturity feel like strength.

7

In Search of a Godfather: Why the Immature Demand a Strongman

BLUF: EXPLORES THE PSYCHOLOGICAL APPEAL OF AUTHORITARIAN FIGURES AND THE SYSTEMS THEY SUSTAIN. EXAMINES HOW EMOTIONAL IMMATURITY, FEAR OF FREEDOM, AND DEVELOPMENTAL ARREST LEAD PEOPLE TO IDOLIZE LEADERS WHO PROMISE CERTAINTY IN EXCHANGE FOR OBEDIENCE—REVEALING HOW THESE SYSTEMS ARE BUILT NOT JUST BY THOSE IN POWER, BUT BY THOSE WHO ABDICATE IT.

t's easy to look at patriarchy and blame men. After all, they're often the ones in charge. They're the ones passing laws, leading corporations, shaping doctrine, commanding families. Their faces are on the money, in the pulpits, at the podiums. They're the ones doing the shouting. And often, the silencing. And no doubt about how in patriarchy, the system is rigged to benefit them.

But this book is not about blaming men. Because modern men are not the architects of this system—they are its assigned standard bearers. Just as women are conscripted into impossible ideals of femininity, men are conscripted into the punishing role of embodying the system itself.

Raised to be the face of control, the enforcer of hierarchy, the performer of certainty, men are groomed to carry the flag of patriarchy. And that role, too, is a prison. It demands performance over presence. Image over integrity. Power over connection. Invulnerability over self-awareness. It tells them: "You must be the one who knows. You must never falter. You must never question your role. You must never feel." And when they fail to meet this inhuman standard—as they must—they are shamed. Or they are defended at all costs. Or both.

Patriarchy doesn't just assign women to be less than. It assigns men to be more than human—and then punishes them for not being gods.

This isn't about toxic masculinity. Masculinity is not toxic. Men are not toxic. It's the system that is toxic—because it demands that men become symbols instead of selves.

In the narcissistic family system of patriarchy, men are cast as the Golden Child—idealized, projected upon, expected to uphold the illusion. But that idealization is not love. It is a trap.

And women? Women are often the standard bearers of femininity, but not of patriarchy's *identity*. They are tasked with submission, with virtue, with pleasing—but they are not told they are the system. Men are—which is why the backlash against male vulnerability is so ferocious. Why male dissent of patriarchy is often met with contempt and sneering. Why men who step off the pedestal are attacked just as surely as women who refuse to kneel.

Because patriarchy doesn't actually revolve around gender, but rather around a personality type—the Big Daddy, the Godfather, the Domineering Figure who embodies power without accountability. A way out of the burden of self-definition. A bypass around the work of individuation. A shortcut that replaces the struggle to become with the comfort of obedience.

It's easier, in the short term, to follow the Big Daddy than to become fully oneself. But there is a cost. There's always a cost.

Growing up is painful. It requires grief, responsibility, and confrontation with reality. But not growing up is more painful still. It costs us our clarity. Our creativity. Our inner life. Our power. And often our relationships. And it asks us to worship illusions that cannot hold us—and carry standards we were never meant to bear.

So, this is not a war between men and women. It is a refusal—by the sane—of a system that asks all of us to play parts that betray our humanity.

SECTION I: THE GODFATHER ARCHETYPE — FANTASY, PROTECTION, AND OBEDIENCE

> *BLUF: Introduces the psychological and cultural appeal of strongman figures. Frames the Godfather not just as a person, but as an archetype that offers false safety in exchange for obedience.*

Somewhere deep in the psyche of every uninitiated adult lives a wish: that someone else will manage it.

The mess.

The money.

The decisions.

The danger.

The responsibility of being a person with agency, complexity, and consequences.

For those who never fully crossed the threshold into adulthood—either because they weren't supported and/or because they refused to do the work —the longing for a parent never goes away. But it often changes form. It shapeshifts from a literal mother or father into a symbolic figure: a Big Daddy, a Godfather, a sovereign with the answers. Someone powerful enough to tell them what to do, who to be, how to think—and who will take the blame if it all falls apart.

This is the perpetual parent fantasy—a bypass around adulthood, and the foundation of every Godfather system.

God the Father, the Mafia Don, the Family Patriarch, the Cult Leader. These figures may look different on the surface, but their structural appeal is the same. They offer what the unformed self craves:[54]

- ❖ Protection from uncertainty

- ❖ Certainty in place of nuance

* A ready-made identity and place in the world
* A clear hierarchy with no internal compass required
* Relief from the burdens of choice, contradiction, and consequence

Whether it's "God the Father" in a high-control religion, a charismatic cult leader who demands loyalty, or a father who rules the home or the nation like a king, these figures function as substitutes for individuation. They replace the difficult, often painful process of growing into a full self with the comforting simplicity of obedience.

And for many—especially those shaped by trauma, neglect, or emotional chaos—this feels like safety.

This fantasy of a powerful, all-knowing parent figure doesn't arise out of nowhere. It emerges when key developmental tasks are left incomplete.

Erik Erikson described adulthood as the stage of identity and intimacy—where a person is called to form a cohesive self and take responsibility for their life. Winnicott spoke of the "good enough mother" whose job is to gradually disappoint the child just enough that they begin to develop their own inner resources. And Fromm warned that freedom itself can provoke deep anxiety in those who have not developed the internal strength to carry it.

When these developmental tasks are disrupted—by trauma, overprotection, neglect, enmeshment, or rigid ideology—adulthood never fully arrives. The individual remains psychologically young, seeking an external authority to guide, protect, and validate them. The Godfather archetype then becomes not just appealing, but necessary. He serves as a psychological prosthetic, a way to manage the terror of freedom by outsourcing the responsibilities of adulthood.

THE STRONGMAN'S TIME —
GOLDEN PAST, GUARANTEED FUTURE

Immature psyches don't just outsource authority. They also distort time. Instead of holding past, present, and future as boundaried concepts, they collapse into what psychologists call the child's world of living in the "eternal present"—where only immediate comfort, grievance, or need exists.

Strongman cultures turn this inner distortion into a political weapon. They rewrite the past as a purified "golden age" where everyone knew their place, roles were clear, and authority was never questioned. Real history—the exploitation, the violence, the stolen land, the unpaid labor, achievements of women, the silenced voices—is scrubbed away. What remains is a nostalgic cartoon: men as protectors, women as contented helpers, outsiders as either invisible or happily subordinated. Any attempt to name the harm of the past is cast as disloyalty or attack.

At the same time, the future is either denied or promised as a reward. Climate collapse becomes a hoax. Generational harm becomes "overreacting." Changing gender roles become a "threat to civilization." The Strongman pledges that if we only return to the "natural order" as he defines it—if everyone will obey and play their assigned roles—then every problem will melt away. This is not vision. It is future-faking: a grandiose fantasy that trades real responsibility for magical restoration.

To maintain this fantasy, emotion itself has to be controlled. Grief, shame, and moral complexity would puncture the dream, so they must be repressed or projected. The Strongman culture narrows the emotional spectrum: anger and dominance are sanctioned for those on top; cheerfulness and compliance for those beneath. Any discomfort that leaks through is redirected outward onto "outsiders": women, minorities, dissenters, immigrants, or whoever is cast as the threat of the week. This is scapegoating as emotional regulation.

Instead of integrating pain, the system exports it. Instead of owning guilt, it projects it. Instead of feeling the ache of history and the responsibility of the future, it blames someone else for disturbing the fantasy. In this way, the Strongman is not just a political figure; he is the archetype of dangerous ease. He grooms his followers while holding out the promise of the fantasy of a permanent Child world—a purified golden past, a promised future golden paradise, and a present stripped of complexity and consequence. It is everything the Eternal Child longs for: someone else to think, someone else to blame, someone else to carry the burden of becoming. But grooming is always a deception. The door that opened so invitingly now slams shut and locks from the outside. And by the time followers reach for the handle they discover they can no longer leave.

SECTION II: THE PSYCHOLOGY OF SURRENDER — WHY SOME PEOPLE WANT TO BE RULED

> *BLUF: Explores why some individuals are drawn to authoritarian figures—examining fear of adulthood, unresolved dependency needs, and the longing to avoid personal responsibility.*

Emotionally immature systems tell a simple story:

"You don't have to figure it out. Just trust me."
"You don't have to grow up. Just stay loyal."
"You don't have to carry the weight. I'll do it for you—if you obey."

This is seductive. Especially for someone whose early life was marked by betrayal, confusion, or absence. The Big Daddy archetype offers what every frightened child longs for: a safe adult who knows what's best. But the promise is false. Because the Godfather figure is not grounded in wisdom or care. He is grounded in dominance, emotional manipulation, and projection.

He appears strong not because he is whole—but because he has demanded the obedience of everyone around him. His power is not earned. It is enforced.

A SHORTCUT AROUND BECOMING

To grow into a full adult is to undergo a series of difficult initiations:

- To make mistakes and take responsibility for them.
- To live with contradiction.
- To feel the sting of rejection, the ache of loneliness, the weight of freedom.

- ❖ To build an internal compass rather than outsourcing morality.
- ❖ To confront your shadow and differentiate from the collective.

Godfather systems offer a shortcut: Don't build a self. Just play your part. Don't hold your own ground. Just follow the one who does.

But what looks like shelter is a cage. What feels like relief is repression. And the longer we stay under the illusion, the harder it becomes to remember that we were meant for something more. Because this isn't just a longing for safety. It's a longing to never grow up. And that longing keeps the Godfather system alive.

Every Godfather system runs on a simple, seductive lie:

Obey, and you will be protected.

This is not an explicit contract. It's rarely spoken aloud. But it is understood—psychologically, emotionally, and often spiritually.

The offer is compelling, especially for the emotionally immature or the traumatized:

"Let me carry the burden of decision-making."

"I'll keep you safe—as long as you don't question me."

"Stay in line, and nothing bad will happen."

At first, it feels like a gift. Someone else has the answers. Someone else will take responsibility. Someone else will protect you from the chaos, the complexity, the crushing weight of freedom.

But like all bargains with power, this one comes at a cost.

THE CURRENCY IS OBEDIENCE

In exchange for perceived safety, followers must hand over something precious:

- ❖ Their critical thinking
- ❖ Their internal authority
- ❖ Their full emotional range
- ❖ Their evolving self

They must silence their doubt. They must suppress their instincts. They must perform loyalty even when the system is failing or the leader is clearly corrupt.

This is the psychological protection racket:

The Godfather offers safety—but only from dangers he defines.

And when you stop playing the game, that "safety" disappears. The same system that promised to shelter you suddenly becomes the thing you need protection from.

THE HIDDEN COST OF COMFORT

What begins as comfort becomes coercion.

And over time, the follower pays not just with obedience, but with:

- **Emotional constriction** (Don't feel that. Don't say that. Don't be that.)

- **Identity diffusion** (Who am I without this role? This leader? This community?)

- **Moral outsourcing** (I no longer discern truth. I just echo what I'm told.)

- **Stunted development** (I stop growing—because I'm never allowed to step into full adulthood.)

The longer a person remains in this dynamic, the more their agency atrophies. Like unused muscles, the parts of themselves that once reached toward freedom become weak, uncertain, disoriented.

And when they finally begin to question the system, they may feel like they've lost the capacity to choose.

This is not accidental. This is how the system is designed.

WHY THE SYSTEM NEEDS OBEDIENCE TO SURVIVE

Godfather systems don't run on truth. They run on compliance. The leader doesn't need to be right. He needs to be obeyed. The structure doesn't need to serve life. It needs to be preserved.

And so, the entire system depends on followers who have:

- Abandoned their discernment

- Suppressed their doubts

- Traded their voice for a seat at the table

In this way, the price of protection is self-abandonment. It's a slow, subtle erosion—not of the body, but of the soul.

THE FALSE PROMISE OF 'YOU'LL BE TAKEN CARE OF'

In emotionally immature systems, this is the core lie:

"You don't need to grow. Just follow. Just serve. Just believe."

It feels easier than individuation. It feels safer than confrontation. But eventually, the bill comes due.

Because the Godfather is not God.

He is a man—flawed, frightened, often manipulative—propped up by the projections of those who refuse to lead themselves. And the longer we obey, the harder it becomes to remember we were ever meant to be grown up, to be free.

TRAITS OF THE GODFATHER FIGURE

The Godfather archetype is not about gender—it's about psychology. It's a pattern of behavior, a structure of control, and a performance of strength designed to mask emotional immaturity. At its core, the Godfather figure offers certainty without substance, dominance without accountability, and safety that always comes at a price.

This figure is not limited to mafia dons or patriarchs in traditional families. It shows up in pulpits, political rallies, corporate boardrooms, social media empires, and even in spiritual or wellness communities. What defines him (or her) is not his title, but the emotional system he creates around himself: one of dependency, loyalty, projection, and fear.

THE MASK OF STRENGTH

The Godfather performs certainty. He performs invincibility. He performs clarity. He cultivates an aura of confidence so unwavering that followers begin to doubt their own instincts in his presence. His certainty becomes the gravitational force around which others orbit—because it promises relief from confusion, from contradiction, from the terrifying ambiguity of adult life.

But that strength is often a mask.

Beneath the surface, the Godfather figure:

❖ **Cannot tolerate dissent** because it destabilizes his illusion of omnipotence.

❖ **Refuses accountability,** because admitting error would collapse his persona.

❖ **Controls narratives** because he must shape reality to stay in power.

❖ **Represses vulnerability** because it threatens the image of infallibility.

He is not whole. He is curated. A persona crafted to absorb the projections of those who are unwilling to lead themselves.

NARCISSISTIC AND ANTISOCIAL TRAITS IN DISGUISE

What followers experience as charisma is often a cocktail of narcissism and antisocial traits—traits that would be glaring in a partner or parent but are reframed as "leadership" in a Godfather.

Common traits include:

❖ **Grandiosity**—He presents himself as larger-than-life, the only one who can save, fix, or lead.

❖ **Entitlement**—He expects unquestioning loyalty, admiration, and resources.

❖ **Lack of empathy**—Others are tools, pawns, or mirrors—never equals or worthy of consideration.

- **Deceit and manipulation**—He spins stories to fit his narrative, even at the expense of others' truth.

- **Punitive control**—Disagreement is met with humiliation, exile, or spiritualized threats.

- **Image obsession**—Reputation is everything. He will sacrifice people to preserve perception.

- **Authoritarianism**—He demands obedience and calls it trust, order, truth, or even love.

He doesn't just demand control—he erases complexity.

He doesn't just punish difference—he pathologizes it.

And because his followers haven't built the inner structures of emotional adulthood, they mistake his dominance for stability.

SECTION III: INNER WEAKNESS, OUTER PROJECTION — HOW THE STRONGMAN REFLECTS THE FOLLOWER'S INNER WORLD

> *BLUF: Strongman figures gain power not through personal strength but through projection—by embodying the denied traits and unmet needs of their followers. This section unveils how Godfather systems aren't isolated phenomena, but collective projections of developmental avoidance. These systems exist because people refuse to do the work of emotional maturity—and prefer to orbit around someone who performs strength.*

Here's the devastating irony: The Godfather is not admirable. He is familiar. He mirrors the exact qualities that emotionally immature followers have yet to face or develop in themselves:

- Their fear of failure and reluctance to accept responsibility.

- Their fear of uncertainty.

* Their wish for a perfect authority.

* Their desire to bypass individuation.

* Their unresolved wounds around power, safety, and dependency.

The Godfather looks like a leader. But he is actually a mirror.

A mirror for those who fear they are not enough and want someone else to carry the burden of becoming.

The most dangerous systems are not imposed from the outside. They are accepted—because they mirror what already lives inside us.

Patriarchy, cults of personality, authoritarian regimes—these are not anomalies. They are reflections. They are the outward manifestation of unresolved emotional immaturity, dependency, fear, and projection. And they persist not only because of those who lead them, but because of those who follow.

When we have not done the work of individuation, we look for someone to do it for us. When we haven't cultivated internal authority, we outsource it. When we cannot bear complexity, we gravitate toward simplicity—even if it's cruel. When we are afraid to know ourselves, we idolize someone else. This is the engine of the Godfather system: mutual evasion masquerading as structure.

WE GET THE LEADERS WE'RE WILLING TO FOLLOW

A system led by the Godfather archetype is not created by one man alone. It is built, sustained, and reinforced by every individual who agrees to the trade: "I will give you my agency, my discernment, my truth . . . in exchange for safety, identity, and direction."

And the more people make that trade, the stronger the illusion becomes. Not because the leader is strong—but because he has been collectively entrusted with power no one else wants to claim.

Godfather systems are not based on consent. They are based on abdication. This abdication—this surrender of inner authority—is not simply a moral failing. It is often the result of developmental arrest. As Erik Erikson noted, adulthood requires the integration of identity and the capacity for intimacy—tasks that cannot be completed without both internal stability and self-trust. Winnicott taught that true maturity emerges only when the child is allowed, over time, to experience the frustration and ambiguity of life without being rescued or engulfed. And Fromm warned that freedom, without psychological grounding, becomes a source of terror rather than joy.[63]

When those foundational structures aren't built—whether through trauma, overcontrol, emotional neglect, or cultural conditioning—the psyche remains unequipped for self-leadership. And so, it seeks a stand-in. A Godfather. A proxy for the strength it never got to build. These systems, then, are not anomalies. They are natural outgrowths of developmental gaps. They exist because too many of us never got to finish becoming whole.

They work because people prefer obedience to uncertainty, projection to responsibility, fantasy to grief. And as long as the Godfather plays his role—and the followers play theirs—the illusion feels stable.

But it is not stable. It is brittle. And it begins to fracture the moment even one person sees it for what it is.

Every Godfather system reflects what it was designed to conceal:

- **Emotional immaturity** beneath charisma

- **Dependency** beneath loyalty

- **Disempowerment** beneath structure

- **Fear** beneath devotion

- **Suppression** beneath peace

The Godfather is not the cause of arrested development. He is the consequence of it. He arises in systems where people have been taught *not* to grow up. He thrives in cultures where obedience is framed as virtue. Where critical thought is punished. Where freedom feels unbearable.

He is what shows up when people abandon the project of becoming—and outsource the burden of adulthood to someone who promises they'll never have to carry it again.

SECTION IV: THE THRESHOLD WE CROSS — WALKING AWAY FROM THE FANTASY

> *BLUF: Names the inner threshold between collusion and adulthood, showing how walking away from the Godfather—despite the anxiety of freedom—is the quiet, seismic act that begins to dismantle dominance systems.*

We have already seen how freedom carries its own kind of ache—the anxiety of standing on our own feet without a parent, leader, or system to hide behind. Patriarchy exploits that ache. Godfather systems offer us a bargain: "Give up your inner authority, and I'll spare you the weight of adulthood."

But when we refuse to grow up, we don't avoid the cost of adulthood— we just pay it in a different currency: dependency, borrowed identities, and obedience to people who are more interested in managing us than in loving us. As children, we rightly depend on structure, authority, and care from others. As adults, that dependence is meant to shift. If we are to become whole, sovereign, and alive, we must eventually carry what once belonged to someone else: our choices, our consequences, our values, our truth.

Freedom is not comfort. It is responsibility. It is the risk of standing for something when no one tells us what to believe; the risk of becoming someone when no one defines us; the risk of failing with no one to rescue us; the risk of discovering who we are without a role to hide in. That unease is the anxiety of freedom—and many people evade it by clinging to roles, systems, and authorities that promise certainty in exchange for obedience.

When we refuse to grow up, we don't escape adulthood—we outsource it. We pay with dependency, with borrowed identities, with obedience to figures who do not care for us but who are more than happy to manage us.[57] The fantasy of the Big Daddy—the Godfather, the protector, the knower— is seductive. He promises to carry the weight of adulthood for us. And in return, he asks only for our loyalty and obedience to him.

But this is not leadership. This is mirrored immaturity; he has not grown up either. He simply play acts adulthood better than we do. He has learned to dominate rather than to self-govern, to control rather than to become.

And the bond we form with him is not love—it is collusion.

He protects our fantasy. We protect his illusion. And no one grows.

There comes a moment in every life when the cost of staying small outweighs the risk of becoming whole.

> *"And the day came when the risk to remain tight in a bud*
> *was more painful than the risk it took to blossom."*
> —Anaïs Nin

That tipping point—the moment where we stop waiting to be rescued and start showing up for ourselves—is the beginning of emotional adulthood. To walk away from the Godfather is an act of rebellion—but it's more than that.

It is an act of individuation. It is an act of accountability.

Most of all, it is an act of liberation.

Because accountability and liberation always walk hand in hand.

When we cross the threshold, we surrender the illusion of effortless provision—the Edenic dream where nothing is asked of us, nothing is needed from us but faith.

But we pick up something far more powerful: our own lives.

We stop outsourcing authority. We stop looking for someone to carry us.

And we begin to say:

"I will carry the weight of my life."

"I will make peace with uncertainty."

"I will own my failures—and my triumphs."

"I will own my choices—and their consequences."

"I will take the risk of being seen—so that I can finally be real."

"I will do the labor of clarity—and carry the courage of seeing."

It may not look like a revolution. It may not be loud. But it is seismic. Because when we grow, we stop serving what was built to keep us small. We stop upholding systems that center fragility and demand obedience. We stop mistaking control for stability.

And then we see it clearly: The emotionally immature don't just long for a Godfather. They build him a throne. And around that throne, they build systems. In healthy systems, power exists to protect and provide for the vulnerable. Parents care for children. Leaders serve the group. Elders pass down wisdom for the benefit of all. But in dominance hierarchies, that equation is reversed. Power no longer protects—it extracts. Those at the top do not serve the group; the group is compelled to serve them.

These systems manufacture obedience—not through consent, but through fear, indoctrination, dependency, and myth.

At their core, they are engineered to reverse the natural order of care. We see them in:

* Narcissistic families, where the child is parentified to meet the emotional needs of the adult.

* Cults, where followers provide money, labor, and sex to elevate the leader.

* Theocracies, where religious obedience enriches a few and silences the rest.

* Nationalism, where identity and loyalty are weaponized to benefit the ruler and his allies.

* Patriarchy, the most sprawling of them all—where every structure bends to provide the spoils of domination to the Godfathers and their proxies.

These are not separate systems. They are variations on a theme. And that theme is domination disguised as order. Control disguised as morality. Immaturity scaled into architecture.

Dominance hierarchies elevate the emotionally immature, the grandiose, and the coercive—not by accident, but by design. They reward loyalty over conscience, submission over wisdom, and performance over truth. They are allergic to feedback and fatal to dissent. They cloak themselves in biology, history, tradition, or religion—but at their core, they are extraction systems.

They do not evolve to serve life.

They evolve to serve themselves.

And they only survive when we stay small. But when we walk away—when we choose growth over obedience, clarity over fantasy, and accountability over avoidance—we don't just leave something behind.

We become someone new.

It's not easy. Crossing the threshold always has a cost. You may lose comfort. You may lose belonging. You may lose the illusion that someone else is coming to save you. And what you gain is not just for you—it's for the world you will now help shape. Because when you walk away from systems designed to keep you small, you don't just leave.

You begin to build clarity and capacity—the emotional adulthood that is denied, discouraged, and dismantled by every system built on immaturity.

You begin to create what those systems fear most: a human being who knows their worth, lives by their own compass, and refuses to orbit around power. And that is where true revolution begins. Not with anger. Not with rebellion. But with a quiet, seismic choice: to grow.

Because when enough people grow, the Godfather loses his throne. The cult loses its gravity. The system loses the things it depends on most:

Your compliance.

Your silence.

Your willingness to stay small.

The Godfather offers structure, certainty, and external rules—an outer scaffolding meant to spare us the inner work of becoming our own authority. He is the father of control: he promises protection from chaos, direction without discernment, order without growth.

But the work of adulthood isn't finished when we walk away from him.

For just beyond his fortress waits another figure in patriarchy's theater—the Eternal Mother—keeper of warmth, empathy, and the spark of life itself. If the Strongman is our externalized authority and externalized control, she stands for our externalized vitality and the externalized responsibility to develop our inner potential.

Both exist because the Eternal Child has not yet learned to cultivate those forces from within.

The next chapter turns toward her: the one who carries the system's current, who keeps the machine alive, and who must decide whether to keep feeding it—or reclaim the power to generate life for herself.

8

The Fairy Godmother of Patriarchy — The Life Force It Can't Survive Without

BLUF: BUILDING ON THE LAST TWO CHAPTERS, THIS CHAPTER MAPS THE ARCHETYPE OF THE FAIRY GODMOTHER/ETERNAL MOTHER—THE FIGURE PATRIARCHY RELIES ON TO SUPPLY THE VITALITY, CONSCIENCE, AND GROWTH IT EXCUSES MEN FROM CULTIVATING.

SECTION I: THE PATRIARCHAL CONTRACT — BORROWED VITALITY, STOLEN ALIVENESS

> *BLUF: Domination cannot generate the warmth, empathy, and aliveness a culture needs to function—so patriarchy siphons these from women and rebrands the extraction as "the natural order."*

Every culture built on domination depends on something quieter to keep it alive. The Strongman may stand at its center—commanding, rigid, self-contained—but his grandeur is mechanical. His power moves with the stiff precision of gears. His certainty clangs like metal on stone. He can impose order, but he cannot generate life.

Behind the armor lies only hollowness. Lifeless. Cold. Colorless. Soulless. A system that moves but never breathes.

And yet even the most rigid regimes hunger for aliveness. They need pulse and color, warmth, and continuation. They need the energies that create, nourish, sustain, and protect and give meaning and bring color to life. The Strongman cannot generate this. He must take it from others.

Domination always requires a split in the human energies of life. A system built on control must outsource everything it cannot generate—warmth, empathy, flexibility, relational intelligence, moral imagination.

Patriarchy survives by separating power from care, authority from attunement, domination from the very energies that make life livable—and then extracting those energies from women. History shows this clearly.

The Third Reich—one of the most obvious Strongman cultures ever constructed—reduced women's roles to a three-word slogan: *Kinder, Küche, Kirche* (children, kitchen, church).[58] Its propaganda exalted women for producing future soldiers, restricting them to cooking, childbearing, and reinforcing ideology. It pushed marriage and childbirth with financial rewards, prohibited contraception, and abortion providers could be punished with death. It awarded medals to "honored mothers" even as it barred women from education and professions it considered "male."

The message was unmistakable: the puppet regime's vitality must be supplied by women, even as the regime drained their own and their children's.

This is the deeper pattern.

Every culture requires a flow of aliveness—the human capacity to nourish, enliven, create, relate, imagine, and sustain it. But cultures shaped around domination divide up those capacities along rigid lines. They split the world into hardened categories: those who command and control and those who energize, those who seize resources and those who nourish, those who take and those who give life.

The result is always the same.

A wooden, hardened, unfeeling structure—machine-like in its movements—leaning on others to supply the heart, warmth, color, and spirit it cannot generate on its own.

And because such a system cannot bear the contrast—its own lifelessness reflected beside another's vitality—it must also diminish and dehumanize those who feed it. It strips them of personhood to justify the extraction of their energy, and it strips them again to avoid seeing its dependency: a cold body animated by someone else's warmth.

It is a soul-starved culture that must borrow soul—must steal life.

And so, to understand what it truly means to come alive—to move from stiff woodenness to full humanity—we turn to an old story.

Long before growth had theories and charts, the tale of Pinocchio taught the oldest truth of all: aliveness is earned through effort, and realness is forged on the journey. And so, the story begins again, as it always has —with a wooden figure, a single wish, and the journey that alone can bring a heartless, hollow body to life.

SECTION II. A WOODEN BEGINNING – PINOCCHIO AND THE ANCIENT TRUTH OF BECOMING REAL

> *BLUF: Pinocchio reveals the ancient truth patriarchy evades realness is earned through inner effort, not bestowed by another's love, devotion, or magic.*[59]

Long ago in Italy, there lived a woodcarver named Geppetto. He worked happily during the day, but at night he felt a deep loneliness. One evening he carved a wooden puppet shaped like a boy, dressed it carefully, and laid it gently in a small bed. Looking up at a bright star, he whispered, "If only I had a real boy of my own."

That night, the star shimmered into the form of a Blue Fairy. She touched the puppet with her wand. "Little wooden Pinocchio," she said, "open your eyes. Tomorrow you will walk and speak like a real boy. And if you prove yourself brave, truthful, and unselfish, you may become real." She appointed a wise cricket to guide him, then vanished into the night.

In the morning, Geppetto was astonished to find Pinocchio awake and talking. Overjoyed, he embraced him and called him his son.

Pinocchio longed to go to school. Though he had little money, Geppetto traded his warm coat to buy schoolbooks. The next day, Pinocchio set off proudly with Jiminy Cricket on his shoulder. But on the way, a sly Fox and Cat convinced him to go to a fair instead. Ignoring the Cricket's warnings, Pinocchio sold his schoolbooks for a ticket and entered the fairgrounds.

Inside, he leapt onto a puppet stage and dazzled the crowd. The puppet master, seeing an opportunity, locked Pinocchio in a birdcage. When the Blue Fairy appeared and asked how he had ended up there, Pinocchio lied —and his nose grew longer with every false word. Only when he finally told the truth did his nose return to normal. The Fairy freed him, returned his books, and warned him to choose wisely from now on.

Back on the road, Pinocchio accepted a ride from a Coachman who promised him a place called Pleasure Island, where boys could do whatever they liked. Ignoring Jiminy Cricket again, Pinocchio went. At first the island seemed full of delights—candy, games, and endless fun—but soon the boys began turning into donkeys. Pinocchio sprouted ears and hooves himself. Horrified, he fled with Jiminy Cricket's help and reached a seaside village.

There he learned that Geppetto, searching for his lost son, had sailed out to sea and never returned. Blaming himself, Pinocchio leapt into the ocean to find him. A giant whale soon swallowed him whole. Inside the dark belly of the whale, Pinocchio found Geppetto alive. Overjoyed, they embraced.

Pinocchio quickly planned: he built a smoky fire to make the whale sneeze. With one tremendous blast, the whale expelled them into the sea, and they washed ashore. But Pinocchio lay motionless on the beach.

In a flash of light, the Blue Fairy appeared. "Pinocchio," she said, "you saved your father. You have proven yourself brave, truthful, and unselfish." She touched him with her wand, and Pinocchio became a real boy.

Awakening with soft arms and legs, he cried, "Father, look—I'm real!" Geppetto wept with joy. And so, Pinocchio and Geppetto lived many happy years together.

THE LESSON OF PINOCCHIO'S TALE

The tale of Pinocchio tells the truth about becoming human with genuine heart.

To be real, we must meet life with courage, tell the truth about our choices, and relate to others as separate beings with needs and limits of their own. Integrity becomes relationship; unselfishness becomes evidence of real connection.

Pinocchio also shows that transformation is always an inside job.

Outer events may shake us awake, but no one can make us real on our behalf. Even the Blue Fairy could only open the door—Pinocchio had to choose to walk through it.

And the work is demanding.

The belly of the whale is the story's pressure chamber: a place of consequence, containment, and truth. It shows that becoming real requires facing limits, accepting responsibility, and rising to challenges we did not choose. Courage, truthfulness, unselfishness—these cannot be borrowed, gifted, or wished into place.

This is why some people, and some cultures, resist transformation.

They don't want the pressure, the limits, the containment, or the effort needed in the belly of becoming. They want someone else to animate them from the outside while they remain unchanged characters—enlivened with novelty delivered to their door, celebrated into significance, loved into being, and free to linger forever on Pleasure Island.

Pinocchio exposes this evasion for what it is: a refusal to develop a heart and come alive. And from here—from this tale of wooden beginnings and earned aliveness—we turn to another ancient metaphor of transformation: the pregnant belly. The original container. The original pressure. The clearest image we have of what real initiation demands: a willingness to be changed on the inside long before anything shows on the outside.

Yet to the immature mind, pregnancy can also become a tempting misreading—a symbol of transformation without inner work. A fantasy that becoming alive is simply the result of pleasure, contact with ecstasy, or the "magic" of union, rather than the long, disciplined labor of growth, character, and becoming.

THE PREGNANT BELLY — THE FIRST SYMBOL OF TRANSFORMATION

Before humans understood conception, pregnancy looked like pure magic.

A woman's body quietly swelling with unseen life.

A heartbeat emerging where there had been none.

A child formed out of invisibility and emerging into the visible world.

From the outside, it appeared effortless: no machinery, no instruction manual, no conscious work from the one being transformed. A woman received a man, time passed, and a human being appeared—whole, complete, and unmistakably real. In many cultures this mystery was interpreted as divine intervention. Gods breathed life into women. Spirits overshadowed them. Light, wind, water, dreams, and blessings were said to spark conception.

The womb became the earliest symbol of transformation without visible effort—a chamber where the invisible becomes visible, where potential becomes personhood, where magic seems to happen on its own.

Of course, every woman who has ever carried life knows the truth: pregnancy is not effortless at all. It is labor long before labor. It is pressure, containment, risk, rearrangement, and consequence—an inner crucible of becoming.

But from the outside, especially in pre-scientific eras, pregnancy could look like creation that requires nothing from the one being created. The fetus is transformed without conscious effort; the mother does the work.

It is from this ancient mis-seeing—this illusion of effortless transformation—that many of our cultural fantasies are born. The idea that one person can be changed *for* another. That transformation is bestowed, not earned. That realness descends from above like a blessing, instead of arising from within like a discipline.

And while most fairy tales tell stories of challenges met and learning undertaken, some fairy tales do show the fantasy of magical transformation without effort. Perhaps the illusion of effortless fetal transformation seeded the cultural fantasy of transformation without work.

SECTION III: FAIRY-TALE LOGIC — HOW PATRIARCHY SELLS TRANSFORMATION WITHOUT EFFORT

> *BLUF: Patriarchal fairy tales claim men change through women's devotion while women are rescued through men's desire—naturalizing one-sided emotional labor and marketing eternal childhood to both.*

Some of the most enduring fairy tales—Snow White, Cinderella, Sleeping Beauty—teach a specific dream: transformation from without.

The girl does not go on a journey. She does not face trials. She does not develop character.

She is discovered.

She is rescued.

She is kissed awake.

She is chosen.

A prince happens upon her in the woods, sees her across a ballroom, or kisses her out of sleep. His attention alone—his desire, his recognition of her beauty—is framed as the engine of her new life.

In these tales, he animates her.

And she "lives happily ever after" in a world where roses bloom forever, nothing decays, and her needs are endlessly and adoringly met.

THE ETERNAL CHILD QUEEN

Patriarchy does not only promise boys the life of the Eternal Child King—it also sells girls the fantasy of the Eternal Child.

Just be beautiful.

Just be good.

Just wait.

A Prince will come.

He will rescue you from drudgery.

He will transform your life.

You will never have to grow up or change.

He will adore you forever.

And like all fairy tales, the story ends at the wedding—as if marriage were the culmination of her arc rather than the beginning of her real one.

But if we follow the story beyond the final page...

We arrive not in a kingdom of eternal roses but in the land of adulthood.

Patriarchal marriage will ask things of her it will never ask of him:

- Her name will change, his will not.

- Her legal status shifts; his remains intact.

- Her daily labor expands from one person to two or more.

- Her economic captivity closes in on her.

- Her body will stretch, swell, bleed, and recover to bring forth children.

His body does not change.

His labor often does not change.

His social standing usually rises.

Before marriage, he relates to her to win her hand.

After marriage, she must relate to him to sustain the home, the family, and the relationship.

Sex and marriage will transform her life; they may or may not transform his.

This is the fairy tale's hidden ending: she will change—he may not.

But just as patriarchy sells women the promise of eternal girlhood, it also sells men the promise of being transformed without effort.

THE FROG PRINCE — TRANSFORMATION BESTOWED FROM WITHOUT

In the popular retelling of *The Frog Prince*, the princess kisses the frog, and he instantly becomes a prince.

He does nothing to change.

Unlike the female arc in fairy tales, the magical rescue does not rely on his good qualities but on her willingness to look past obvious ugliness. Her acceptance—her patience, her openness—is treated as the magic of his transformation.

This pattern appears in countless "enchanted bridegroom" tales:

A man turned into a beast or monster is freed when a woman:

- ❖ sees his inner beauty,

- ❖ marries him,

- ❖ sleeps beside him,

- ❖ remains loyal,

- ❖ or performs some act of obedience or affection.

He is transformed. She performs the labor—whether that labor is epic or as small as a single kiss.

The message is unmistakable: A woman's devotion is the wand that changes him.

BEAUTY AND THE BEAST – A DANGEROUS NARRATIVE

Beauty and the Beast introduce a darker, more seductive version.

This is not instant magical transformation.

It is the story sold to millions of women:

"If you love the Beast enough, he will want to change."

"If you see the goodness beneath his brutality, he will soften."

"If you hold on long enough, he will become the prince you glimpsed in the beginning."

This is the fantasy that traps women in marriages of neglect, volatility, emotional unavailability, or covert and overt abuse.

She keeps hoping the early "princely" version will reappear.

She keeps believing that more patience, more empathy, more softness, more forgiveness will inspire him to grow.

She keeps waiting for the transformation patriarchy promises is just around the corner.

But in the tale—as in life—she is told the curse will not break until she works for it.

THE PATTERN BENEATH THE STORIES

Across these tales, the same cultural logic repeats:

Women are transformed merely by men's desire for them.

Men are transformed by women's effort on their behalf.

Men do not have to transform to earn the relationship.

Women must transform to sustain it.

Patriarchy does not require men to grow.

It requires women to grow—and then to use that growth as a magic wand on his behalf.

This is the oldest promise:

- ❖ Love alone will change him.

- ❖ Devotion will make him devoted.

- ❖ Forgiveness will make him caring.

- ❖ Indulging his comfort on Pleasure Island will eventually inspire maturity.

- ❖ Bearing his children will automatically make him responsible.

Meanwhile—until these fairy-tale promises materialize—she provides everything:

- ❖ understanding

- ❖ emotional labor

- ❖ sexual energy

- ❖ aliveness

- ❖ home-building

- ❖ meaning

- ❖ relationship glue

- ❖ the spark that makes him feel significant—all in the belief that this will make him real.

The girl may be kissed awake—but only to become the Fairy Godmother with her magic wand.

The Eternal Boy receives the magic.

And the tale never asks what becomes of the woman whose life is spent animating someone else's becoming.

THE CONTRADICTION: WOMEN AS BOTH TOO MAGICAL AND NOT MAGICAL ENOUGH

Patriarchy teaches two opposite beliefs simultaneously:

1. ***Women's magic is dangerously powerful.***

    Her sexuality is a spell.

    Her beauty a snare.

    Her presence the cause of male desire and male crime alike.

    Her magic is so great it can overpower his will.

2. ***Women's magic is necessary because men lack will.***

    Her love is expected to regulate him.

    Her goodness to cleanse him.

    Her devotion to animate him.

    Her empathy to cheer him on.

So, women are: punished for being "too powerful," and blamed when their "power" fails to transform him.

It is a double distortion that leads to the final fantasy: patriarchy teaches both men and women that women's love, labor, sexuality, and goodness are a kind of supernatural force—powerful enough to transform anything but not powerful enough to demand reciprocity. And from this confusion emerges the final illusion: the belief that men are entitled to magic itself.

SECTION IV: ENTITLEMENT TO MAGIC — THE ETERNAL BOY'S DEMAND FOR A WAND, NOT WORK

> *BLUF: Patriarchy convinces men they are entitled to transformation without effort, relying on women's bodies, emotions, and labor as the wand that makes them feel alive.*

At the heart of patriarchy lies a hidden expectation: that women carry a magic wand, and that their bodies are places of transformation.

A wand that:

- turns houses into homes
- turns chaos into celebration
- turns sex into transcendence
- turns relationships into meaning
- turns "me and you" into "we"
- turns men into husbands, fathers, leaders
- turns emptiness into aliveness

This is not imagined as partnership. It is imagined as entitlement.

To the Eternal Boy, magic is his birthright.

SEXUAL MAGIC — HIS TRANSFORMATION, HER LABOR

Nowhere is this clearer than in sexuality.

In patriarchal scripts, sex is framed as:

- her turning him on
- her getting him off
- her facilitating his transcendence

He receives the ecstasy.

Her body is the vessel for the alchemy.

In orgasm he experiences the temporary transformation of *la petite mort*—a momentary dissolving of ego that feels like rebirth.

But for her?

- he is often indifferent to her pleasure except when it flatters his ego
- her orgasm is optional
- her erotic experience is secondary
- her body is treated as conduit and container

His desire is treated as sacred.

Her desire is treated as negligible.

This is the real engine of patriarchal lust:

Lust is not intimacy—it is the hunger to feel changed without changing.

And because it meets neither the inner self nor the other person, satisfaction is fleeting.

Unsatisfied, it grows only more ravenous.

Demanding, greedy, insatiable, it devours whatever it touches—and tastes nothing.

And the demand for her transformational magic only becomes more gluttonous.

PLEASURE ISLAND – PATRIARCHY'S HOME ADDRESS

Pleasure Island is not just a scene in *Pinocchio*.

It is patriarchy's natural ecosystem.

A world where:

- magic arrives without effort
- novelty entertains without cost
- women's labor appears "effortless"
- holidays and celebrations "just happen"
- homes maintain themselves
- relationships work without anyone working on them

The Eternal Boy wants:

- the magic
- the ecstasy
- the glow
- the meaning
- the home
- the connection

… without giving anything that creates them.

He wants the *effects* of adulthood—status, pleasure, importance—

without the *ingredients* of adulthood—effort, responsibility, reciprocity. He wants the benefits of becoming real while refusing the belly-of-the-whale journey that makes anyone real.

EMOTIONAL MAGIC — UNDERSTANDING, FORGIVENESS, AND EXEMPTION

Beyond sex and domesticity lies another form of magic he expects: the magic of emotional absolution—unconditional love, unconditional positive regard, unconditional understanding.

He wants:

- to be endlessly understood
- to be sympathetically explained
- to be excused from consequences
- to be forgiven without changing
- to be admired without effort
- to be comforted without vulnerability

Forgiveness is meant to be recognition of transformation already done. But in patriarchy, forgiveness becomes absolution without accountability.

Understanding becomes:

- a way to rewrite his cruelty as stress
- a way to soften his indifference into "he meant well"
- a way to turn harm into accident
- a way to protect his ego with her empathy

Her emotional labor becomes the wand that swishes away any need for his reform—and the publicist for his image.

And these entitlements—unlike the Eternal Boy—grow.

They become demanding. Greedy.

He gives less and expects more.

Fairy tales give us unambiguous teachings about what happens to those who grow greedy.

FAIRY-TALE MORALITY VS. PATRIARCHAL MORALITY

In fairy tales, when someone misuses magic and becomes greedy, consequences follow:[60]

- The Fisherman's Wife loses everything.
- The Sorcerer's Apprentice floods the house and is humbled.
- Aladdin's laziness nearly costs him the lamp and the princess.
- King Midas turns his world—and his daughter—to gold and begs for reversal.

The rules are clear:

Treat magic as entitlement or shortcut, and the story destroys the one who misused it.

But in patriarchy's upside-down moral universe, the opposite happens. The one who gets greedy is rarely the one who pays the cost. Instead, the consequences become:

- unwanted pregnancy
- too many children
- endless domestic and emotional labor
- economic dependence—and abandonment
- social stigma
- caretaking responsibilities
- dismissive, devaluing, demeaning treatment
- abuse
- legal retaliation
- cleaning up others' messes
- physical illness and injury
- moral injury
- mental exhaustion

And the ones who bear the burden are:

- women
- children
- the vulnerable
- the dependent

Patriarchal morality flips fairy-tale morality on its head: In fairy tales, misused magic is punished. In patriarchy, misused power is protected—and those harmed by it foot the bill.

SECTION V: THE ETERNAL MOTHER — THE WOMAN BEHIND THE WAND

> *BLUF: What looks like effortless feminine "magic" is actually skill, labor, foresight, and emotional intelligence—and patriarchy survives by mistaking her work for nature.*

From the outside, it looks like magic.

Dinner appears on the table—hot, balanced, seasoned to the tastes of everyone present and timed to their schedules. Clothes return clean and folded to drawers. Doctor's appointments are made. Birthdays are remembered. A house becomes a home—warm, inviting, expressive, alive. Children grow and thrive under a web of invisible labor so constant and competent it becomes mistaken for nature itself.

To the Strongman or Eternal Boy, it seems uncomplicated, effortless. *What does she even do all day?*

But none of it is magic. It is attunement, foresight, planning, decision-making, and continuous work—the same ingredients required for any transformation.

She sees what is needed.

She holds the whole in mind.

She anticipates, organizes, and initiates.

She carries the pressure.

She absorbs the consequences.

She does the work.

In the childish logic of patriarchy, men's work is treated as "real"—planned, intentional, measurable—while women's work, from childbirth to holiday magic to the daily labor of making life livable, is treated as effortless enchantment. Not something requiring skill, learning, or mastery. Something that "just happens," not something that is *made* to happen.

It is no different from the moment a child realizes Santa isn't the one eating the cookies or placing the presents under the tree. The magic was carefully orchestrated. Someone wrote the note in careful handwriting. Someone wrapped the gifts at midnight. Someone saw what everyone needed and created joy out of thin air.

Behind every Fairy Godmother is an Eternal Mother—the woman trained to provide the cumulative effect so others can lounge in and enjoy the ambiance.

And behind the Eternal Mother is something harder to name: a remnant of the Eternal Girl, the part of her that learned early that love required over-functioning. That harmony depended on adaptive agreeableness. That safety came from foresight. That being "good" meant being indispensable.

This is how one-sidedness becomes normalized.

THE ONE-SIDED DYNAMIC — APPROPRIATE FOR CHILDREN, IMMATURE FOR ADULTS

A parent–child relationship is one-sided by design. In this time-stamped relationship, the parent exists for the child's welfare and well-being and to provide a home in which the child can grow into adulthood. The child does not exist to provide the parent with companionship, validation, collaboration, or anything that would be expected from another adult.

The parent gives; the child receives. The child may offer little bouquets of effort and love—a scribbled drawing, a half-made bed, a spontaneous hug—and these gestures are rightly celebrated as growth.

But inside a partnership, adulthood requires reciprocity: cooperation, collaboration, shared responsibility, mutual effort, and mutual growth.

You are not owed another person's body, labor, servitude, or self-erasure.

You *are* owed partnership.

You *are* owed consideration.

You *are* owed respect.

You *are* owed reciprocity of effort and commitment.

But when someone never outgrows one-sided behavior, we do not find mature collaboration. We find the Eternal Boy, who wants the praise a child receives for token effort—a chore attempted, a mood improved, a moment of attention—treated as substantive contribution. He wants recognition without responsibility, reward without reliability. What is natural in a child becomes disturbing in an adult.

And on the other side of this dynamic is the over functioning Eternal Mother, who is often the Puella Aeterna—the Eternal Girl—in grown-up clothing. The girl who was parentified too early and trained to assume responsibilities that belonged to others; who learned to manage what adults neglected; who absorbed consequences that were never hers; who became indispensable before she became empowered.

She grew up believing that love meant foresight, that safety meant smoothing, and that her value lay in compensating for other people's refusal to be mature.

THE GIRL IN THE ETERNAL MOTHER

Her task of maturing is the opposite of his.

He must take personal responsibility that belongs to him.

She must stop taking responsibility for what does not belong to her.

Her initiation is learning to contain herself—not the world. To step out of the reflexive mothering role. To stop adjusting, smoothing, compensating, rescuing, and shouldering consequences that belong to others. To endure the discomfort of people's disappointment when she stops making magic on demand.

This is the counterintuitive maturation of the Eternal Girl:

- ❖ To be the container of her own power.
- ❖ To hold boundaries without collapsing into caretaking.
- ❖ To stop transforming people who refuse to transform themselves.
- ❖ To refuse to bring vitality to those who drain and diminish.
- ❖ To stop explaining herself to people uninterested in understanding.
- ❖ To refuse the one-sided relationships patriarchy offers and insist on *adult* ones—or none at all.

She becomes "the good enough mother" to herself: one who disappoints others in healthy ways, who lets reality do its work, who lets consequences fall where they rightly belong, who recognizes that love cannot redeem someone else's refusal to grow, and who accepts that grief is sometimes the price of adulthood.

THE MAGICAL BELIEF SHE MUST RELEASE

She must release the enchanted idea that she is the key to his potential.

"Behind every great man is a great woman" is both acknowledgment and trap. It appears to honor her invisible contribution while keeping her in his shadow—sculpting his destiny while neglecting her own.

She is the one who midwifes what is latent.

She is the one who sees the angel in the marble and keeps carving.

She is the one who keeps sculpting long after it should be his turn to pick up the chisel.

Letting go of this magical thinking is not bitterness; it is adulthood.

And it requires beginning to sculpt away everything that does not belong to her and finding her own individuality.

THE EMOTIONAL LOGIC OF REFUSAL — HOPE AS A DEFENSE AGAINST GRIEF

Why does she stay in these old patterns?

Because leaving means mourning.

To stop coddling the Eternal Child or defending the Strongman means facing the truth that love did not transform him—that her devotion could not materialize potential he refused to develop. That she could not grow what he would not. That is not failure. It is reality.

But reality feels like loss, and loss feels like death.

So, she keeps hoping. Keeps forgiving. Keeps turning her pain into proof of loyalty. Hope becomes her narcotic—her final defense against despair.

Yet each rescue postpones her own rebirth.

Each self-erasure deepens the pattern.

Her tenderness becomes complicity; her empathy becomes a leash.

Her tolerance becomes not compassion but a refusal to accept reality and to grieve.

THE MATURATION: CHOOSING EQUAL RELATIONSHIPS

Her adulthood begins when she demands reciprocity.

When she relates only to other adults as adults.

When she stops being the invisible partner behind a man's shine.

When she steps into the public sphere with her own name, her own contributions, her own authority.

When she becomes the protagonist of her own life.

She initiates herself.

She chooses change.

She no longer waits to be chosen or rescued or transformed by anyone else.

She transforms herself.

SECTION VI: PATRIARCHY'S MISPLACED BATTLE — FIGHTING THE MIRROR

BLUF: Instead of facing their own arrested development, patriarchal men fight the women who reflect it—attacking the mirror rather than confronting the self.

Every real transformation requires an adversary. In every mythic arc, the hero must face the Dragon that represents:

- his smaller self
- his fear
- his resistance
- his unclaimed potential
- the part of him that must die for something new to grow

But patriarchy refuses this inner battle.

The Eternal Boy and the Strongman may look like opposites, but psychologically they are two sides of the same developmental arrest:

- **The Eternal Boy** avoids adulthood. He is soft where he should be formed, bendable where he should stand firm, unable to tolerate the weight of consequence.

- **The Strongman** overcompensates for avoiding adulthood. He is rigid where he should be flexible, brittle where he should be strong, armored to hide an inner hollowness.

One collapses inward.

The other calcifies outward.

But both are terrified of pressure, accountability, and growth.

They are two masks worn by the same undeveloped self.

And because neither can face the fear of change, both relocate the battle outward.

The true antagonist is the immature self—the inner child who resists adult responsibility.

But instead of confronting that opponent, patriarchy teaches men to fight the person who represents the demand for maturity.

The woman.

The boundary.

The truth-teller.

The mirror.

She becomes the reflection of everything he refuses to face in himself.

WHY THE BATTLE IS MISPLACED

A mature psyche can and will confront itself.

An immature psyche will not—and eventually cannot—because the ego is too fragile to withstand truth.

Patriarchy's core psychological features make self-confrontation unbearable:

- **Fragile ego:** even gentle feedback feels like annihilation.

- **Childish logic:** cooperation feels like submission.

- **Entitled dependency:** women are expected to hold maturity for both adults.

- **Binary thinking:** he is either perfect or humiliated—no middle ground.

- **Fear of freedom (Fromm):** responsibility is terrifying, so he clings to familiar hierarchies.

- **Avoidance of individuation:** patriarchy hands him a ready-made identity—*collective manhood*—that demands no self-definition, only loyalty to the myths and silence about its wrongs; break either, and his "manhood" is revoked.

A system built on these traits cannot tolerate introspection.

So, it finds an enemy outside itself—because it cannot bear to meet the one within.

And—like every child frightened by his own reflection—he attacks the mirror.

The Eternal Boy's true foe is the man he refuses to become. But patriarchy teaches him that whoever holds the mirror must be defeated.

HOW THE MIRROR BECOMES THE ENEMY

When she asks for reciprocity, he hears inadequacy.

When she asks for problem-solving, he hears criticism.

When she asks for respect, he feels emasculated.

When she asserts boundaries, he feels threatened.

When she mirrors reality, he accuses her of being "too sensitive" or "the problem."

In his emotional logic:

- Her request is a demand.
- Her boundary is an accusation.
- Her growth is a rebellion—an indictment of his stagnation.
- Her disappointment is unfair.
- Her clarity is an attack.

He fights her because he will not fight the part of himself that would rather hit the snooze button forever.

And patriarchy reinforces this inversion.

It tells him:

- You are already enough.
- You already know best.
- You are the natural leader.
- You are the chosen one.
- You are the Golden Child of culture—no need to grow.

And it rewards his evasion of adulthood. It grants him:

- status
- exceptionalism
- authority
- excuses
- spiritual permission
- and a cultural boys' club

. . . for staying underdeveloped.

THE BOYS' CLUB —
THE COLLECTIVE REFUSAL TO GROW UP

The Dragon on the journey is not women obstructing male individuation.

It is the opposite:

Men, collectively avoiding leaving the boys' club.

The price of joining adulthood—accountability, reciprocity, self-reflection, sobriety—feels too high compared with the perks of remaining in collective childhood.

So, patriarchy builds a world where men never have to face the stillness and the pressure of the mirror—the kind of pressure where all real growth originates.

Protected from the world outside themselves—women's knowing, women's experiences, women's contributions, women's individuation, women's perspectives—they never have to leave the safe camaraderie and the echo chamber of the boys' club.

And beneath it all lies a collective fear—rarely named aloud:

- If men individuate from patriarchy's identity, they might lose the benefits it bestows.

- If they face themselves, they might lose the grandiosity and special status of the Golden Child.

- If they grow up, they cease to be exceptional.

Not all men of course—only those who refuse to grow out of patriarchy.

And so, patriarchy creates a haven for this refusal: a cultural frat house where extended adolescence is the norm—where teasing, demeaning, taunting, and using are treated as camaraderie, and where women are expected to run the gauntlet of emotional, domestic, and psychological projection.

Eternal boys dressed as Strongmen.

Women and society are expected to tiptoe around the fragile collective ego of men to keep the system intact—to give a wide berth to the debauchery, incompetence, and danger of the frat-house mindset.

And so, the battle remains misplaced.

The boys' club dons its togas, raises prop swords, and fights the "dragon lady" who dares to call them to graduate.

She becomes the obstacle.

She becomes the test.

She becomes the enemy they must defeat to preserve the illusion of mastery.

He and his buddies wink and wage war—not against their immaturity, but against the mirror they call the dragon lady.

SECTION VII: THE COLLAPSE OF THE SPELL — WHAT HAPPENS WHEN SHE STOPS CARING

> *BLUF: When women stop caring and stop over functioning, patriarchy's immaturity is exposed and the system panics—prompting it to get her back in line by calling her "crazy."*

Patriarchy's survival depends on women caring about everyone else—because if she were to stop, the system's immaturity would not merely be exposed; it would be unable to function.

The machinery of daily life would seize: homes, communities, workplaces, and institutions would feel the sudden absence of the invisible labor they've always mistaken for nature.

Women already know the world can go on without men because they've had to keep going through abuse, dysfunction, addiction, discrimination, laziness, violence, and men quitting on families they created.

What patriarchy cannot fathom—what terrifies it most—is women behaving the way the system has long behaved toward them: not caring.

Women refusing to overfunction.

Women handing back responsibility.

Women refusing to pretend that charm is care.

Behind every patriarchal structure are women softening intent by performing invisible alchemy—reframing domination into "order," selfishness into "stress," indifference into "misunderstanding."

Her role is to provide the soul, the spark, the warmth, the relational intelligence.

Her softness is the insulation that makes a cold system survivable.

Her empathy is the padding that keeps the culture from impaling itself on its own sharp cruelty.

She is the one who humanizes what would otherwise be unbearably inhuman. Her task is to make the patriarchal system appear stable, humane, moral, and life-giving.

Without her ability to feel, soothe, interpret, and forgive, patriarchy would be experienced for what it is: a dystopian, barren landscape of entitlement, self-interest, cruelty, and moral indifference.

And so she is charged with reflecting back the image patriarchy's fragile ego needs to see and needs to believe in order to function: to reflect the system as caring, capable, moral—even when she knows it is not; to mirror vitality, goodness, warmth, color, humanity—even when they do not exist.

Patriarchy feeds on empathy even while discrediting it.

It calls softness, compassion, and creativity weakness—and hardness and moral indifference strength.

But it needs her softness, so it does not have to confront its hardness. It needs her understanding, so it does not have to cultivate a conscience. It wants her aliveness, so it does not have to face the emptiness inside itself.

And when she stops providing this emotional electricity—when she withdraws her softness, her kindness, her forgiving interpretations—the system reacts because it cannot afford to lose the idealized reflection she supplies.

It cannot tolerate the truth she now names.

Patriarchy can dish it out—but it can't even take feedback.

Patriarchy does not challenge men to become better, it silences women who point out what's out of integrity, immature, unfair, or unjust.

It wages war on the reflection, without any conscience.

And patriarchy issues men the simplest weapon of all: Discredit her.

Call her irrational. Call her unstable. Call her crazy.

This is not an accident—it is a tactic of war designed to destabilize her, to make her doubt what she knows.

The next chapter steps directly into that mechanism: how cognitive dissonance becomes traumatic when an entire culture insists that women should not trust their own perception.

9

"She's Crazy" — Traumatic Cognitive Dissonance and the Manipulation of Reality

BLUF: PATRIARCHY RUNS ON ENGINEERED INNER CHAOS. IT DELIBERATELY DESTABILIZES PERCEPTION—ESPECIALLY WOMEN'S—THROUGH CHRONIC CONTRADICTION, USING THE RESULTING DISORIENTATION TO DISCREDIT REALITY AND WEAPONIZE CONFUSION. THIS KEEPS PEOPLE OFF-BALANCE, SELF-DOUBTING, AND EASIER TO MANIPULATE. THE SYSTEM GASLIGHTS WOMEN, DOUBLE-CASTS MEN AND WOMEN IN CONTRADICTORY ROLES, AND TURNS CONFUSION INTO CONTROL—WHILE HOLLOW MEN ARE INFLATED AS LEADERS BY THE VERY PEOPLE THEY DESTABILIZE.

SECTION I: WHAT COGNITIVE DISSONANCE FEELS LIKE — THE PERSONAL TRAP

BLUF: Traumatic cognitive dissonance is not confusion—it is a psychological assault that destabilizes a person's ability to trust their own perception, creating the conditions for control.

Imagine someone you love dearly telling you, "I love you" and "I hate you," in the same sentence.

Now, feel what happens inside your mind as it ricochets between those two opposing realities, trying to land on which one is true. Imagine the mental chaos. Imagine the emotional chaos. Feel how frantic, trapped, and disoriented you would become as your brain tries to solve a puzzle that cannot be solved. You believe they love you—because they say so—but they're also telling you they hate you. And your nervous system begins to split itself trying to hold both truths at once.

That is cognitive dissonance.[61]

Now imagine you have marriage vows with this person—so you must make sense of it.

They say they love you, and sometimes even act like it: they do small favors, smile at you in public, play the role of the good partner. But there is a second, constant, quieter message running underneath—one that says: "I don't like you."

When you're sick, they seem irritated. When you ask for help, they're suddenly exhausted. When you reveal your pain, they mock you, then accuse you of being "too sensitive." When you try to explain clearly and calmly what hurts, they pretend not to understand, or insist your tone is the real problem. *She's just a friend,* they say, though the texts sound like more than friendship. And sometimes, if you catch the angle exactly right, you see the smirk—the satisfaction in your confusion.

But they also hold your hand sometimes. They say the right words, insist they love you.

And so, you tell yourself: *I must be imagining it. I must be expecting too much. I must be the problem.*

"He's a good guy," you repeat like a spell against your own instincts.

The pattern becomes the trap: the contradiction is never resolved, so you turn the blade inward.

You begin to think you must be crazy.

He hints that you are.

Maybe he's right.

Dr. Peter Salerno names this experience for what it is: Traumatic Cognitive Dissonance. Not just confusion—a sustained psychological assault through contradiction, denial, and emotional reversals so relentless they destabilize the brain itself and the nervous system. It is, he writes, "crazy making, brutal, and unrelenting"—a form of trauma far more disorienting than ordinary stress because it destroys the ability to trust one's own sense of reality. He adds:

> "Traumatic cognitive dissonance is one of the most debilitating trauma conditions that can occur after being involved with a disordered personality. Unfortunately, it is almost completely undetected, overlooked, misunderstood, or even denied by the vast majority of mental health professionals who specialize in treating trauma. It is more often than not misattributed to co-dependency, poor boundaries, or early attachment wounds by misinformed professionals."[62]

Salerno documents a thorough list of fallout symptoms: loss of cognitive control, insomnia or hypersomnia, dissociation, memory disorientation, emotional paralysis, mental paralysis, feeling like an imposter, feeling like a failure, feeling like you're going crazy, hyper vigilance, inability to trust your instincts, and suicidal ideation.

The body begins to malfunction because the mind has been forced into an impossible double-logic: love / hate, safe / unsafe, wanted / resented— no exit, no clarity.

And this is the hinge. Because patriarchy runs on this exact mechanism. Not accidentally. Not occasionally. Systemically.

Patriarchy is built on the engineering of contradiction as control.

SECTION II: THE DOUBLE ARCHITECTURE — HOW PATRIARCHY MANUFACTURES CONTRADICTION

> *BLUF: Patriarchy is engineered through pairs of contradictions—double standards, double binds, double messaging—that keep reality unstable and people self-policing.*

The double structure of contradiction prevents reality from stabilizing and that instability keeps obedience in place. Here are some of the doubles that produce destabilizing contradictions.

DOUBLE STANDARDS

Different rules for different people

→ "Boys will be boys" / "Girls must be pure"

DOUBLE BINDS

No acceptable way to win or punished no matter what you do

→ "Speak up and you're aggressive; stay silent and you're complicit"

DOUBLE SPEAK (DOUBLESPEAK)

Language that hides, reverses, or distorts truth

→ "Discipline" for abuse, "protection" for control

DOUBLE IMAGE / TWO-FACED PERFORMANCE

Public persona vs. private reality

→ The Strongman in public, the Eternal Boy in private

DOUBLE MESSAGE

What is said versus what is meant

→ "I'm only joking" as cover for hostility

DOUBLE VALUATION

Same behavior judged differently depending on who does it

→ Assertive man = leader; assertive woman = bitch

DOUBLE BINDING NARRATIVES

Two opposite stories supported at once

→ "Women are emotional and irrational" + "Women must regulate men's emotions"

Patriarchy is not built on one lie, but on pairs of lies held together—double standards, double binds, double images—creating a hall of mirrors where truth can never land.

It keeps people trapped not through overt abuse or violence alone, but through cognitive dissonance so chronic it becomes self-policing.

We won't delve into all these doubles. But let's look at the primary Double—the one that anchors all the others. To do so we point to the archetypal roles we've already explored: the Eternal Child, the Strongman, and the Eternal Mother, and see how pitting these roles against each other in contradiction is the core engineering that underpins patriarchy itself. Then we'll look at how ordinary men and ordinary women have been trained to embody these contradictions and keep the system running across millennia:

- ❖ Men as Strongman in public but Eternal Boy in private
- ❖ Women as Eternal Child in public but Eternal Mother in private

These contradictions are damaging for everyone: for men, for women, for children raised in patriarchy and they are poison for adult relationships where individuation and equality is the basis for true collaboration and partnership. And while this cognitive dissonance serves to control both men and women it does not affect them equally.

MEN IN PATRIARCHY COGNITIVE DISSONANCE

Empowered to assume a Strongman persona while secretly depending on the Eternal Mother

Men are trained to believe:

- ❖ "You are the leader" / but you depend on women to provide a chore list of what needs to be done

- ❖ "You are the provider" / but she does paid work, and is still expected to cater to "the provider"

- ❖ "You are the authority" / but the "authority" can avoid responsibility and accountability

- ❖ "You are independent" / but dependent on the relational, logistical, and emotional labor outsourced to women

- ❖ "You are in charge" / but need someone else to carry the consequences of one's choices and behaviors

Public role: Strong, stoic, in control

Private reality: Emotionally dependent, unskilled at self-regulation, expecting to be mothered

Men *live inside contradiction* and are shaped by it—but they are not the primary target of the contradiction. And they are damaged by the message to not show vulnerable emotions, develop rational skills, or repair skills, but patriarchal dissonance primarily serves to keep their power, not dismantle their sanity.

WOMEN IN PATRIARCHY TRAUMATIC COGNITIVE DISSONANCE

Cast as the Eternal Child in public (incompetent, emotional, inferior) while secretly functioning as the Eternal Mother (responsible, hardworking, hyper-competent, stabilizing)

Women are trained to believe:

* "You are childlike, irrational, and fragile" / but you must regulate men's emotions and keep the family stable

* "You need a man to lead you" / but you are the one with the executive skills at home (and often at work), leading everyone without credit

* "You are protected and provided for" / but you must sacrifice your dreams, health, and safety—and often defend yourself from the very man calling himself protector

* "You're lucky he takes care of you" / but you are the one doing the caretaking

* "You are too emotional to lead" / but you must absorb everyone else's emotions and never falter

Public role: *Dependent, lesser, ornamental*

Private reality: *Responsible, competent, emotionally laboring adult*

So, women live inside a crazy-making contradiction: treated like a child / expected to function like a parent

But unlike men, women are:

* punished for naming the contradictions

* blamed for reacting to it

* expected to carry the emotional, logistical, and relational cost of it

* told they are *crazy, dramatic, overreacting, ungrateful, or misperceiving reality*

That is what turns cognitive dissonance into traumatic cognitive dissonance:

→ *the contradiction is weaponized*

→ *the target is disoriented on purpose*

→ *the system erodes their capacity to trust their own perception it labels them crazy.*

SECTION III: 'SHE'S CRAZY' — TARGETING SANITY

> *BLUF: Calling women "crazy" is not descriptive—it is a tactic to invalidate perception, discredit truth-telling, and keep women from trusting their own reality.*

HOW WOMEN ARE CALLED 'CRAZY'

Women are framed as crazy in both overt and covert ways—and every version serves the same purpose: to undermine credibility, dismiss perception, and destabilize sanity. The labels are not descriptions; they are silencers.

Let's begin with the granddaddy of them all: *"Men are logical and women are emotional."* That is simply a socially acceptable way of saying: "Men are rational. Women are crazy. Their perspectives don't count."

DIRECT LABELS

crazy, dramatic, drama queen, overreacting, hysterical, unhinged, unstable, imagining things, paranoid, "you need help," too emotional, too sensitive, "calm down"

RELATIONAL SMEARS

my crazy ex, she went psycho, she's obsessed, needy, "she likes drama," impossible to please, impossible to reason with, "you know how she gets," "she's nuts"

GASLIGHTING REFRAMES

that never happened, you're remembering it wrong, you're reading into things, you can't take a joke, you took it the wrong way, you're being irrational

AND THEN THE SILENT VERSION

the look, the smirk, the eye roll, the pitying tone, the fake calm, the "she's unhinged" glance shared with another person

Men call women crazy with their faces long before they call them crazy with their words.

These cues say:

"You're not rational."
"Your mind is the problem."
"The issue isn't what happened—it's who you are."

They don't argue. They don't rebut.
They reframe her sanity in real time—without ever needing evidence.

HOW MEN ARE CALLED 'CRAZY'

Men are called crazy too—but it is not used to discredit their perception or invalidate their anger. It is used to mark danger, volatility, or rebellious power: loose cannon, went off the rails, out of control, ticking time bomb, wild, unhinged, madman genius, "crazy like a fox," "he doesn't play by the rules."

It is often admiring or a warning, not erasure.

Men are almost never called "crazy" for noticing a pattern, having emotions, or reporting harm. When men are called crazy, it's about action—violence, risk, rule-breaking—and often said admiringly.

When women are called crazy, it's about perception: memory, intuition, reality-testing.

Women get called crazy for naming contradictions—for naming reality.

Men get called crazy for defying reality—or for refusing its rules.

THE CORE DISTINCTION

For men, patriarchy's contradictions may be uncomfortable, but they are often rewarding.

For women, the contradictions become captivity.

And here's where the system hides itself.

SECTION IV: THE GOOD GUY — PATRIARCHY'S TROJAN HORSE

> *BLUF: Patriarchy's most effective enforcer is the "good guy" whose chronic non-cooperation is framed as innocence, leaving women carrying the entire load while doubting their own judgment.*

Patriarchy is not sustained primarily by monsters, tyrants, or the cartoon villains of misogyny.

The good guys sustain it—the ones who don't see themselves as part of the problem, who sincerely believe they are fair, respectful, and kind, and yet still live out the script of patriarchy because they have never had to step outside it.

The most effective delivery system for domination is not the man who boasts about it—but the man who *doesn't recognize he's benefiting from it.*

He does not shout, threaten, or strike. He shrugs, delays, forgets, excuses, withdraws, and lets her carry the load.

He believes in equality in theory, while quietly depending on inequality in practice.

He is the man who says:

"Of course, I support women"—while never adjusting his comfort.

"I'm not like those other guys"—while benefiting from the same unpaid labor.

"Just tell me what you need"—and then resenting being told.

"I would help if you asked"—but punishing the ask.

"I don't control you"—he simply refuses to take part unless things go his way.

Like a Trojan Horse, he arrives looking like a gift wrapped with affection, charm, good intentions, and "not all men" decency—but once inside the walls of shared life, the old architecture unfolds.

He is not the Strongman face of patriarchy.

He is the *carrier.*

And in every system—legal, political, relational—the carrier also bears responsibility.

Many men want the benefits of patriarchy without the accountability. They want to laugh at the sexist jokes, talk over women's voices, vote for the misogynist, benefit from unequal pay and workplace discrimination, and reflexively defend every serial sexual assaulter as "wrongly accused"—but are outraged at being held responsible for their participation.

They drive the getaway car and howl when they are charged with the robbery.

The legal system is clear:

If you drive the getaway car, you are charged with the crime.

If you participate in a robbery where someone is killed, you are charged with murder—even if you didn't pull the trigger.

If you cover up the crime, aid the criminal, or receive stolen goods, you are an accessory after the fact.

This is not radical feminist theory.

It is basic legal reasoning.

And the critique of "not all men" and of the "good men" who passively stand by follows this same logic.

You cannot receive the stolen benefits of a system that strategically disadvantages women—protection, privilege, exemption, leniency, default leadership, social deference—and declare yourself uninvolved.

Patriarchy does not need all men—or even most men—to be violent to survive. It only needs enough "good men" who refuse to grow—and enough women trained to feel guilty for noticing.

The tragedy is not that the Good Guy intends harm.

The tragedy is that he assumes his comfort is the natural operating system of the relationship—and her discomfort is simply the cost of doing business—and calls that love.

WHEN REFUSING TO COOPERATE IS SOLD AS MANHOOD

In healthy development, individuation means becoming an internally re-sourced adult—someone who can think, decide, contribute, carry respon-sibility, and bring something of substance into shared life. Real adulthood isn't about doing everything alone, but about being able to participate as an equal rather than as a dependent.

Patriarchy short-circuits that process. Instead of developing an inner adult, it hands men the *appearance* of independence while excusing them from the work that makes independence real. The developmental labor—frustration, skill-building, accountability, shared responsibility—is by-passed. What replaces it is not maturity, but defiance where cooperation should be.

Dr. Peter Salerno describes this antagonism to collaboration as a defin-ing trait of severely disordered personalities: "... they display an unwilling-ness to cooperate even at the most basic level in relationships, all while feigning earnest collaboration and cooperation."[63]

Most men are not severely disordered, but many echo this feigning cooperation while being antagonistic to it. Because patriarchy trains even "good guys" to imitate this same relational stance—not through violence or overt domination, but through chronic non-participation disguised as confusion, forgetfulness, or laid-back temperament.

This is the version many women live with:

The man who "doesn't know how"

The man who "didn't hear"

The man who promises later, delivers never

The man who waits until she gives up and does it herself

The man who offers "help" when the work is already done

The man who becomes helpful only when others might see it

The man who watches her struggle and feels no need to assume an equal share.

This is not inability.

It is non-cooperation presented as innocence.

And when he is asked directly—or held to a shared expectation—the mask slips: irritation, defensiveness, accusations of nagging, withdrawal, or a flat refusal framed as "not being controlled."

He is not confused. He did hear. He didn't forget. He is entirely capable. He simply does not care enough to interrupt his comfort—and that indifference is the point, not the accident.

His passivity is not neutral. It is a strategy that ensures she carries the mental load, the household load, the emotional load, and the consequences.

The goal is not to avoid one chore.

The goal is to train her out of requesting partnership at all. To make asking cost more than doing it alone. To turn competence into a trap.

So, she spends years believing the problem is her delivery:

maybe I wasn't clear

maybe I should've said it differently

maybe I'm too sensitive

maybe I need to be more patient

maybe he'll help if I don't sound upset

maybe love means carrying more so he doesn't have to

Meanwhile, he does not adjust—because the imbalance benefits him exactly as it is.

WHY PATRIARCHY REWARDS THIS

Patriarchy defines masculinity as never being answerable to a woman—not even in a shared life. So, refusal is reframed as independence. Withholding becomes strength. Non-participation is treated as authority. Dependence on a woman's labor is recast as leadership over her.

The man who refuses to cooperate will often congratulate himself for being "self-reliant," while other men quietly admire him for not letting a woman "tell him what to do."

He is not self-sufficient.

He is supplied—by the very person he dismisses.

This is the architecture of pseudo-individuation: he performs adulthood from the recliner—remote in hand, shoes still on the floor where he left them—while the woman he calls his partner keeps the world running around his station. Not because she wants to mother a man, but because the alternative is failure, disorder, or harm.

That is what adults do: they do what needs to be done, even when they're tired, even when it's not fun, even when no one praises them.

And often, he mocks her for having standards, for "making things hard," for "caring too much," for not outsmarting adulthood the way he has.

The Eternal Mother exists so he can pretend he has grown up—without doing the work that growth requires.

Her active maturity is framed as *aggression*.

His passive immaturity is framed as *integrity*.

This reversal is not accidental.

It protects the person who is refusing adulthood and penalizes the one absorbing the cost of that refusal.

So, when she asks for partnership, he calls it "nagging." When she sets a boundary, he calls it "emasculation." When she asks him to change in response to changed circumstances—marriage, children, illness, aging—he calls it "trying to control him." All while insisting that being exactly the same person he was at twenty is a sign of steadfastness or strength.

Refusing to evolve when you enter a relationship or have children is not principled bravery. It is an open admission that you are lazy and self-centered, and that no one else's well-being matters as much as your comfort.

And the more responsibly she adapts to reality, the more she is mocked for her conscientiousness. The more competent she becomes the more she is told that she's simply better at it so she should be the one to do it.

That is the cognitive trap: the person doing the adult work becomes the problem, and the person avoiding the work becomes the one who must be protected from "unfair expectations."

The result is a chronic mind-bending reality inversion: the person who matures carries the burden of change, and the person who refuses growth claims the authority to judge it.

SECTION V: DENIAL, REVERSAL, AND THE COGNITIVE DISSONANCE OF DISMISSING PATRIARCHY

> *BLUF: Denying patriarchy requires a cognitive split—insisting the system isn't real while emotionally defending it—revealing benefit disguised as disbelief.*

There is a peculiar modern contradiction in which people insist patriarchy is a myth while living inside—and benefiting from—its structures every day. They deny that men as a group hold disproportionate power, even as nearly every nation, religion, corporation, military, legislature, and historical archive reflects male dominance. They deny that women face systemic barriers, even as those same barriers are coded into law, wages, medicine, religion, and culture. The mind must split to keep this denial: *"If I don't see it, it must not be real,"* even while walking on the floor the system built. This is cognitive dissonance as self-protection: the comfort of fiction over the discomfort of recognition.

An even stranger contradiction appears when someone denies patriarchy exists—yet leaps to defend it. If there is no patriarchy, why defend it? Why insist it's "natural," "necessary," "traditional," or "good for society?" Why resent its critique if there is nothing to critique? This is the giveaway. The emotional intensity reveals what the argument tries to hide: not only does patriarchy exist, but it is also *felt* to be threatened. The mind must hold two incompatible beliefs at once: *"It isn't real"* and *"Don't you dare change it."* That is not logic. That is self-interest dressed as denial.

TRAUMATIC SYMPTOMS OF CHRONIC COGNITIVE DISSONANCE

So, let's refresh our memory of the traumatic symptoms of chronic cognitive dissonance.

1. Self-Doubt as Default

* "Maybe I misunderstood."
* "Maybe I'm overreacting."
* "Maybe my memory isn't accurate."
* "Maybe he's right and I'm the problem."

When reality can no longer be trusted, the self cannot be trusted either. The internal compass is shattered, and that is the point.

2. Speech Paralysis (or the Over explaining Loop)

* The trauma exists but cannot be named.
* The words don't match the experience.
* The harm doesn't "look like harm" from the outside.
* "I can't explain what's happening" turns into "I must be making it up."
* And sometimes the opposite happens first: you explain and explain and explain—piling on detail, context, proof, examples—because you're trying to *earn* belief.
* But when even over explaining fails, speech collapses into silence.

A person who cannot narrate their experience—or cannot get it *believed*—loses the ability to resist it.

The voice doesn't disappear because there's nothing to say.

It disappears because saying it has proven pointless, costly, or dangerous.

3. Dissociation and Freeze

When the nervous system cannot resolve contradiction, it shuts down:

- ❖ autopilot
- ❖ numbness
- ❖ going along
- ❖ zombie compliance
- ❖ emotional flattening

Obedience looks like consent from the outside, but it is neurobiological survival.

4. The "I Must Be Crazy" Loop

The system denies the abuse.
The abuser denies the abuse.
The culture denies the abuse.
So, the only explanation left is, *I must be broken.*
This is not accidental. It is a narcissistic inversion weaponized at cultural scale.

5. No Outside Reality Check

In a closed system—a cult, a dictatorship, or patriarchy at scale—there is:

- ❖ no neutral witness
- ❖ no shared language for the harm
- ❖ no counter-narrative
- ❖ no social mirror that reflects truth back
- ❖ no "outside" for the mind to stand on

The victim is not isolated by accident, but by architecture. When there is no one to reality-test with, the lie becomes the only world available.

So far, we've mapped the cognitive trauma patriarchy causes.

Now we must ask the question almost no one says out loud:

Was the trauma a side effect—or the point?

What if we've been centering the wrong character?

SECTION VI: THE TRAUMA LOOP — MISDIAGNOSED, MISATTRIBUTED, AND MISUNDERSTOOD

BLUF: Abuse is not simply childhood trauma spilling over; often it is intentional exploitation. The trauma loop that sustains patriarchy is maintained in the victim, not the abuser.

Now, we shift from what it feels like to what it means.

And here we reach a conceptual tension—not between individual scholars, but between two dominant explanations for repeated harm.

In Chapter 1 we explored several scholars' assertions of patriarchy as arising out of the trauma of a climate crisis and clinician Christine Forner's description of patriarchy as a self-perpetuating trauma system, a trauma loop that harms everyone in it.

The idea is that systems like patriarchy reenact unresolved wounds (in men) across generations, and that abuse is what happens when pain goes unhealed.

On the other side of the work of clinicians like this is educator-author Dr Peter Salerno (PsyD), who has studied and written widely about disordered and exploitative personalities and cognitive dissonance—and he is unequivocal: the research shows that most traumatized people do not become abusers—and that many abusers show patterns of empathy impairment with neurological or genetic roots.

This doesn't mean their behavior is outside their control—only that it is not caused by trauma. Trauma may appear in their history, but Salerno is clear: it is not the source of the exploitation—it is often the excuse for it.

Acknowledging this distinction does not deny the impact of trauma—

it prevents us from confusing injury with exploitation, and compassion with naiveté.

In other words: harm can be intentional, calculated, and self-serving—not the overflow of a wound, but the weaponization of one.

The first lens is a widespread belief that explains abusive behavior as a byproduct of injury to the abuser.

The second lens debunks this belief and shows harm can be a strategy—intentional, self-serving, and repeatedly rewarded.

These are not simply different explanations. They lead to entirely different moral conclusions about how abuse works, who benefits from it, and how it sustains itself.

And this is where patriarchy comes into view in a new light.

What if both lenses are true? What if patriarchy is a trauma loop *and* it is intentional in harming? What if we've been centering the wrong character and the wrong assumption?

The long-held assumption has been that the trauma loop belongs to *the abuser.* That the reason he harms others is because he himself is in pain. That "hurt people hurt people." That if we just understood his wound, the violence would make sense. That empathy for him, not clarity about his behavior, is what's missing.

But what if that is the cognitive error Salerno warns about?

What if, in our refusal to imagine intentional harm, we project our own conscientiousness—our own good intentions—onto people who do not operate from conscience at all?

What if the trauma loop is real, but it does not originate in the abuser?

What if it is the victim's trauma that keeps the system alive?

What if the key to patriarchy is not that it expresses trauma, but that it *feeds on* trauma?

What if the abuser's power comes not from his wound, but from his ability to weaponize *ours*—our confusion, our unhealed wounds, our self-doubt, our human desire to be loved and genuinely cared about, our longing for repair, our fear of abandonment, our inherited scripts about duty, loyalty, forgiveness, and second chances?

What if what he hungers for are the very qualities he has disowned, devalued, demeaned, and assigned to the "feminine" sphere—empathy, care, accountability, relational intelligence, mutuality, and fairness?

What if the abuser's behavior comes not from his damaged inhumanity, but from his lack of humanity?

What if the "cycle of abuse" has been misread all along—not a cycle inside the abuser, but a cycle he induces in others to keep control?

An intentional targeted destabilization?

SECTION VII: ENGINEERED DESTABILIZATION — CHAOS AS A WEAPON

> *BLUF: Abusers destabilize others on purpose; confusion, collapse, and self-doubt are not accidents—they are engineered conditions that give the abuser power and emotional supply.*

Destabilization doesn't just give the abuser control—it also gives him emotional *supply.*

The disorientation, the tears, the shock, the self-doubt, the "what just happened?"—those *reactions* are part of what he feeds on.

Not just your labor, but your emotional distress becomes fuel.

There is a name for this: duping delight[64]—the rush the abuser feels when you fall for the lie, when you explode, when you collapse, when you freeze, when you doubt yourself.

He is not laughing at a joke. He is laughing at *your distress—at your disarray.*

Most people don't comprehend what happened in the moment—but they remember the look that flitted across his face.

Not the words.

The sly pleasure.

Or the blank faced, shocking absence of caring as you fall apart.

And that reaction—the smirk, or the cruel void—deepens the shock. It compounds the destabilization.

And destabilization has a second function: it isolates.

When you are scrambling internally to make sense of what just happened, you're too busy to reach for help, too unsure to trust your instincts, too disoriented to recognize the pattern. Chaos is not just control—it is containment. It traps you inside your own mind.

Abusers do not fear chaos. They create it.

Not because they are overwhelmed by suffering, but because confusion is a ripe opportunity to take advantage of others.

Chaos is not a symptom of their trauma—it is a weapon they deploy.

Abusers destabilize others to create the very conditions in which they thrive:

If you are disoriented, he becomes the reference point.

If you doubt yourself, he becomes the authority.

If you are dependent, he becomes the controller.

If you feel threatened, he suddenly appears as a protector—even when he created the danger.

This is not accidental turbulence. It is engineered disorientation—a psychological fog that keeps others off-balance, apologizing, second-guessing, and trying harder.

And here we must correct one of patriarchy's most persistent lies: that the feminine is the source of chaos, and the masculine the force of order.

No.

There is nothing inherently chaotic about women or the feminine.

And there is nothing inherently orderly about the masculine.

What we call "chaos" in patriarchal systems is often the symptoms of the intentional destabilization created by someone else's manipulation.

The true source of chaos is not the feminine—it is the abuser who destabilizes reality and then poses as its only interpreter.

He shatters the equilibrium, then declares himself the only steady hand. He causes the storm, then insists you cling to him for shelter. He manufactures confusion, then offers "leadership" as clarity.

And to be clear, we aren't going to traffic in reverse gender essentialism: abusive behavior is not "the masculine" either. It is disordered characters performing authority.

And this is why the cycle of abuse keeps spinning. Not because the abuser is trapped in a trauma loop, but because others are trapped in the behavioral, emotional, and cognitive trap he engineers.

If that is true, then patriarchy is not a tragic inheritance of generational pain. It is an organized extraction system that harvests trauma responses the way a parasite harvests nutrients from a living host.

It is not a cry for help. It is a strategy.

It is not "hurt people hurting people." It is empty people feeding on strong people they ambush.

And that insight changes everything.

Because the question is no longer: *What happened to him?*

The question becomes: Why does he need you to stay confused, destabilized, forgiving, doubting, or small?

What does he gain from your trauma that he cannot generate for himself?

SECTION VIII: THE THEATRE OF PATRIARCHY — APPEARANCE VS REALITY

> *BLUF: Patriarchy is theatrical: hollow men appear powerful only because everyone around them is forced to kneel; once the performance stops, their supposed authority collapses.*

Before we leave Part I, there is one last reality we must see without flinching: Patriarchy is not held up by truly powerful men.

It is held up by *empty* men who require a system to inflate them so they can impersonate power.

The man at the center—the Strongman, the Patriarch, the Godfather, the "natural leader"—is not what the theatre makes him appear to be. Strip away the entourage, the deference, the obedience, the myth, and the fear, and what remains is not strength but hollowness:

No inner authority
No genuine convictions
No emotional maturity
No capacity for reciprocity
No gravitas, only costume
No self-governance, only control of others

He cannot collaborate because he has too little to contribute, so he defines cooperation as domination and submission. He cannot engage in real intimacy because equality exposes the empty core. He cannot grow because growth would reveal how long he has avoided it.

He is not dangerous because he is strong.

He is dangerous because he will do anything to keep his weakness from being exposed.

That is why patriarchy must recruit others into the web of corruption.

Not because the patriarch is mighty, but because he is inadequate without an audience, a loyal circle, a narrative, a supply chain, and a buffer zone of defenders.

The poser needs publicists and PR
The hollow needs inflators
The incompetent needs doers
The fragile needs protectors
The fraud needs fixers
The predator needs camouflage
And the myth needs believers

Patriarchy is not a single man on a throne—it's a production in which the Strongman only looks tall because everyone else is required to kneel.

Men are double cast as rulers in public and boys in private.

Women are double cast as children in public and parents in private.

The contradiction is the script.

And the illusion only works as long as everyone keeps performing their assigned roles.

When enough people stop playing along, the set collapses, the lights come up, and the "powerful man" is revealed for what he has always been: a small figure propped up by staging, not substance.

Power was never in him—it was in the people who believed the performance.

And that brings us to Part II—the technology of the illusion. In Part II, we explore these extraction systems in detail—not just how they operate, but how they grow, how the systems are built, and what they want to extract from us all.

Because immaturity, when left unchecked, does not stay small—it scales into families, cultures, and governments that frame control with care.

THE SYSTEMS THAT GROW WHEN WE REFUSE TO

When emotional immaturity is left unchecked, it doesn't just damage individuals or relationships—it becomes architecture. Part II traces how the behaviors of psychological immaturity—entitlement, avoidance, manipulation, and control—are scaled into systems of extraction and domination. These chapters reveal how patriarchy operates not as reasoned leadership, but as a culturally sanctioned disorder: a pathocracy built from emotional arrest, enforced compliance, and moral distortion.

Reader Note:
We can talk about hard things.
We can name what hurts—and choose clarity over comfort on our way to something more whole.
We can grieve the loss of illusions, even as we reclaim truth.
We can look honestly at the systems that shaped us—not to shame ourselves or others, but to liberate ourselves.
We can hold complexity. We can grow. We can make different choices.
You don't have to agree with everything in these next chapters.
But I invite you to stay present.
Let the discomfort be data. Let the clarity do its quiet work.

10

Extraction Systems: Designed to Feed the Center

BLUF: INTRODUCES THE ARCHITECTURE OF NARCISSISTIC, PATRIARCHAL, AND CULT-LIKE SYSTEMS AS DOMINANCE HIERARCHIES BUILT NOT FOR GROWTH, BUT FOR EXTRACTION. EXPLORES HOW THESE SYSTEMS FUNCTION EMOTIONALLY, PSYCHOLOGICALLY, AND STRUCTURALLY TO DRAIN THE MANY FOR THE BENEFIT OF THE FEW—AND HOW THEY REVERSE REALITY TO PRESERVE THEIR POWER.

After exploring how the emotionally immature construct dominance hierarchies to serve themselves, we now turn to how those hierarchies operate—not just in families, but across entire cultures.

This chapter begins with a map of extraction systems, followed by a deeper exploration of how they form, how they function, and how they shape the people inside them.

Not all systems are built for growth. Some are built for extraction. These systems—whether a narcissistic family, a high-control religious cult, or the sprawling structure of patriarchy—are dominance hierarchies organized not to serve the many, but to feed the emotional, material, sexual, and psychological needs of those at the center.

They are survival-based, not growth-based. Control-based, not collaboration-based. They do not evolve. They do not uplift. They maintain. They hoard. And they survive by convincing others that submission is love, that loyalty is morality, and that tradition is truth.

The more disordered these systems become, the more they reverse reality: claiming that domination is protection, that obedience is empowerment, that inequality is the natural order. But systems do not lie. They reveal their purpose in what they consistently produce.

Follow the money. Follow the power. Follow the sex. Follow the recognition. These trails always lead to the truth: Who benefits the most? Who is extracted from? Who labors, and who receives the rewards?

SECTION I: THE EMOTIONAL ARCHITECTURE OF EXTRACTION — BUILT TO CONSUME NOT TO EVOLVE

> *BLUF: Defines extraction systems as emotionally immature hierarchies centered on a dominant figure or group whose needs shape the entire structure. Reversing the parent-child dynamic. Others are recruited not for collaboration, but to serve and regulate the center.*

These systems are built around a central figure or elite class whose needs define the purpose of the group. Others are recruited not for collaboration, but for extraction—of time, energy, admiration, labor, sexuality, and attention. Emotionally immature at their core, these systems operate like a child demanding the entire household orbit them, where the group exists to regulate, validate, elevate, and protect the central figure.

Examples include:

- A narcissistic parent in a family

- A cult leader surrounded by "true believers"

- The patriarchal father figure upheld by political, legal, and religious institution

These systems mimic the early parent-child dynamic but distort it.[65]

The central figure is infantilized—never questioned, never confronted, never told no, while others are adultified—expected to anticipate needs, suppress their own, and provide constant emotional regulation. The result is a parentified environment, where those in the outer rings exist to serve those in the inner.

And, crucially, reality is reversed.

The more disordered the system, the more aggressively it insists it is virtuous, claiming to protect those it harms, to elevate those it exploits, and to serve those it drains.

Common tactics include:

- **Sentimental language:** "We're a loving family," "This is God's will," "We're doing this for your own good."

- **False benevolence:** Abuse framed as discipline, domination framed as leadership.

- **Moral inversion:** The abuser is seen as the protector; the one who resists is labeled disloyal, dangerous, or unstable.

SECTION II: THE MARKERS OF AN EXTRACTION SYSTEM

BLUF: Offers a diagnostic framework—through key questions like, "Who is allowed autonomy?" and "Who is punished for walking away?" —to identify systems organized around the extraction of labor, emotion, and loyalty.

You can identify these systems not by what they say, but by what they do consistently.

Question	Follow the Trail
Who is getting their needs met?	Who is being centered? Who is regulated?
Who is doing the emotional labor?	Who is soothing, accommodating, explaining, and apologizing?
Who is allowed autonomy?	Who is permitted to set rules, break boundaries, or demand loyalty?
Who is being asked to sacrifice?	Whose dreams are deferred? Whose voice is silenced? Whose labor is hidden?
Who is free to leave?	Who is punished for walking away? Who is made to feel guilty for outgrowing the system?

At the heart of every narcissistic family, cult, or patriarchal structure lies a single operating principle: feed the center. These are not systems designed for mutual flourishing, but for extraction. The emotional, material, psychological, and even sexual resources of the many are systematically drained to support the insatiable needs of the few.

Whether it is a narcissistic parent, a cult leader, or a dominant class of patriarchs, these systems operate like inverted pyramids—with all the labor and loyalty of the group funneled upward to sustain one central, controlling entity. In return, followers receive only the illusion of safety, purpose, and identity.

These systems thrive not only on dominance, but on delusion. They are built on a reversal of reality—a web of lies, half-truths, manipulations, omissions, and projections that confuse the mind and twist the soul. Behind every sleight of hand, there is always a core truth waiting to be seen.[66] And it is this: If you follow the money, the power, the sexual entitlement, and the recognition, you will always find who the system was really built to serve. Because dominance hierarchies and all extraction systems feed on the followers, the stragglers, the naïve, the vulnerable, and the faithful.

PREDATORS AND THE INVERTED MORAL PYRAMID

The more disordered a system is, the more it rewards predators. And the more it must reverse reality to excuse its abuses.

At the top of the dominance hierarchy are not wise leaders, but intentional extractors. Predators. These are individuals who take without giving, dominate without conscience, and exploit the confusion of others to maintain power.

But one predator cannot maintain a system alone. Like the narcissistic parent in a dysfunctional family, they must recruit others into abuse-by-proxy.[67] This is where the system begins to assign roles.

- Some become **enablers**, justifying the predator's behavior and silencing dissent.

- Some become **scapegoats**, absorbing the collective shadow and blame.

- Some become **golden children**, rewarded for loyalty and mimicry.

- And some become **flying monkeys**, acting out the predator's will, sometimes without even realizing they're being used.

These roles create a self-reinforcing loop. Each person's identity becomes tied to the system. Dissent is punished. Loyalty is rewarded. And slowly, moral clarity is replaced with moral ambiguity to accommodate the slippery slope of increasing depravity.

Extraction systems cannot survive without permission structures. These are the social, psychological, and cultural mechanisms that allow depravity to flourish in plain sight.

- A degrading comment is brushed off as a joke.

- A violent outburst is explained away as stress.

- A blatant abuse of power is defended as leadership.

These small permissions accumulate. And soon, people find themselves standing in support of things they once would have condemned. They lose their grip on right and wrong. They begin to equate morality with loyalty to the predator rather than loyalty to truth, decency, or conscience.[68]

This is not accidental. It is a feature of the system. Permission structures operate at the individual, group, and cultural levels—creating what we might call a moral greenhouse for predators.[69]

SECTION III: LOSS OF MORAL AGENCY IS INEVITABLE IN EXTRACTION SYSTEMS

> *BLUF: Highlights how people lose their moral compass in exchange for safety, identity, or belonging. Over time, they become tools of extraction themselves—using language, money, sex, and coercion to uphold the system.*

Perhaps the most tragic element of extraction systems is the way they corrupt agency. People enter the system in search of meaning, safety, or belonging. But through a series of gradual self-betrayals, they abandon their own inner compass.

They trade self-trust for ideology. They trade discernment for obedience.[70] They trade empathy for alignment with power.

And in doing so, they become instruments of the very system that is draining them. As their own clarity and conscience erode, they are handed tools—technologies of extraction:

- **Language**, to confuse, manipulate, and dominate.
- **Money**, to control and withhold access.
- **Sex**, to soothe, shame, or punish.
- **Coercion**, to enforce roles and silence dissent.

These are not random abuses. They are strategic distributions of power, designed to keep the center fed.[71]

Every system has a bottom line. And if someone can manipulate you into relinquishing your moral agency—your basic sense of fairness, humanity, and right and wrong—then they own you. Not just your behavior. But your mind. Your compass. Your soul. Your family. Your community. Your nation. Your future.

This is how extraction systems work. Not just through violence, but through confusion. Through false promises, subtle indoctrination, and emotional blackmail. Through keeping people so lost in survival, so invested in their role, that they forget they have the power to say: *No more.*

Because the truth is this:

The more you feed a narcissistic individual, group, or structure, the more voracious and bold it becomes.

The dominator's biggest lie is this: Feed it, and it will be satisfied.[72]

But it's never satisfied. It only grows more entitled. More depraved.

We are not here to appease it.

We are here to outgrow it—and to starve the beast.

These extraction systems don't operate through brute force alone. They operate through language—words designed not to clarify, but to confuse. To coerce. To recruit others into the lie.

The first technology of control is not violence.

It is persuasion.[73]

11

Words as Weapons:
The Hijacking of Communication

BLUF: EXPLORES HOW EMOTIONALLY IMMATURE SYSTEMS USE LANGUAGE AS A TOOL OF DISTORTION, DOMINATION, AND ROLE ENFORCEMENT. INTRODUCES FIVE CATEGORIES OF MANIPULATIVE COMMUNICATION AND EXAMINES HOW LANGUAGE BECOMES EMOTIONAL CAMOUFLAGE, CASTING SPELLS THAT CONFUSE, COERCE, AND EXTRACT. WHEN COMMUNICATION IS WEAPONIZED, IT PAVES THE WAY FOR DEEPER FORMS OF CONTROL—INCLUDING FINANCIAL AND REPRODUCTIVE MANIPULATION.

THE SPELLS WE LEARNED IN THE CRADLE

Before we learned grammar, we learned magic. We learned how words could open worlds—or close them. How language could soothe or shrink, liberate, or bind.

As children, we experienced the magic of language firsthand. A bedtime story could open entire worlds—worlds of magic, of good witches and dark spells. And we learned about the spells our family cast. How words carry energy. They can hurt or heal, encourage or punish.

A loving voice could calm our tears. A harsh word could shrink us. A cold silence could isolate us. A lie could make us question what we knew to be true.

Words are the original technology. And when wielded with emotional immaturity or malice, they become tools of domination.[74]

In the hands of a dominator, language is not used to connect—it is used to control.

SECTION 1: HOW WORDS BECOME WEAPONS

> *BLUF: Introduces the five core categories of manipulative communication (Seduction, Confusion, Defense, Punishment, and Control) and describes how language becomes a primary tool of domination in narcissistic and patriarchal systems.*

In narcissistic, coercive, or patriarchal systems, communication is not a tool for connection, but rather a tool of domination. Instead of words being used to build trust or understanding, they are used to seduce, confuse, control, and punish. Language becomes a technology of extraction, manipulating emotions, rewriting reality, and recruiting others into roles they didn't choose.[75]

Once a dominator can control the story, controlling the resources becomes much easier.

At the heart of all of it is the lie. Some lies are direct, some are hidden beneath charm, and still others arrive wrapped in scripture, tradition, or "common sense." But make no mistake: in a system built on emotional immaturity and power-hoarding, everything is some form of a lie.

And as the oxygen of narcissistic systems, these lies must be constantly supplied, rehearsed, and repeated—because if truth ever enters the room, the entire illusion begins to collapse.[76]

THE MANY FACES OF THE LIE: CATEGORIES OF MANIPULATIVE COMMUNICATION

There are countless tactics used to manipulate language—but they nearly always fall into one of the five categories that follow. Understanding these categories can help you see what's really happening beneath the surface of words.[77]

1. *Seduction Tactics: Getting You to Let Your Guard Down*

These are the love-bombs, the flattery, the promises of safety or special-ness. The goal is to lower your defenses and bypass your instincts.

COMMON TACTICS:

> Love bombing and praise
>
> Faux concern and over-helpfulness
>
> Manipulative intimacy or "soul talk"
>
> Future faking and false promises

2. *Confusion Tactics: Making It Hard to Think Straight*

These tactics are meant to destabilize you, make you second-guess your-self, and keep you emotionally disoriented. Confusion is power in these systems.

COMMON TACTICS:

> Word salad and over-intellectualizing
>
> Gaslighting and contradiction[78]
>
> Double talk, double binds, and mixed messages
>
> Whataboutism, bothsidism, and deflection

3. *Defense Tactics: Avoiding Responsibility*

These are the linguistic gymnastics used to dodge accountability. The aim is to reverse blame, redirect attention, or protect the system from exposure.

COMMON TACTICS:

> DARVO (Deny, Attack, Reverse Victim & Offender)[79]
>
> Lying and lying by omission
>
> Goalpost shifting
>
> Projection and scapegoating
>
> Bothsidism (flattening moral distinctions)

4. *Punishment Tactics: Using Words to Harm or Silence*

These are aggressive or passive-aggressive tactics meant to intimidate, shame, humiliate, or isolate. They hurt on purpose.

COMMON TACTICS:

> Demeaning, devaluing, degrading
>
> Faux joking or sarcasm
>
> Smear campaigns and gossip
>
> Silent treatment and stonewalling
>
> Interrogation disguised as curiosity
>
> Poke and provoke (to trigger a reaction)
>
> Rejection of fact—denial of observable reality

5. *Control Tactics: Enforcing Power and Roles*

These tactics reinforce hierarchy and obedience. Their goal is to reinforce a pecking order and make submission feel like virtue.

COMMON TACTICS:

> Mansplaining and one-upmanship[80]
>
> Interruption and over-talking
>
> Thought-stopping phrases and clichés
>
> "Helpfulness" as control (weaponized chivalry)

Emotional withholding—the withdrawal of affection, not as a boundary but as a manipulative tool to induce fear, shame, or compliance.

Monopolizing definitions of truth, morality, or reality—framing dissent as delusion and loyalty as virtue."

Note: Some of these behaviors—like overexplaining or emotional withdrawal—can emerge from trauma, not from manipulation. In abusive systems, survivors learn to explain everything, anticipate criticism, or protect themselves with silence.

The key difference is *intent* and *power*. Manipulative language is used to dominate others. Defensive language is used to protect the self. Clarity helps us tell the difference—and to make choices rooted in truth rather than reflex.

SECTION II: THE CHILD MIND WITH THE GROWN-UP VOCABULARY

> *BLUF: Explores how emotionally immature individuals use adult-sounding language to express immature motives—either pleading for comfort or controlling others. These contradictory behaviors scale upward into systems that reward compliance and punish clarity.*

In emotionally immature systems—especially those organized around narcissism, domination, or patriarchal control—language becomes a mask. It is emotionally insecure on the inside but smoothly glib and confident on the outside. The result is a disturbing paradox:

The speaker sounds adult, even eloquent. But the communication serves the function of a frightened or controlling child: to dominate, deflect, avoid, manipulate, or soothe themselves at your expense.[81]

This disconnect is what makes such communication so destabilizing. The tone sounds reasonable. The words may be calm. But the function of the message is immature and self-serving.

TWO FORMS OF IMMATURITY, ONE SOPHISTICATED MOUTHPIECE

The words of emotionally immature individuals can follow two patterns—sometimes alternating rapidly between them.

1. **The Child Archetype** – pleading, self-pitying, blaming, catastrophizing, fawning, manipulating for comfort or care.

2. **The Bully Archetype** – shaming, belittling, threatening, demanding, controlling the narrative to avoid accountability.

These aren't always obvious. Sometimes they're cloaked in calm language, religious references, therapy-speak, intellectualism, or charm.[82]
But underneath, the logic remains childish:

"If you loved me, you wouldn't hurt me by telling the truth."

"You made me do this."

"Only I get to decide what's fair, what's true, what's allowed."

FROM INTERPERSONAL HARM TO SYSTEMIC CONTROL

What begins in personal relationships—at the dinner table, in the workplace, in romantic dynamics—scales upward into entire social systems. The same emotionally immature logic becomes embedded in institutions and ideologies.

And once embedded, language becomes a tool of role enforcement and emotional control:

If you comply, you're "good," "loyal," "humble."

If you resist, you're "difficult," "dangerous," "deluded."

These labels are not descriptive—they are prescriptive. They are meant to discipline behavior, silence resistance, and maintain dominance.[83]

LANGUAGE AS SPELLCASTING IN THE SYSTEM

The emotionally immature speaker is not just talking—they are casting a spell:

- A spell to erase nuance.

- A spell to disguise domination as love

- A spell to enforce conformity.

- A spell to invert victim and perpetrator.

And because the language is so emotionally charged, listeners often internalize the message on a gut level—before their intellect even has a chance to intervene.

This is why communication becomes a technology of extraction: It doesn't just express dominance—it manufactures consent for it.

But distortion doesn't just confuse individuals—it sustains entire power structures. And to preserve those power structures, language must assign roles and disguise harm.

SECTION III: WORDS AS COSTUMES — ENFORCING ROLES AND MASKING HARM

> *BLUF: Shows how language is used to assign roles, disguise abuse, and create confusion between behavior and identity. Explains how personas and flattering language can obscure domination, silencing those who dissent or question the system.*

Language doesn't just describe reality—it *constructs* it. In narcissistic family systems, cults, and patriarchal cultures, language becomes a tool for assigning roles, reinforcing submission, and disguising abuse.

- You're the troublemaker if you name the abuse.
- You're the selfish one if you ask for fairness.
- You're the ungrateful one if you step outside your assigned role.

But language doesn't only mask the harm—it also masks the harm-doer. Dominators craft carefully curated identities through words:

* The concerned father figure
* The well-intentioned authority
* The pillar of the community
* The innocent man falsely accused
* The generous helper
* The spiritual guide

These personas function like emotional camouflage.[84] They make it hard to connect words to actions, hard to reconcile behavior with reputation. This is how predators are protected—by the masks they wear, and the stories they spin. When language becomes a costume, the truth disappears beneath the performance. When control of language is monopolized, truth itself becomes distorted. And once perception is captured, domination becomes much easier to enforce.

To reclaim our power, our agency, we must reclaim language and our ability to name reality—as naming what's been hidden breaks the spell.[85] When we learn to hear clearly, we learn to see clearly—and from that place, we choose differently, which leads to agency, boundaries, and freedom.

Here are a few tips for recognizing spells woven through words—and how to break them.

* Ask yourself: Does this language bring clarity or confusion? Connection or control?
* Trust your internal signals: the nausea, the tightness, the fog—that's your body whispering, *This doesn't feel right.*
* And above all, remember: Language was meant to connect, not to cage.

Words are the first enchantment, which makes communication the gateway manipulation—the original breach through which all other extractions flow.[86] Once language is used to distort perception, shame dissent, and weaken boundaries, it becomes easier to entangle people in more overt forms of control. What begins as a fog of confusion often escalates into full seizure of agency. You don't even realize your energy, time, and loyalty have been captured—until you try to say no and find you've forgotten how.

The next tool in the dominator's arsenal is money and reproduction. Like language, money can connect or control, support freedom or buy submission. And in systems of extraction, it is rarely neutral, rather it becomes a lever of dependency, a gatekeeper of survival, and a scoreboard of power. Once communication is weaponized, it lays the foundation for more concrete control. In other words, the manipulation of perception makes it easier to manipulate resources, meaning if you can control the money, you control the freedom and resources of the targets.

12

Economic Entrapment: Money, Motherhood, and the Extraction of Labor

BLUF: EXPLORES HOW PATRIARCHAL AND NARCISSISTIC SYSTEMS USE FINANCIAL CONTROL AND REPRODUCTIVE MANIPULATION TO ENFORCE DEPENDENCY, EXTRACT LABOR, AND UPHOLD DOMINANCE. REVEALS HOW TRADITIONAL ROLES, WORKPLACE DISCRIMINATION, AND THE WEAPONIZATION OF MOTHERHOOD AND FATHERHOOD FUNCTION AS STRATEGIC TOOLS OF ENTRAPMENT—NOT SUPPORT. CLOSES WITH THE WARNING THAT SYSTEMS REQUIRING YOUR POWERLESSNESS ARE NOT JUST—THEY ARE ABUSIVE BY DESIGN.

At the heart of every narcissistic or patriarchal system is a core strategy: create a group of designated losers so others can be winners.[87] It is not an oversight—it is the design.

Language manipulates perception. Money manipulates autonomy and survival. Together, they form the double-bind that traps people inside systems never built for their thriving.

SECTION I: ECONOMIC ENTRAPMENT AND DEPLETION

> *BLUF: Introduces how narcissistic and patriarchal systems sabotage financial independence through unpaid labor, rigid gender roles, and economic discrediting. Highlights the systemic erasure of women's work and the structural extraction of care.*

Narcissistic family systems, cults, and patriarchal structures maintain control by undermining the financial agency of those they wish to dominate. Economic manipulation ensures a steady supply of labor, care, and emotional attention flowing to the center of power.

These systems:

- ❖ Discourage financial independence in women while assigning them most of the unpaid domestic and caregiving labor.

- ❖ Use rigid gender roles and religious ideology to normalize economic dependency.

- ❖ Hinder access to higher-paying roles through discrediting competence and qualifications.

- ❖ Reward domination and hoarding in men, while penalizing autonomy and ambition in women.

This isn't about personal hardship. It's systemic sabotage that devalues women's contributions to the paid workforce and erases the financial value of the unpaid work itself—about three-quarters of which is done by women worldwide.[88]

Analyses drawing on Oxfam/UN data estimate that if women were paid at each country's minimum wage for their unpaid care and domestic work, they would have contributed about $10.9 trillion to the global economy in 2020. Forbes notes this is more than twice the size of the global tech industry that year and that this unfair burden affects women's health.[89] And that unpaid labor isn't just daily care—it also includes the mental, emotional, and physical load behind "holiday magic": birthdays, celebrations, and family rituals that are disproportionately organized and executed by women. (Examples: planning, purchasing, decorating, hosting, cleanup—much of which is invisible and uncounted.)

Yet this work is excluded from GDP and largely ignored in public policy—despite being foundational to economies. (National accounts treat it via "satellite" measures rather than core GDP).[90]

Global evidence shows the burden's impact: women perform at least 2.5 to 3 times as many hours of unpaid care and domestic work as men, which reduces time for paid work or forces longer total workdays that combine paid and unpaid labor.[91]

In narcissistic systems, money is never just money. It is safety, mobility, freedom, and power—and that's exactly why dominators want to control it. Communication is the gateway manipulation, but money is the lock on the door. Words confuse. Money entraps. In systems like patriarchy, financial dependence is not an accident—it's an outcome by design. The structure makes it easy to fall into dependence and hard to climb out. And any system that is easy to enter but difficult to leave is not one of love or integrity. It is one of control.

SECTION II: THE WEB TIGHTENS — HOW FINANCIAL CONTROL DEEPENS DEPENDENCE

BLUF: Patriarchal systems use overlapping financial structures to trap women in cycles of dependency. Framed as tradition or devotion, unpaid caregiving and systemic workplace discrimination leave women economically vulnerable and overburdened. These conditions are not accidental—they are engineered to extract labor while limiting choice.

DEPENDENCY DISGUISED AS DEVOTION

For centuries, women have been assigned the role of unpaid caregivers—responsible for home, children, and emotional labor—while men assumed the role of breadwinner. This arrangement has been romanticized as "traditional," "natural," or "complementary," but in practice, it functions as economic entrapment.

Even when the intent is not malicious, the outcome is the same: women's earning potential, retirement savings, career trajectory, and financial independence are systematically eroded.[92]

THE SETUP

* Women are expected to step out of the workforce during childbearing years "for the good of the family."

* Re-entry into the workforce is difficult—caregiving years are not seen as valuable work experience.

* Their unpaid labor underwrites the economic success of the household—but none of that labor builds personal equity.

THE CONSEQUENCES

* Lack of personal income means lack of freedom to leave abusive or neglectful relationships.

* Women may have no credit history of their own and limited access to joint funds.

* Divorce, widowhood, or financial betrayal can leave them economically stranded.

Dependence isn't safety—it's vulnerability disguised as tradition.

WORKPLACE DISCRIMINATION AS SYSTEMIC SABOTAGE

The Illusion of Opportunity

Even when women pursue education and careers, the workplace is riddled with invisible traps:

- Underpayment for equal work
- Overburdening with emotional and administrative labor
- Exclusion from promotions or hiring in favor of less qualified men
- Undermining through infantilization or tokenizing praise

Discrediting Competence to Preserve the Hierarchy

- Highly competent women are treated with suspicion: "Was she hired because she's qualified—or because she's a woman?"
- Cultural smear campaigns paint successful women as "cold," "difficult," or "lucky," while men are called "stars."
- Women must constantly prove what men are presumed to be.

In patriarchy, male competence is assumed. Female competence must be endlessly defended.[93]

THE LITERAL AND SYMBOLIC DEVALUATION OF WOMEN'S WORK

How Women's Labor Is Minimized, Erased, and Exploited

"Pink collar" jobs are devalued not because they require less skill—but because they're associated with women. Unpaid caregiving labor is excluded from the GDP, though it sustains the entire economy, and even in dual-income homes, women do most of the domestic labor—subsidizing their partner's economic productivity.

STAT SNAPSHOT:

- Women globally perform over **75%** of unpaid care work.[94]

- In 2019, compensating women for unpaid labor in the US at *minimum* wage would total **$1.5 trillion**—nearly **130 times Amazon's net income** that year.

- In the US, that unpaid labor is worth **$1.5 to $2.5 trillion** annually.

- Globally, it could account for **up to 9% of GDP**—more than manufacturing.

- In **Spain**, unpaid work accounts for **53%** of GDP.

- In Latin America, it's **21.4%** of GDP.

- Women retire with **30–40% less** in savings than men, due to time spent caregiving.

According to Silvia Federici: "They say it is love. We say it is unwaged work."[95] But one thing is certain: when women's labor is deliberately unvalued so it can be unpaid, it isn't free—it's stolen.

MANIPULATION OF SELF-WORTH AND FINANCIAL COMPETENCE

Systems of control don't just trap people emotionally. They deplete, entangle, and disempower them materially. They slyly devalue, discredit, and minimize women's contributions and manipulate their perception of their contribution—their self-worth. And they shape society's perception of the value of women's labor, as well as their social, political, historical, creative, and scientific contributions.

Tactics of Financial Entrapment:

Depletion: Overwork, caregiving, emotional labor that leaves no time for agency or reflection.

Financial Exhaustion: devaluing and discrediting women's work so they work for free or for less. The net result is the ability to survive but not thrive, as well as exhaustion.

Financial Infantilization: "I'll take care of everything"—until you're trapped.

Strategic Undermining: Sabotaging ambitions, careers, or networks.

Control Disguised as Care: "You wouldn't have any of this without me."

Scarcity as Punishment: Financial threats or silent sabotage when you assert independence.

Debt as Entrapment: Shared accounts, manipulated obligations, or confused financial records.

Co-opted Labor: Taking credit for your work, controlling how your earnings are used.

The system isn't just abusive—it's expensive.[96] All of this leads to one final form of economic entrapment: reproduction.

Because once a woman is financially dependent and also responsible for caring for children—she is, in the system's eyes, locked in. And the same system that tells her motherhood is sacred will fight viciously to deny her the resources to survive it.

Let's look at how this system manipulates not just money, but motherhood itself.

SECTION III: REPRODUCTIVE ENTRAPMENT — WHEN BIOLOGY BECOMES A LEVER OF CONTROL

BLUF: Reveals how patriarchal systems weaponize parenthood—using children, custody, and forced birth to control women's autonomy and entrench male dominance. Includes an analysis of reproductive control as both economic and psychological captivity.

In patriarchal systems, reproduction is not simply a biological process—it is a mechanism of control.[97]

From laws and religious doctrines to cultural norms and economic structures, the ability to bear or provide for children is systematically exploited to reduce autonomy, tighten dependency, and ensure compliance. Women are expected to give everything to their children, while men are expected to sacrifice everything to provide for them. But the system that enforces these expectations offers little real support to either.

It is not parenthood that is the problem—it is how parenthood is weaponized to entrap.

FOR WOMEN: MOTHERHOOD AS ECONOMIC ENTRAPMENT

Routinely, patriarchal systems exploit women's reproductive capacity to enforce financial dependence, social isolation, and long-term vulnerability.

Paternal Ownership of Children in Patriarchal Societies

In highly patriarchal cultures, children are legally and symbolically considered the property of the father. They bear his name, inherit his lineage, and default to his custody if a woman leaves—regardless of abuse or maternal fitness.

Examples include parts of Afghanistan, Iran, Saudi Arabia, and some ultra-conservative religious sects, where mothers risk losing access to their children entirely if they attempt to leave the marriage or defy male authority.[98]

And even in supposedly egalitarian societies:

- Fathers are often assumed to be more credible in court.

- Patriarchal norms grant men greater access to legal representation.

- Equal custody may be granted despite documented abuse— justified by a court's desire to "preserve co-parenting."

In these systems, the price of leaving may be losing one's children—or financial ruin.

Custody as a Weapon, Not a Responsibility

For many dominators, custody is not about nurturing—it's about punishment and power.

Custody battles are used to reduce child support, avoid financial settlements, or prolong control after separation.[99]

Women are forced to remain in coercive or violent relationships to protect their children from being taken or mistreated.

The legal system often enables this, cloaking male control in the language of paternal rights.

FORCED BIRTH AS FINANCIAL AND PHYSICAL ENTRAPMENT

In patriarchal cultures, reproductive control is not about protecting life. It's about controlling women.

- Abortion bans and restricted access to birth control are not just moral postures—they are tools to enforce dependency.

- Forced birth derails education, employment, and the ability to leave abusive situations.[100]

- Once a child is born, patriarchal systems withdraw their performative concern—leaving the mother to carry the physical, emotional, and financial burden alone.

The system demands that women care deeply for the children it forces them to bear—while offering them no protection or support once the child is born.

The Sadism of Forced Birth

When pregnancy is framed as a "consequence" of sex, we are no longer in the realm of morality—we are in the realm of punishment.[101]

- The logic is not "protect the unborn." It is: *you chose this, now suffer for it.*

- Forced birth becomes a form of state-sanctioned retribution—a sadistic assertion that women must "pay" for their sexuality.

- The fetus becomes a weapon to control all women.

This is not about life. It's about power.

Bodily Sovereignty Is the Baseline

Patriarchy claims the right to regulate women's bodies in ways it would never tolerate for men. It enshrines a false moral authority—one that denies the most basic ethical truth: every man and every woman have the right to sovereignty over their own body.

No man—and no woman—has entitlement to sovereignty over another person's body. Even a parent does not own a child's body. And so, outside of urgent medical necessity, no one has the ethical right to command another person's body—especially not in ways that violate their consent, personhood, or long-term wellbeing.

Bodily sovereignty is not gendered.

It is the baseline of personhood.

And any system that denies it—especially in the name of virtue—is not protecting life. It is denying personhood to enforce domination.

SECTION IV: FOR MEN — REPRODUCTION AS IDENTITY TRAP AND FINANCIAL NOOSE

BLUF: Explores how patriarchy also exploits men, forcing them into provider roles, suppressing emotional autonomy, and using shame-based scripts to enforce compliance. Shows how fear of irrelevance fuels control over women.

Just as patriarchal systems reduce women to reproductive vessels, they reduce men to providers—their humanity and agency sacrificed on the altar of masculine duty.

1. *Forced Provider Role: Masculinity Tied to Earnings*

In patriarchy, a man's worth is not in who he is—but in what he produces.[102]

> *"Real men provide."*
>
> *"A good husband never lets his wife work."*
>
> *"Your paycheck is your value."*

This script pressures men to:

> *Stay in soul-killing jobs they cannot afford to leave.*
>
> *Burn out in silence to maintain an image.*
>
> *Shame themselves and their wives if she pursues work or independence.*

Who benefits? The system. It gets free labor from women—and compliance from men.

2. *Shame-Based Compliance: Fatherhood as a Trap*

When family size is glorified and contraception is restricted:

> *Men are pressured into having more children than they can support.*
>
> *They are told to trust God, accept blessings, or leave it in His hands.*

Rather than mutual planning or conscious partnership, fatherhood becomes conscription.

> *Dreams are deferred.*
>
> *Autonomy is sacrificed.*
>
> *Financial strain becomes lifelong.*

3. *Weaponized Duty: Emotional Leverage Disguised as Honor*

Men are emotionally manipulated with messages like:

"If you leave, you're destroying your family."

"Real men don't walk away."

"A stable home is your responsibility."

Even in toxic environments, they are told that endurance is masculinity. Like women, men are not seen as people—they are seen as roles.[103]

4. *Fear of Feminine Autonomy*

In systems that demand male dominance, women's independence is framed as a threat:

"If she earns, will she leave?"

"If she doesn't need me, am I still a man?"

"If I'm not the head of the household, who am I?"

Patriarchy doesn't just suppress women—it terrifies men with the idea of no longer being needed and thus not "being a man."

FINAL REFLECTION: IF A SYSTEM NEEDS YOU POWERLESS, IT ISN'T JUST

A just system does not:

Require women to choose between survival and autonomy.

Demand men sacrifice their dreams for obedience.

Use children as pawns to extract labor, devotion, or silence.

In systems of extraction, reproduction is not about nurturing life. It is about maintaining control. And a system that needs you to be dependent, ashamed, or financially trapped to remain stable is not a system of order. It is a system of abuse—dressed in the language of morality, family, and love.

If You Follow the Money, You See the Trap

Patriarchal systems have always insisted they are about "order," "tradition," or "the good of the family." But when you follow the money, the power, and the unpaid labor—it becomes clear: these systems are not designed to support people. They are designed to extract from them.

The more dependent a person becomes—financially, emotionally, re-productively—the easier they are to manage, and the easier they are to guilt, shame, silence, trap and coerce.

This is not an accident. It is a design.

We see it in traditional marriage roles that erode women's financial independence. We see it in workplaces that sabotage women's credibility and underpay their efforts. We see it in laws that regulate reproduction and punish autonomy. And we see it in the insulting suggestion that men's only worth is in what they provide financially.

A system that cannot function unless you are depleted is not a system of support. It is a machine that runs on your sacrifice.

These are not private struggles. They are engineered dependencies, passed off as love and duty.[104] And when someone tries to escape—when they say no, claim their agency, stop feeding the machine—the system retaliates.

But financial control is rarely enough to maintain the illusion. Eventually, someone begins to resist. And when they do, the system must find someone to blame. Someone to carry the shame, the blame, the darkness the system cannot admit to itself.

Enter: the scapegoat.

13

The Scapegoat Mechanism: Shame, Blame, and the Expendable Other

BLUF: EXPLORES HOW EMOTIONALLY IMMATURE SYSTEMS PRESERVE POWER BY OFFLOADING GUILT, SHAME, AND FAILURE ONTO DESIGNATED SCAPEGOATS. TRACES THE HISTORICAL ORIGINS OF SCAPEGOATING FROM RITUAL SACRIFICE TO MODERN SOCIAL SYSTEMS, REVEALING HOW PATRIARCHAL CULTURES STRATEGICALLY SHAME WOMEN AND OTHERS DEEMED INCONVENIENT. EXPOSES PROJECTION, INTROJECTION, GENDERED MORAL LABOR, AND SPIRITUALIZED BLAME AS TOOLS OF EMOTIONAL OUTSOURCING—AND ENDS WITH THE LIBERATING POWER OF REFUSAL.

SECTION I: THE SIN EATER AND THE GOAT — PRIMITIVE SOLUTIONS TO AN EVOLVING PROBLEM

BLUF: Explores ancient scapegoat rituals as early psychological attempts to manage guilt and shadow. Frames scapegoating as developmentally immature but once culturally adaptive—and explains why patriarchal systems continue to cling to it.

Humanity has been growing—emotionally, morally, and psychologically—for millions of years. As our collective consciousness evolves, so too does our ability to manage discomfort, complexity, and responsibility.

Today, we understand that maturity requires the integration of shadow: the ability to acknowledge our faults, own our impact, and repair what we've broken. We know that this process isn't shameful—it's essential. It's how we grow, create, and relate with integrity.

But early human societies did not yet have this capacity. Like young children who blame-shift when they break something or lash out when they feel guilt, ancient communities struggled to metabolize their own moral mistakes. They didn't know how to take responsibility—so they externalized it.

They created rituals—primitive, sacred, brutal rituals. And among the oldest of these was the rite of the scapegoat.[105] These ceremonies weren't just superstition. They were developmentally appropriate attempts to manage a psychological truth: people needed to offload shame, guilt, and fear—both to preserve the fragile ego of the group and to explain what they couldn't yet understand.

Much like children, these early societies had not yet developed the cognitive or emotional tools to process failure, imperfection, or contradiction. When a rupture occurred—famine, illness, interpersonal conflict—the community needed a narrative. And often, the narrative pointed to someone else: a witch, a foreigner, a disobedient woman, a corrupted soul.

In some early Hebrew traditions, two goats were chosen. One was sacrificed on the altar. The other—the escape goat—was driven out into the wilderness, symbolically carrying the sins of the entire community. The message was clear: our guilt, our fear, our failures—we will not carry them ourselves. We will load them onto another.

We see echoes of this pattern all over the world. In Celtic tradition, the sin-eater was a poor outcast paid a few coins and fed a piece of bread and ale to "absorb" the sins of the dead—so the family could remain clean and spiritually unburdened.[106] In parts of Africa, Asia, and South America, ritual human sacrifices were performed to preserve "order," "fertility," or "favor with the gods." Scapegoating was, for a time, a way of managing what people couldn't yet understand.

But we know more now. And we are capable of better.

Across cultures, one theme repeats: someone must be chosen to carry the darkness. But in emotionally immature systems, this pattern never evolves.[107] Instead of learning to carry their own shadow, immature individuals and systems cling to this primitive solution. They need someone to blame. Someone to banish. Someone to bear the guilt they refuse to feel.

That person becomes the scapegoat.

Thankfully, human consciousness has evolved, and our emotional maturity has deepened. Just as children eventually learn to say, "I'm sorry" and make things right, so too can adults and societies grow beyond primitive rituals of blame.

We now understand the concept of the shadow—the parts of ourselves we would rather not see. And we know that maturity doesn't mean never making mistakes. It means recognizing them, repairing the harm, and growing wiser because of them. This is not a shameful process. It is the foundation of creativity, growth, and true moral leadership.

But in patriarchal systems—where emotional development is often frozen in place—this evolution is interrupted. Patriarchy, like the narcissistic family or cult, cannot tolerate internal fault. It cannot say, "We were wrong." And so, it must always find someone else to carry its darkness. It must find a scapegoat.

For much of human history, scapegoating was considered sacred. But we now see it for what it is: the tool of those who are scared.

Scared of their own shadow.

SECTION II: SCAPEGOATING IN EMOTIONALLY IMMATURE SYSTEMS

> *BLUF: Defines scapegoating as a key tool in narcissistic and patriarchal systems that refuse internal accountability. Introduces the scapegoat as an emotional and moral dumping ground used to preserve dominance hierarchies. Examines the systemic targeting of women as default carriers of cultural shame. Highlights how patriarchal narratives cast women as the problem.*

What happens in ancient ritual still plays out in modern dynamics. The narcissistic family. The cult. The corporate ladder. The patriarchal nation.

In systems that lack emotional maturity—where the ego refuses to be humbled, where apologies are seen as weakness—someone must absorb the discomfort and take the blame and pay the consequences.

Scapegoating is not just a dysfunctional habit—it is a core technology of system preservation.[108] Like language and money, it becomes a tool to keep dominance hierarchies intact. It protects the central power by outsourcing shame and diverting attention from the system's deeper failures.

In short: the scapegoat is assigned the job of carrying what the system refuses to confront. Mistakes. Rage. Shame. Insecurity. Injustice. Weakness.

Rather than metabolize these internally, immature systems find someone to symbolically drive into the wilderness or to sacrifice for others' behavior.

THE PURPOSE OF THE SCAPEGOAT IN PATRIARCHAL SYSTEMS

Patriarchy is not just a hierarchy of dominance—it's a moral pyramid scheme. A dominance hierarchy disguised as virtue, engineered to extract not just labor and loyalty, but also moral absolution for those at the top. It only works if someone else is always "below," someone else always "to blame."[109]

Scapegoating serves many critical purposes:

❖ **Maintains the illusion of moral superiority** for those in power.

❖ **Distracts from structural failures** by blaming individuals.

❖ **Reinforces the hierarchy** by showing what happens to dissenters.

❖ **Binds the group** by giving them a shared enemy.

❖ **Protects the ego** of the leader by offloading shame.

And in patriarchy, there is a default scapegoat: women.[110] They are the sin-eaters cast as:

The temptress who causes men to stray or rape.

The hysteric who can't be trusted with leadership.

The bad mother who causes her children's dysfunction.

The ungrateful wife who destroys the family by wanting more.

The witch, the whore, the too-much, the never-enough.

When systems fail—when men are violent, when children suffer, when communities break down—the question becomes:

What did she do wrong?

What's more, patriarchy demands that women carry not only their own pain, but also the unresolved trauma, shame, and rage of the men around them. And when they refuse? When they name the harm or walk away?

They are cast out and labeled disloyal. Man haters. Dangerous. Damaged. Rejected for refusing to eat one more ounce of sin.[111]

SECTION III: FROM GOAT TO WOMAN — HOW SCAPEGOATING EVOLVES

BLUF: Reframes scapegoating as a modern psychological and cultural technology. Analyzes projection, introjection, and gender essentialism as key mechanisms of moral outsourcing.

Primitive cultures had literal goats. Patriarchal systems have figurative ones.

In emotionally immature systems, we no longer drive animals into the wilderness or sacrifice them on altars. We sacrifice people—often the most emotionally honest, morally courageous, or inconvenient people in the room. And most often those people are women.

Scapegoating has evolved into a psychological and cultural technology, one that assigns blame and unprocessed shame to others to preserve the self-image of the system, by offloading the burden of accountability to maintain the illusion of virtue.

Let's break down how this works.

THE MECHANICS OF MODERN SCAPEGOATING

Projection: The Mirror Reversed

What we cannot bear in ourselves, we see—and punish—in someone else.

- An angry man accuses a woman of being "too emotional."
- A leader who lies regularly accuses truth-tellers of deceit.
- A society built on domination accuses women who speak up of being "hysterical," "crazy," or "divisive" or of wanting to control men.

Projection is not just a personal defense mechanism. In immature systems, it becomes institutionalized.[112]

Introjection: Carrying What's Not Yours

Projection cannot exist without its twin: introjection.

When someone projects their unowned shame or aggression onto you —and you internalize it—that is introjection. You begin to wonder: Am I the problem? Am I too much? Am I wrong?

Scapegoats are often the most psychologically aware, emotionally sensitive, or morally honest people in a system. And that's exactly why they're targeted. They won't play along with the lies. So, the system makes them the problem.

Gender Essentialism: Shame and Shadow Assignment

In patriarchal cultures, shame-shifting is deeply gendered.

Men are assigned strength, logic, leadership.

Women are assigned emotion, chaos, manipulation.

Then, women are held responsible for managing, cleansing, or redeeming the very harm patriarchy creates, becoming the emotional laundromats of culture—expected to forgive, absorb, nurture, and heal everyone else without complaint.

This often sounds like: she must "rise above." She must "be the bigger person." She must "forgive and forget"—even when no one has taken responsibility.[113] Women aren't just blamed. They're expected to clean up what patriarchy won't even admit to spilling.

MODERN SCAPEGOATS: NOT JUST IN FAMILIES

Scapegoating isn't confined to family systems. It shows up across every structure shaped by patriarchy:

In Religion

Eve as the original sinner. Mary as the silent, suffering redeemer. Women must carry the sin—or erase it—but never name its source.

In Media

Ambitious women are "emasculating." Victims are "lying for attention." A woman's tone, expression, or confidence is enough to make her suspect.[114]

In Politics

Women who seek power are called "witches," "bitches," "monsters," or "whores." They're either too emotional or too cold to be likable.

In Families

The truth-teller is cast as the destroyer.[115] The child who names abuse is blamed for "tearing the family apart."

INTERSECTIONALITY: ACKNOWLEDGING THE LAYERS

While this chapter focuses on patriarchy's scapegoating of women, it's important to briefly acknowledge that the dynamic deepens at the intersection of race, class, sexuality, and ability.

Women of color, queer women, and disabled women are often scapegoated more harshly, more publicly, and with less cultural protection. The more marginalized someone is, the more weight they are expected to carry—not only of their own suffering, but of everyone else's projections.[116]

SECTION IV: MODERN SCAPEGOATING TACTICS — A FIELD GUIDE

> *BLUF: Provides concrete, named tactics such as anticipatory blame, spiritualized martyrdom, group scapegoating, and empathy exploitation. Helps readers recognize how systems assign shame to avoid growth.*

Scapegoating today is subtler—but no less destructive. Here are modern masks the scapegoat is made to wear.

Moral Panic & Group Scapegoating

Used to justify mass control, exclusion, or violence.

Examples: Satanic panic, anti-LGBTQ+ hysteria, attacks on single mothers or "welfare queens," or immigration panics.

Purpose: Shift collective anxiety or guilt onto a symbolic "other." These moments often coincide with periods of cultural or economic instability, where leaders look for a target to unify the group through fear.[117]

Scapegoating Through Distraction

When a scandal or failure threatens those in power, a scapegoat is sacrificed to preserve the illusion of accountability.

> **Example:** Firing one employee for "isolated misconduct" in an abusive work culture.

> **Effect:** The system claims moral high ground, but nothing changes.

Biological & Pathologizing Scapegoating

Labeling someone's existence as inherently defective, dangerous, or disordered.

> **Examples:** Diagnosing women with "hysteria," pathologizing neurodivergent children or survivors of abuse as "too sensitive" or "unstable."

> **Effect:** Their pain is dismissed as inherent dysfunction, not a response to harm.

Spiritual Scapegoating

Assigning others the responsibility to cleanse, forgive, or purify the community.

> **Examples:** Women being asked to forgive public abusers "for the sake of unity," or Black communities expected to be gracious after state violence.

> **Effect:** Emotional labor and moral burden are offloaded onto the wounded.

Burdening the Empath

In emotionally immature systems, the person with the most empathy often becomes the scapegoat because they care enough to name the harm. Their compassion is exploited, and their pain is reframed as instability or selfishness.

Effect: Their attunement becomes a liability. Their emotional clarity is rewritten as emotional dysfunction.[118]

Preemptive Scapegoating (Anticipatory Blame)

Blaming someone in advance for a rupture that hasn't even happened yet.

> **Examples:** "If this relationship fails, it'll be because you're so dramatic," or "Don't ruin Thanksgiving like you always do."
>
> **Effect:** Locks the target into a role they can't escape, and gaslights them preemptively.

The "Healing" Scapegoat

Spiritualized forms of scapegoating that frame the target as the "wounded healer" or "sacrificial lamb" who must transmute pain for the group.

> **Examples:** Assigning one person the role of family therapist, truth-teller, or generational curse-breaker while others continue to harm or avoid accountability.
>
> **Effect:** Emotional martyrdom becomes their identity—while the system avoids change.

Each tactic allows the system to maintain control while avoiding responsibility. When seen clearly, they become impossible to justify—and easier to name.

SECTION V: THE LONG – TERM TOLL ON THE SCAPEGOAT

> *BLUF: Details how scapegoating corrodes personal identity and agency. Highlights the psychological impact—and how stepping out of the scapegoat role becomes a revolutionary act of self-clarity and systemic disruption.*

Scapegoating isn't just painful—it warps one's sense of reality and erodes identity over time:

You begin to question your perceptions.

You may feel ashamed for existing.

Observable (External) Costs

Social exclusion and ostracism: Scapegoats are often erased from family systems, group dynamics, and community narratives. Invitations disappear. Relationships fracture. Their very presence becomes unwelcome.

Reputational damage: Smear campaigns and whispered narratives paint the scapegoat as unstable, disloyal, or dangerous—often leading to professional exclusion, lost opportunities, and public doubt.

Exclusion from jobs or industries: Particularly in religious, academic, or niche professional settings, scapegoated individuals may be quietly blacklisted or lose entire career paths due to false narratives or misaligned power.

Financial and legal fallout: Scapegoats often lose access to housing, inheritance, employment, or custody as systems rally around the dominant narrative.

Chronic overwork to prove legitimacy: To compensate for false accusations or character assassination, many scapegoats spend years over-functioning, being perfectionistic, and trying to earn back dignity that should never have been taken.

Hidden (Internal) Toll

Chronic trauma symptoms: Prolonged invalidation can lead to depression, anxiety, panic, dissociation, C-PTSD, and chronic shame.

Distorted sense of reality: Scapegoats may question their memories, emotions, and even basic instincts—wondering if they really are the problem.

Identity erosion: The constant narrative of being "wrong" or "bad" begins to seep into the self-image—often sabotaging confidence and voice.

Dissociation or collapse: When over-functioning fails to bring relief, many scapegoats shift to under-functioning—shutting down, withdrawing, or disappearing.

Relational mistrust: After being betrayed by those closest, scapegoats may struggle to form safe, trusting relationships in the future.

Community-Level Damage

Stigma and groupthink: Scapegoating reinforces binary thinking in systems: one person must be bad so the others can feel good. This creates echo chambers of denial and cruelty.

Silencing of truth-tellers: Those who name harm are punished—not for lying, but for breaking the trance of complicity.

Perpetuation of the system: When the scapegoat is driven out, the system feels stabilized—but only because it has offloaded its shadow.

But here's the quiet revolution: Refusal is Power.
The moment a scapegoat says:
"That shame is not mine."
"That guilt belongs to the one who harmed."
"I will not carry this for you anymore."
That moment changes everything. It restores reality. It restores sanity.
It's the moment Giséle Pelicot, a French woman who was drugged into unconsciousness by her husband and raped by him and more than seventy men for over a decade, refused silence. She insisted the trial be open to the public—not just to expose her husband, but to confront the entire web of complicity that allowed it. "Shame must change sides," she said.[119]

It's the moment survivors of celebrity abusers stood up and said, "Me Too," refusing to be isolated, erased, or blamed. It's the moment a child abuse survivor names the priest who hurt him and says, "You don't get to be holy and hidden anymore."

These moments fracture the ritual. They end the silence. They stop the lie. The spell is broken when the scapegoat steps out of the circle and says:

"I see what you're doing. And I will not play this role anymore."

When the scapegoat refuses to carry what is not theirs, the entire system begins to unravel.

But breaking the spell doesn't come without consequence.

Refusing the role of scapegoat often means facing betrayal—sometimes from the very people who once claimed to love us most.

It's not just exile. It's a reckoning. And yet, for many, that betrayal becomes the doorway. The crossing into clarity.

The moment when survival ends—and initiation begins.

14

The Guardian at the Threshold: Betrayal as Initiation

BLUF: EXPLORES THE PHENOMENON OF BETRAYAL BLINDNESS—WHY WE SOMETIMES CANNOT SEE THE HARM WE ARE LIVING THROUGH UNTIL WE ARE EMOTIONALLY READY. FRAMES BETRAYAL AS AN INITIATORY THRESHOLD MOMENT THAT SIGNALS THE END OF INNOCENCE AND THE BEGINNING OF MATURE SIGHT. INTRODUCES THE MYTHIC IDEA OF DESCENT, THE SYMBOLIC GUARDIAN AT THE THRESHOLD, AND PREPARES THE READER FOR THE NEXT CHAPTERS ON COERCIVE CONTROL AND THE DARK TETRAD—TOOLS OF DOMINATION THAT EMERGE WHEN SYSTEMS SCALE IMMATURITY INTO CONTROL.

SECTION 1: WHEN SEEING BECOMES DANGEROUS — THE NATURE OF BETRAYAL BLINDNESS

BLUF: Introduces betrayal blindness as a survival response to protect relationships we depend on. Clarifies that not-seeing is often a strategy, not a failure, and describes how patriarchal systems rely on internalized silence and loyal roles to maintain power.

We do not always miss the truth because we're naïve. Sometimes, we miss it because we are not yet safe enough to see it.

When betrayal comes from someone we love—or need, or depend on —our mind may flinch. Our body may freeze. Some truths arrive too early, too raw, too destabilizing to hold. So, we tuck them away. We shrink the facts. We rewrite the memory. We make excuses. We love harder. We try to be better.

This is not weakness. This is survival.

And it is deeply human.

There is a name for this: *betrayal blindness*—a term coined by psychologist, Dr. Jennifer Freyd.[120] It describes what happens when awareness of abuse, coercion, or harm would threaten a necessary relationship. We go blind—consciously or unconsciously—because knowing the truth would break the very bond we depend on.

It is the blindness that protects a child who cannot afford to see that their parent is unsafe. It is the silence of a partner who senses something is wrong but fears the cost of knowing. It is the civic loyalty that covers our ears when the country we love commits violence in our name.

And yes, it is the spell we fall under in patriarchal systems that depend on our devotion to roles that deplete us.

We don't just protect those we love. We protect the stories we need to believe to feel safe.

THRESHOLD CROSSINGS: THE SOUL'S SECRET READINESS

In nearly every myth, there is a threshold—a point at which the seeker must descend into darkness to rise.

This descent is not a failure. It is an initiation.

In myth and mysticism, this crossing is often guarded. A lion at the gate. A riddle. A shadowy figure who demands something in exchange. This is not punishment. It is protection. You cannot enter new realms of freedom and consciousness until you are strong enough to carry the truth.

And the truth is this: betrayal is one of life's great initiations.

We rarely choose it. We don't consciously want it. But it happens. And when it does, it marks the end of innocence—not because we've done something wrong, but because we are finally ready to see what we couldn't see before.

Initiations require descent. The underworld. The disillusionment. The grief. They require letting go of false safety to find real inner ground. And that means seeing—not just what others have done to us, but how we adapted to survive. How we dimmed, denied, defended, or delayed knowing what we were not yet ready to know.

And now, perhaps, we are ready.

"We see what we can bear. We silence what we must, in order to stay bonded to those we need."[121]

THIS IS A THRESHOLD MOMENT

This chapter marks a turning point in the book.

Everything that comes next—Coercive Control and Dark Tetrad—will walk directly into the underworld of intentional deception, manipulation, and domination. These systems are not simply misguided. They are methodical. And for many, the realization of their full intent will be painful, perhaps horrifying.

So, take a breath. You do not need to cross that threshold today.

You can pause. You can close the book. You can come back later.

This, too, is maturity: knowing when to press forward and when to rest.

You weren't blind because you were weak. You were blind because the cost of seeing would have shattered something you weren't yet ready to rebuild. But now . . . maybe you are.

WHAT IS BETRAYAL BLINDNESS?

Betrayal blindness is not denial for denial's sake. It is an adaptive response to impossible conditions.

For example, when a child depends on a parent for safety, love, food, or survival—and that parent harms or neglects them—awareness itself becomes dangerous. To fully know that someone you rely on is also hurting you would create a psychological rupture too overwhelming to hold. So, the mind does what it must: it hides the truth, even from itself.

This is betrayal blindness.

Dr Freyd introduced the term betrayal blindness to describe the unconscious unawareness of abuse, coercion, or injustice when acknowledging it would threaten a necessary relationship or identity.

And it doesn't just happen in childhood.

It happens in marriages where one partner senses something is deeply wrong but fears the loss of home, security, or community.

It happens in religious institutions that groom followers to ignore abuses committed by spiritual authorities.

It happens in nations where citizens cling to myths of freedom or virtue while the system quietly exploits, excludes, or brutalizes them or others in their name.

And it happens within patriarchal systems, which depend not just on obedience, but on loyalty—to roles, to stories, to identities that make us feel stable, even when they cost us our wholeness.

Judith Herman, in her book Trauma and Recovery, says: "Secrecy and silence are the perpetrator's first line of defense." And what the perpetrator needs to maintain his image and claim of innocence is exactly what will be demanded of his victims—silence, and often maintaining silence means maintaining unawareness."[122]

Betrayal blindness is not stupidity or weakness. It is a strategy of the psyche—an ingenious one, really. It allows us to function in the presence of contradiction. To survive in the presence of danger. To stay bonded to people or systems that may be harming us—because we don't yet see another way to survive without them.

And this is why it must be treated with tenderness.

You weren't blind because you lacked intelligence.

You were blind because you needed the bond more than you could afford the truth.

SECTION II: THE COST OF NOT KNOWING — SELF-DOUBT, NUMBING, AND SYSTEMIC SILENCE

BLUF: Explores how betrayal blindness corrodes self-trust over time. Describes the psychological, emotional, and somatic costs of protecting harmful bonds—and the ways systems exploit our silence to manufacture compliance.

Betrayal blindness protects us. But protection always comes at a price. When we cannot fully see what's happening, we cannot fully trust ourselves. We second-guess our instincts. We gaslight ourselves before anyone else has to. We build stories to make the unacceptable feel acceptable— until we can no longer tell what's true.

This is the slow corrosion of self-trust.

At first, the price is invisible. We tolerate the mood swings. We explain away the lies. We shrink around the tension and tell ourselves:

"They didn't mean it."

"It's not that bad."

"I'm probably just overreacting."

But over time, the toll grows heavier:

- You begin to **numb out**, disconnect from your body, your desires, your knowing.

- You become **emotionally flattened**—unable to name what you feel, or why.

- You feel **foggy, confused, unsure** whether what happened actually happened.

- You **anticipate criticism**, explain yourself constantly, and walk on eggshells in your own life.

- You become **estranged from your own clarity**—because clarity would cost too much.

This isn't just psychological. It's physiological. The nervous system adapts to betrayal by living in a low-level state of hypervigilance or shutdown, which often results in you feeling exhausted but wired. Disconnected but anxious. Calm on the outside, chaos underneath.

And it's not just personal. Entire systems rely on betrayal blindness.

It is probably no surprise at this point that patriarchal systems do not want you to ask too many questions. They want your loyalty, not your clarity. They want your obedience, not your discernment. They want you to believe that being "good" means being quiet, unquestioning, and endlessly forgiving,[123] when all the while they feed you sanitized versions of harm, saying things like:

"That's just how things are."

"He means well."

"Family is everything."

"Boys will be boys."

"Don't talk about it—it'll make things worse."

But these phrases don't just mask harm. They manufacture compliance. "Silence doesn't just hide the betrayal. It helps it grow."[124]

But one day—perhaps quietly, perhaps suddenly—the silence begins to crack. And that's when the seeing begins.

SECTION III: HOW WE BEGIN TO SEE — GUT KNOWING, SYMBOLIC SIGNALS, AND THRESHOLD MOMENTS

> *BLUF: Names the ways awareness begins to return—through body signals, recurring dreams, language shifts, and outside reflections. Frames these moments as initiatory awakenings that mark the beginning of individuation.*

The truth rarely arrives all at once. It comes in glimmers. In gut feelings. In contradictions we can no longer explain away. A moment that doesn't fit the story. A sentence that stings more than it should. A child's question that makes us pause. A memory that resurfaces, uninvited, but sharper than ever before.

At first, we blink it away. We go back to the role. The rationalization. The rhythm of not knowing.

But something is shifting. A part of us is beginning to see. This part is quiet, but persistent. It speaks in body language—tight shoulders, insomnia, a stomach that flips when they walk into the room.

It speaks in symbols—recurring dreams, emotional flashbacks, déjà vu. It speaks in longing—What if this isn't all there is?

And then one day . . .

You overhear a story that mirrors your own—and realize it is abuse. Someone names the dynamic you've been drowning in and suddenly, you can breathe. You find yourself saying, out loud, "That's not okay"—and meaning it.

These are threshold moments. Not because everything changes at once —but because you begin to change. When you can't unsee what you've seen, you realize you can't go back to playing the part without knowing it's a performance.

The challenge, however, is that awakening doesn't feel like triumph. It feels like grief.[125]

Because clarity is a loss:

- The loss of who you thought they were.

- The loss of who you thought *you* were.

- The loss of the story that held everything together.

It may be followed by rage, numbness, shame, or profound disorientation. That's okay. That's normal. That's part of the crossing.

Remember: You weren't blind because you were weak. You were blind because the cost of seeing would have shattered something you weren't yet ready to rebuild. But now . . . maybe you are.

Seeing is not a punishment. It is an initiation. And what you do next will matter—not just for your own liberation, but for everyone still trapped in the story you are outgrowing.

SECTION IV: THRESHOLDS AND INITIATIONS — THE DESCENT BEFORE THE RISE

> *BLUF: Frames betrayal as an initiation into deeper maturity. Connects personal awakenings to the mythic arc of underworld descent and rebirth. Introduces the idea of thresholds as sacred turning points— often painful but necessary for transformation.*

There are moments in life that divide us into *before* and *after*. We don't choose them. They arrive uninvited—through betrayal, illness, loss, rupture, awakening. They shatter our illusions. They pull us out of the stories we were taught to believe. They confront us with truths that will not be unseen.

These are threshold moments. And crossing them changes everything.[126]

In mythology, this crossing is called the *initiation*—a descent into the underworld, the unknown, the unconscious—not a punishment but a passage.

Initiation does not always look noble. It often begins in collapse. Confusion. Darkness. A sudden emptiness where certainty used to live. Not because we are failing—but because we are being invited to see something we've never seen before.

And to see clearly, we must let go of what once kept us blind.

WHAT IS AN INITIATION?

An initiation is a rite of passage into a new level of consciousness, power, or maturity. It is the moment the old self begins to dissolve—and the new self is not yet formed. Said differently: it is the space between stories.[127]

In traditional cultures, initiations were sacred. Young people were guided through rituals that symbolized the end of childhood and the beginning of responsibility, vision, and self-leadership.

But in modern life, our initiations often arrive without ceremony.

We aren't led into them. We fall into them. Or we are thrown.

INITIATION BY BETRAYAL

Betrayal is one of the most brutal initiators. Because it doesn't just break our heart—it breaks the frame through which we understood the world.

It shows us:

- That the person we trusted was wearing a mask.
- That the system we served was built on lies.
- That the story we were handed was not the whole truth.

And once we see it, we can't go back.

This is the spiritual logic of the underworld: You must go down to go up. You must descend into the truth before you can rise into wisdom.[128]

SECTION V: THE GUARDIAN AT THE THRESHOLD — ARE YOU READY TO SEE?

> *BLUF: Uses mythological symbolism to describe the resistance we feel before stepping fully into truth. Prepares the reader emotionally and psychologically for the next three chapters on coercive control, shame dynamics, and the Dark Tetrad.*

In myth, the gate to deeper knowledge is never left unguarded. There is always a dragon, a demon, a riddler, or a fierce sentinel demanding: *Who are you to pass through here?*[129]

That guardian is not your enemy. It is your test. It asks: Are you willing to see what must be seen? To give up the illusions that once kept you safe—but now keep you small?

This chapter is a conversation with that guardian.

You may feel resistance. That's natural. The next chapters—on coercive control and the darkest structures of domination—are not easy terrain. They will not flatter your former stories. But they will show you what is real.

Take Your Time.

Take a breath.

Take your power back.

This is the moment in the myth where the heroine gathers her courage. Where the hero stops running from the truth. Where the soul says: *I'm ready.*

And if you're not ready yet—bless that, too.

Thresholds are not clocks. Initiations unfold in their own time. But if you're here, something in you knows.

You've already crossed many thresholds in this book. You've understood the core nature of patriarchy as immaturity in the disguise of the elder. You've seen some behaviors patriarchy hides. You've named some things this system tries to erase.

And now, a deeper door stands before you.

The next three chapters will take us further into the machinery of domination:

Laziness, Not Leadership—The Hidden Architecture of Control — How coercive control operates through relational laziness, parasitic dependence, and emotional manipulation—not through strength, but through avoidance, erosion, and domination masked as care.

The Mask, the Mirror, and the Shame Dynamic—How shame operates as a control mechanism: internalized, projected, and mirrored back to keep us complicit in roles that diminish us. This chapter reveals the emotional technologies that train us to accept erasure, submission, and self-doubt as love.

The Dark Tetrad—How narcissism, psychopathy, sadism, and Machiavellianism—the dark traits at the heart of misogyny—expose the true nature of patriarchy, especially in its most refined and socially acceptable forms.

These are the darkest places we'll go.

Not because darkness is the goal—but because truth lives there, too.

And truth is always a gateway to freedom.

But only when you're ready.

So, take a breath.

Take a walk.

Take a day or a month if you need to.

You don't have to prove anything. You don't have to be brave all at once.

You're not behind. You're on time.

This is your journey. You get to choose the pace.

If you feel ready, turn the page. If not, I'll be here when you are.

Once scapegoating and betrayal become normalized, coercion becomes easier to justify. The system no longer sees control as harm—it sees it as necessary. Protective. Even loving. And so, control escalates—not as abuse, but as architecture.

15

Laziness, Not Leadership:
The Hidden Architecture
of Control

BLUF: UNPACKS RELATIONAL LAZINESS AND COERCIVE CONTROL AS THE CENTRAL OPERATING SYSTEM OF PATRIARCHAL DOMINATION. UNLIKE PHYSICAL VIOLENCE, COERCIVE CONTROL IS STRATEGIC, INVISIBLE, AND DENIABLE. IT DOESN'T JUST SEEK OBEDIENCE—IT AIMS TO COLONIZE THE SELF. DRAWING FROM BIDERMAN'S FRAMEWORK AND MODERN EXAMPLES, THIS CHAPTER MAPS HOW COERCIVE CONTROL OPERATES ACROSS FAMILIES, CULTS, RELIGIOUS INSTITUTIONS, AND GOVERNMENTS. THOUGH IT OFTEN APPEARS AGGRESSIVE OR COMMANDING, AT ITS CORE, COERCIVE CONTROL RESTS ON RELATIONAL LAZINESS AND A REFUSAL TO GROW UP.

Note to the Reader:

The phrase "relational laziness" is not meant to shame or attack. I recognize that what looks like laziness is sometimes a trauma response, a lack of modeling, or an unawareness of what emotional or relational labor even requires. But whatever the origin—fragility, fear, or entitlement—the impact is the same: someone else in the relationship ends up carrying what you/they are not. Naming this is not about blame. It's about clarity. Because when relational responsibility is chronically one-sided, it becomes a system of extraction—whether or not it was intended that way. And that pattern is not just personal. It is gendered, it is widespread, and it must be named.

SECTION I: THE MYTH OF NATURAL LEADERSHIP VS. THE REALITY OF SELF-LEADERSHIP

> *BLUF: Challenges the patriarchal myth of male leadership by distinguishing dominance from maturity. Introduces self-leadership as the foundation of emotional responsibility and relational integrity.*

Patriarchy has long promoted the myth that men are natural leaders. It's woven into religious texts, state constitutions, marriage vows, and motivational posters. From the earliest ages, boys are taught that leadership is their birthright—that initiative, authority, and rational command flow through their blood.

But leadership is not a birthright. It's not something you inherit by virtue of your gender. And it's certainly not the same thing as dominance.

True leadership—especially self-leadership—is not about commanding others. It's about commanding yourself first.

And that, we must admit, is the very thing patriarchy quietly discourages in its favored sons.

WHAT SELF-LEADERSHIP REALLY REQUIRES

Self-leadership isn't mythic. It's mundane. It doesn't announce itself with fanfare—it shows up in the quiet, unglamorous disciplines of adult life:

Initiative: Doing what needs to be done without being asked or praised.

Accountability: Taking full ownership for your actions, your impact, and your patterns—without deflection or blame.

Emotional regulation: Knowing how to pause, repair, reflect, and grow—especially when you've caused harm.

Situational awareness: Noticing what's happening in a room, a relationship, or a system—and adapting accordingly.

Relational effort: Actively participating in the creation and maintenance of connection, as well as the care and repair of relationships—not as a heroic gesture, but as a shared responsibility and baseline expectation.

Growth orientation: Willingness to learn, develop, and evolve—not just when it's convenient, but when it's necessary.

Self-leadership means cleaning up your own messes—emotionally, physically, relationally. It means being someone others can trust not just in the spotlight, but in the ordinary moments where real maturity is forged.

THE GREAT SUBSTITUTION: PRAISE WITHOUT LEADERSHIP

In patriarchy, however, many men are trained not to lead—but to expect the appearance of leadership to be enough. They are trained to expect praise, devotion, compliance, caretaking, provisions, and servicing, without doing the emotional, relational, or developmental work that earns trust and sustains intimacy.

And more than that, they are trained to believe that this praise is owed to them, no matter their behavior. As if it were part of the contract of manhood.

It's not that men do nothing. It's that even when they do very little, patriarchy teaches them that they are still owed loyalty, respect, admiration, and full-spectrum care—simply because they were born male.

This is not a personal flaw. It's a systemic outcome. The emotional and relational laziness we see in many men is not the result of incapacity—it's the result of conditioning. Of being rewarded for passivity. Of being given power without preparation, credit without cost, and deference without contribution. It's a learned helplessness that masquerades as maturity.

EMOTIONAL IMMATURITY DISGUISED AS STRENGTH

In emotionally immature systems, power is not connected to responsibility—it's connected to entitlement. And so, what gets rewarded is not self-leadership but the projection of competence without the substance of accountability. That's the con. And it is widespread.

It's why so many women find themselves in relationships where they are doing the initiating, the managing, the planning, the improving—and still being told that their partner is "the leader" of the household.

It's why so many men feel insulted when their low effort is questioned but never insulted by the reality of contributing less.

It's why women in emotionally unequal relationships often feel like they are raising a child while being expected to revere him.

And that is the real paradox of patriarchy:

It does not train men to lead—it trains them to expect leadership status while outsourcing the actual leadership to others.

SECTION II: RELATIONAL LAZINESS — THE SOFT CONTROL OF PASSIVE ENTITLEMENT

> *BLUF: Defines relational laziness as a covert form of control based on passivity, guilt cues, and avoidance of emotional, physical, or financial labor. Exposes how patriarchy rewards passive entitlement as masculinity.*

Not all control is aggressive. In fact, some of it is so passive, so entitled, and so embedded that it's nearly invisible—especially in systems that treat one group as natural caregivers and the other as natural recipients of that care.

This kind of soft control shows up as emotional cues designed to trigger guilt, pity, or caretaking—without ever asking directly, as in:

- Sighing heavily instead of saying what's wrong
- Pouting or withdrawing until someone else initiates repair

❖ Hinting at needs—then resenting when they go unmet

❖ Leaving tasks half-done so a partner must finish them

❖ Delaying action until someone else gives up and does it

These behaviors aren't framed as control, but they have a controlling effect, quietly recruiting others into labor without accountability or consent.

Relational laziness[130] is not a term meant to shame—it's a term meant to clarify. It describes a habitual pattern: the desire to receive intimacy, praise, soothing, and domestic stability—without offering the full effort those relationships require.

The relationally lazy person may say "I love you" and even mean it. But their love is maintenance-free. It lacks follow-through, sacrifice, and shared responsibility. What looks like passivity is often something deeper: a refusal of mutuality.

Underneath many expressions of relational laziness is a worldview rooted in child logic. In early childhood, this is developmentally appropriate. Young children cry, pout, charm, or collapse to get their needs met—without considering the caregiver's experience. They are not yet capable of true mutuality.

But when this pattern is never outgrown, it calcifies into a parasitic form of adult intimacy: *You must relate to me. I do not relate to you.*

This is not just laziness. It's a refusal to recognize others as full people—not just functions. And it's often enacted through manipulative behaviors disguised as vulnerability:

❖ Charm to draw in attention without responsibility

❖ Pouting to punish unmet needs

❖ Emotional collapse to provoke rescue

❖ Stonewalling to create pressure

❖ Distress to evoke duty rather than desire

None of these strategies are about connection.
They are about extraction.

TRAITS AND BEHAVIORS OF RELATIONAL LAZINESS

These patterns often go unrecognized, but they leave a clear emotional footprint:

- Avoiding or delaying shared decisions and difficult conversations
- Failing to cultivate situational awareness
- Deflecting responsibility for relational health
- Offering token gestures or shallow apologies without real repair
- Blame-shifting, ignoring, or withdrawing when confronted
- Saying "I care about you" while neglecting core needs
- Resenting sacrifice or shared labor
- Participating at the bare minimum—especially in emotional or logistical care

HOW RELATIONAL LAZINESS FEELS TO THE OTHER PARTNER

Women—or the more emotionally responsible partner—often feel this pattern long before they can name it. It feels like:

- Low effort or disengagement
- Token help with no follow-through
- Emotional distance masked as "being chill"
- Feet-dragging, sloppiness, or delay tactics
- One-sided growth and repair efforts
- Frequent deflection or defensiveness
- Carrying the weight of decisions, care, and communication

These dynamics trap one person in the role of relational leader, therapist, household manager, emotional sponge, and motivator—while the other still claims to be an "equal partner" or even "the head of the household."

This pattern is especially normalized—and excused—for men in patriarchal systems. This is often because culturally, men are taught that emotional labor is women's domain. They may not say, "I expect you to mother me," but their behavior says exactly that.

The bottom line is he does not relate to the woman as a partner. He relates to her as a need-fulfiller. And what appears as helplessness often conceals quiet control, as the main desires:

The soothing without the structure.

The comfort without the effort.

The emotional access without the emotional risk.

The security without the contribution.

The praise without the feedback.

And they want mommy without mother—comfort without correction, devotion without reciprocity.

This dynamic doesn't always stem from malice. But even without ill intent, someone still ends up doing the labor—and it's almost never them.

That's the hidden architecture of relational laziness: It's not just low effort. It's the expectation that someone else will bridge the gap, carry the burden, regulate the conflict, repair the rupture, keep the connection alive.

"You relate to me. I do not relate to you."

This is not love. This is not partnership. This is the emotional logic of a child—weaponized by an adult.

And when this logic becomes overt, unrepentant, or systematized, it evolves into something even more dangerous: coercive control.

SECTION III: STRATEGIC LAZINESS — THE ARCHITECTURE OF COERCIVE CONTROL

BLUF: Reframes coercive control not as impulsive or reactive but as calculated, efficient, and low-effort domination. Reveals how strategic immaturity is used to extract care, sex, loyalty, and power.

If relational laziness is the soft form of control, coercive control is the hardened architecture of captivity.

It's more strategic, more deliberate, more organized. And unlike the passively entitled person, the coercive controller doesn't just want comfort or care—they want domination, psychological leverage, and total access.

DEFINING COERCIVE CONTROL

Evan Stark, who pioneered the term, describes coercive control as a pattern of domination that seeks to strip away autonomy and dignity, creating a state of entrapment and captivity akin to slavery or kidnapping.[131] He emphasizes that coercive control often leaves no physical evidence yet operates with military-grade efficiency to dismantle autonomy and reshape perception.

Dr. Emma Katz builds on Stark's work, showing how persistent, wide-ranging controlling behaviors are used to demoralize victims into permanent obedience, with harms that continue post-separation. She describes how this form of psychological abuse replaces the victim's internal compass with the controller's demands, leaving the victim emotionally captive even in the absence of violence.[132]

Dr. Janja Lalich, who escaped a cult herself, draws explicit parallels between coercive control and cultic systems. She notes that the most effective systems of control don't rely on force alone. They rely on ideological capture—on emotional myths, double binds, and false rewards that extract loyalty, silence, and compliance.[133]

These three scholars map out a chilling reality: Coercive control isn't a spontaneous reaction—it's a pre-engineered system. Not a breakdown of leadership, but a counterfeit form of leadership—crafted to extract without reciprocity.

The abuser is not confused. There's a comforting myth we tell ourselves about abuse: That he lost control. That he snapped. That he didn't mean to hurt her.

But survivors—especially those who've escaped—often come to realize the opposite is true. Abusers don't lose control. They use control—strategically, selectively, and effectively.

They can control themselves at work. They can control themselves in front of the police. They can control themselves around friends, family, or in public. But behind closed doors, they "lose it"? That's not a loss of control. That's a choice. A tactic. A weaponized form of control.

In a powerful article titled "Abusive Men Describe the Benefits of Violence" published in *Voice Male Magazine,* a domestic violence group facilitator recorded the candid confessions of men who were finally honest about what violence and coercive control got them.[134]

The list of benefits these men named filled several blackboards. And they weren't vague about it. They listed what they got—emotionally, materially, sexually, and socially—by controlling, manipulating, and hurting their female partners. Their answers were blunt and revealing.

1. Control Over Others

"Get my way."

"Control her behavior."

"Make her do what I want."

"She shuts up."

"She will look up to me and accept my decisions without an argument."

"Tell kids they don't have to listen to Mom."

Theme: Coercion as a reliable tool to assert dominance and remove resistance.

2. Emotional Gratification

"It makes me feel powerful."

"It relieves tension."

"It's the only thing that works."

"Have someone to unload on."

"She comforts me."

Theme: Violence used as emotional regulation—immature coping externalized as harm.

3. *Avoidance of Accountability*

"She backs off during arguments."

"I don't have to explain myself."

"She won't challenge me."

"Get to write history."

"Convince her she's to blame."

"Convince her she's the problem."

"It's easier than talking."

Theme: Control used to evade vulnerability, dialogue, and responsibility.

4. *Social and Structural Reinforcement*

"My friends think I'm in charge."

"That's how my dad did it."

"I'm just keeping her in line."

Theme: Abuse justified by culture, tradition, and patriarchal modeling. No guilt—just legacy.

5. *Economic and Practical Convenience*

"She doesn't ask for money."

"I don't have to do as much at home."

"I don't get bothered when I want to watch TV."

"Get the money."

"A robot babysitter, maid, sex, food."

Theme: Coercion used to extract labor and maintain comfort with minimal effort.

6. *Sexual Entitlement*

"She has sex with me when I want."

"She doesn't say no."

"Convince her she's unattractive."

"She still sleeps with me, so I must be forgiven."

"I still get sex, and she still cooks my dinner."

Theme: Domination framed as sexual access—possession, not partnership.

7. *Sadistic Pleasure*

"I like to watch her squirm."

"It feels good when she's scared."

"I get a puppet."

Theme: Pleasure taken in the suffering of others. This is not just control—it is cruelty.

From Evan Stark's *Coercive Control* (2007) to Katz's *Coercive Control in Children's and Mothers' Lives* (2022), the conclusion is the same: Coercive control is appealing to emotionally immature and narcissistic individuals not just for power but because it gets results:

Without growth
Without negotiation
Without vulnerability
Without intimacy
Without reciprocity

It's low-effort access to care, sex, labor, and loyalty—a form of relational parasitism camouflaged as structure, spiritualized as protection, and framed as love.

THE EIGHT ELEMENTS OF COERCIVE CONTROL

Adapted from **Biderman's Chart of Coercion**[135], originally created to describe the interrogation tactics used on prisoners of war—is now recognized as the structure for many intimate partner abuse dynamics.

1. Isolation

Cutting off from family, friends, or other influences. Often disguised as protection: "They don't support us," "You're better off without them."

2. Monopolization of Perception

Gaslighting, information control, rewriting history. This mental hijacking keeps a victim confused and off-balance in a constant state of crisis, so they lose sight of the larger picture. The abuser becomes the lens through which all reality is filtered.

3. Induced Debility and Exhaustion

Sleep deprivation, chronic stress, hypervigilance. Chaos. These wear down the body and mind and make resistance seem impossible. This is why so many women in coercive systems describe feeling foggy, tired, or "crazy." They are not crazy. They are exhausted by design.[136] By constant pregnancy, never-ending caretaking of others, one-sided sky-high expectations that shift as soon as you achieve them.

4. Threats

Creates anxiety and despair through intimidation. Note that not all threats are shouted, however; some are whispered, and some are implied. A look. A change in tone. A story about someone else who was "put in their place." Threats of "going to hell," taking your kids, poverty, violence, or ruining your reputation. Threats activate fear—and fear collapses agency.

5. Occasional Indulgences

This is the "breadcrumbing" that confuses victims into staying. The kind word after the tirade. The flowers, the gift after the guilt trip. The unexpected small warmth. This intermittent reinforcement is more powerful than consistent cruelty. It keeps hope alive by thinking, "This time will be different." It makes the victim work harder to earn approval—and blame themselves when they can't.

6. *Demonstrating Omnipotence*

Constant surveillance, "knowing everything," or controlling finances or whereabouts. Controllers assert their power through surveillance, knowledge, and control. They know what you wore, who you texted, how much money you spent. They intercept your emails. They show up unannounced.

7. *Degradation*

Undermining self-esteem to make resistance costly, such as saying, "You're crazy." "You're lucky I put up with you." "No one else would want you." Degradation attacks your identity. It chips away at your confidence until you believe you deserve the abuse—or that it isn't abuse at all. Humiliation, name-calling, minimizing intelligence or competence, often framed as jokes.

8. *Enforcing Trivial Demands*

Compliance training through petty demands, such as arbitrary rules, rituals, or preferences enforced to assert dominance: "Don't look at me that way." "You must answer texts within X minutes." "Don't use that word." Trivial demands serve no practical purpose. Their only function is to normalize submission and to train the nervous system to flinch, to yield, to comply. The more you obey meaningless commands, the harder it becomes to disobey serious ones.

In sum, the purpose of coercive control is total internal takeover. To erase a person's past, rewrite their values, and install a new identity—one that aligns perfectly with the needs of the dominator. To enslave them so thoroughly they no longer recognize their own captivity. To manufacture consent for the destruction of their former self. To fashion a puppet of someone who didn't realize that's what they had become.

FALSE LEADERSHIP, REAL CAPTIVITY

Coercive control is not merely a personal failure to develop self-leadership. It is the deliberate construction of a parasitic leadership style—one that mimics order and concern but operates through entitlement, erosion, and emotional colonization in the form of:

- Leadership without personal growth
- Authority without empathy
- Relationship without mutuality
- Power without accountability

Like the cult leader, the coercive controller is not guiding or growing. He is not the leader of the system—he is the center of it. And the system is designed to ensure that he never has to develop.

He doesn't want reciprocity. He wants access. He doesn't *earn* respect. He extracts it. He doesn't seek genuine intimacy. He demands loyalty.

Coercive control is not what happens when entitlement is denied.

It's what happens when entitlement is institutionalized.

SECTION IV: INTIMACY LABOR – SEX IN RELATIONAL LAZINESS

> *BLUF: Explores how intimacy labor becomes one-sided in immature relationships and systems. Names the emotional exhaustion of building connection with a partner who participates passively. Frames relational imbalance in sexual dynamics as emotional freeloading, not intimacy.*

THE LABOR OF INTIMACY

Intimacy labor is about relating—the work of creating togetherness, the team-building skill of weaving an "us" from "you" and "me," and the ongoing tending of the relationship itself.[137] Unlike other forms of labor, it only succeeds when it's mutual—when both people are invested, attuned, and willing to show up.

In emotionally immature or patriarchal systems, that mutuality is often missing. One partner becomes the emotional translator, the attunement engine, the relational glue—while the other simply absorbs the benefits of closeness without ever cultivating it.

It's like being on a team with someone who won't pass the ball, won't train, won't show up for practice—but still expects to stand on the podium and share the victory. Or worse, it's like losing the game repeatedly because one person was playing for the team, while the other was only playing for themselves.

This is what emotional immaturity in intimacy often looks like: one partner focused on "we," the other on "me." It names what many feel but can't quite articulate: the invisible exhaustion of trying to build connection with someone who doesn't think like a teammate. Here is where we once again see the echo of patriarchy's emotional contract: *"You relate to me. I do not relate to you."*

Intimacy labor is the ongoing emotional, psychological, and sometimes physical work of building and sustaining closeness with another person. It's the invisible architecture of real connection—where vulnerability, trust-building, attunement, and emotional generosity are cultivated over time.

This is not the same as relational labor, which tends to be more logistical: remembering birthdays, initiating plans, managing household tension, kin-keeping. Intimacy labor is internal, attuned, and soul-level, creating the conditions of safety and aliveness that allow two people to show up fully as themselves. And it's not one-size-fits-all. Intimacy labor takes many forms—some spoken, some silent, some visible, some felt only at the level of energy.

Understanding its forms gives us a powerful lens through which to examine the emotional economics of control, care, and extraction.

Relational con-artistry —where one partner receives the benefits of closeness without doing the work

Emotional freeloading —parasitic intimacy masked as connection

False intimacy —created through charm, sex, or trauma bonding, but lacking reciprocal effort or accountability

FORMS OF INTIMACY LABOR IN DEEP RELATIONSHIPS (ALL TYPES)

Whether in friendship, family, or partnership, intimacy labor often includes:

1. ***Emotional Attunement***

   Noticing subtle shifts in mood, tone, or energy

   Asking meaningful follow-ups and staying with hard feelings

   Regulating your own reactions so you can truly show up for theirs

2. ***Deep Listening***

   Receiving someone's truth without interrupting, fixing, or minimizing

   Holding space, even when it's inconvenient or uncomfortable

3. ***Authentic Sharing***

   Offering your truth—not just facts, but feelings

   Risking vulnerability so the other doesn't feel emotionally alone

4. ***Making Meaning Together***

   Reflecting on shared experiences

   Building a shared "we" instead of two parallel lives

5. ***Tending to Rupture and Repair***

   Naming disconnection

   Apologizing, repairing, forgiving, and reweaving trust—without being prompted or guilted

This labor is present in any deep, enduring connection—especially among emotionally mature people. But in many patriarchal systems, women and emotionally attuned partners are expected to perform it alone.

THE 'EXTRA MILE' OF INTIMACY LABOR IN ROMANTIC/ SEXUAL RELATIONSHIPS

In romantic partnerships, all the above remains true—but with the added layer of erotic and emotional vulnerability. In these relationships, intimacy labor extends further.

1. ***Creating Emotional Conditions for Desire***

   Cultivating emotional safety, care, mutual respect, and spontaneity

   Differentiating closeness from control

2. ***Sexual Attunement and Generosity***

   Attending not just to personal arousal, but to the arc of your partner's experience

   Caring about their comfort, pleasure, boundaries, and pacing

3. ***Navigating Power, Shame, and History***

   Recognizing that sex often carries cultural, relational, and trauma-related baggage

   Willingness to work through it together—not override it

4. ***Ongoing Consent and Enthusiastic Participation***

   Seeing consent as a living, breathing process—not a checkbox
   Rooted in care, not compliance

5. ***Carrying the Weight of Meaning***

   In many partnerships, women (or the more emotionally mature partner) carry the symbolic weight of sex—interpreting what it means, whether it was emotionally safe, whether it affirmed or rejected the relationship

   This meaning-making is itself a form of labor—often unacknowledged

WHY THIS MATTERS

When intimacy labor is not mutual—when one person habitually gives and the other habitually receives—it begins to feel less like connection and more like performance. This is why intimacy labor—especially sexual intimacy labor—can feel depleting, invisible, or even violating when it's one-sided.

True intimacy requires maturity—and an equal partner willing to meet you there. What often takes its place is sex as the performance of intimacy, not the culmination of mutual connection.

This deceptive and painful framing isn't just inaccurate—it's injurious. Because no real intimacy labor was done beforehand, one partner may walk away feeling emotionally ecstatic, assuming they've shared something profound—while remaining utterly oblivious to the other's experience of feeling invisible, empty, or used. And worse—she is often expected to perform ecstasy, too: to smile, moan, and affirm the illusion that it was just as good for her as it was for him.

In other words, she is tasked with all the intimacy labor—and then required to pretend that the experience was mutual.

This is the final insult.

Not only must she offer her body—she must protect his ego by performing joy. This is especially true in patriarchal heterosexual dynamics, where sex typically takes place *inside* a woman's body.

That fact alone renders the experience asymmetrical. Letting someone into your body is not the same as showing up at someone else's door. It's the difference between offering sanctuary—and breezing through someone else's home without thought or consequence.

One absorbs the impact. The other enjoys the access.

Yet men are taught to speak of sex as a conquest: Getting some. Doing her. Scoring. And in the most emotionally immature circles of men, the language reveals their distorted thinking:

"She was used up."

"I got some."

"She let me hit it."

Language that frames the act as taking and using, not sharing.

But real intimacy is not about taking. It's not even just about giving. It's about meeting—mutual, conscious, and reciprocal. When these conditions are absent, sex is no longer a place of communion. It becomes a slow-walking desecration. Not necessarily violent or overtly coercive—but hollow, extractive, and eroding to the soul of the one who keeps showing up in good faith, hoping for real connection.

Without mutual care, emotional attunement, and trust—sex is not intimacy. It's access. And access is not connection. And it's certainly not love.

When intimacy labor is absent—or one-sided—and access is mistaken for love, sex becomes not a deeply fulfilling mutual connection but an ongoing site of emotional imbalance, self-soothing, and often injury. Sometimes that imbalance is subtle. Sometimes it's unspoken or unacknowledged.

Other times, it is coercive by design—meaning that sex, in emotionally immature systems, often becomes a form of nervous system regulation for one partner, and emotional abandonment for the other.

SECTION V: GOD SAYS — SEX, COERCIVE CONTROL, AND SPIRITUAL ABUSE

BLUF: Reveals how sex becomes a tool of domination and nervous system, and ego regulation for the emotionally immature dominator. Highlights the role of entitlement, submission, and spiritual coercion in normalizing non-consensual or non-mutual dynamics.

In coercive control, sex isn't used to bond—it's used to bind. For the relationally lazy or the dominator, sex becomes less about intimacy and more about emotional and ego regulation. Like a child seeking comfort at a mother's breast—skin to skin, heartbeat to heartbeat—some men use sex to calm themselves, discharge tension, and reassure their fragile ego. But unlike an infant, these men are not innocent. Their need is fused with entitlement, their dependency cloaked in control.

For them, sex is a strategy—not a meeting of souls, but a method of maintaining power in the following ways:

- ❖ To release rage, stress, or frustration
- ❖ To possess ("You're mine, even when you're angry")
- ❖ To avoid consequences ("If she still sleeps with me, everything's fine")
- ❖ To demand forgiveness ("I apologized—now show me you forgive me")
- ❖ To soothe themselves with her submission

The partner's body becomes a pacifier, a pressure valve, a compliance test. This is not intimacy but containment. This is not love. It's nervous system regulation through domination.

After Hurricane Katrina, interviews with men who had committed rape while sheltering from the hurricane revealed something chilling: *They described it as a way to relieve stress.*[138] This is not confusion. It's entitlement indoctrination. It is the logical endpoint of a culture that teaches men their needs must be met—emotionally, sexually, physically—by the bodies of women.

And coercive control doesn't always begin with pressure from the individual dominator.

GOD SAYS: SPIRITUAL ABUSE AS COERCIVE CONTROL

From emotional coercion to sexual entitlement, the tactics of control often escalate—and the final frontier is spiritual, where domination hides in the language of God.

In many patriarchal systems—especially religious ones—coercive control isn't just emotional or psychological. It's spiritual. And some of the most powerful tools of domination are cloaked in sacred language.

"God says . . ."

"God wants you to . . ."

"The Bible is clear . . ."

These aren't statements of faith. They're weapons of control.

This tactic functions as religious gaslighting—a strategy in which one person claims to speak for God in order to override another person's agency, desire, or understanding of right and wrong. It creates a moral double bind: *to disobey the abuser is to disobey God.*

And this gaslighting is especially effective because it is culturally sanctioned. Even outside fundamentalist faith communities, much of the Western world still runs on the fumes of a religious history that equated female submission with divine order. Our art, law, language, and social expectations still bear the imprint of male-as-God, woman-as-servant.[139] The divine mandate doesn't need a pulpit—it's been absorbed into the cultural bloodstream.

When these religious narratives are fused with fabricated scientific claims, it becomes scientific gaslighting—a pattern where pseudo-facts are repeated until they feel true. Like the widely repeated but debunked claim that "men can't go 72 hours without sex." Or that male sexuality is biologically uncontrollable, while female sexuality is naturally passive.

In this closed system, God is male. Authority is male. Biology is male. And all of them are cited as justification for female submission.

This is how theology becomes coercion in sacred clothing. It hijacks the conscience. It sanctifies domination. It trains women to obey preemptively—not because their partner asked, but because they were taught that God already did.

As author Sheila Gregoire documents in *The Great Sex Rescue*, many Christian women are taught:[140]

That their husband's need for sex every 72 hours is scientific fact

That "sex on demand" is not only marital duty, but divine command

That women must pleasure their husbands even immediately after childbirth

That saying no is selfish or sinful, even if she feels pain or exhaustion

Gregoire calls out these teachings not only as harmful, but as unbiblical, unscientific, and deeply coercive. They train women to believe that their bodies are not their own, but God's gift to men. That being needed is proof of being loved. That denying sex—even in pain or trauma—is a spiritual failure.

But this is not divine will. This is indoctrination. These teachings don't merely justify coercive sexuality—they pre-install it in the minds of women, framing men as helpless victims of biology and women as holy comfort dispensers.

In other words, sex becomes a sacrificial duty, not a mutual joy. And refusal becomes spiritual failure. This is not desire or sacred love. This is discipleship to a lie—and it is evidence of the child who never learned to self-soothe, now in the body of a man with power, violence, and religious permission to use others as comfort objects.

And women are told this is intimacy, that it is proof of being wanted, that being needed like this is romantic. But this is not romance. It's being used—then told it was love.

And it doesn't stop at religion.

The template of divine entitlement—where women exist to meet men's needs—has invaded therapy offices, marriage books, and even progressive spaces under the guise of "neutral" relationship advice. In many couples therapy models, especially those influenced by patriarchal or religious norms, sexual refusal by women is pathologized.[141]

Rather than being seen as having valid reasons to say no, women are seen as withholding. Refusal is reframed as manipulation, and boundaries become framed as punishment. And the therapist? He or she becomes another agent of the system.

Instead of asking, "What are you protecting?" or "What feels unsafe?", women are asked, "Are you meeting his needs?"

Instead of exploring trauma, exhaustion, or unresolved disrespect, women are told to try harder.

Affection is prescribed like a medicine. Sex, a duty. And refusing sex under these models is labeled as:

"Withholding for control"

"Using sex as a weapon"

"Punishing your partner"

But what is being withheld is not a toy. It is the sanctuary of one's body.

And what's being ignored is the *reason* for the refusal:

Emotional neglect

Unmet needs

Disrespect

Trauma

Exhaustion from invisible labor

This is not manipulation. This is a boundary. And calling that boundary manipulation is how patriarchy colonizes even the healing professions.

Thankfully, this is beginning to change. Feminist and trauma-informed therapists are challenging these frameworks by:

Naming the difference between withholding and protective refusal

Reframing consent within long-term relationships

Centering emotional safety—not just performance

Exposing how patriarchal conditioning shows up in libido, desire, and therapeutic bias

As Sheila Wray Gregoire has shown in her critique of evangelical marriage teachings, many women have been taught that their bodies are not their own—and that being used is the price of being loved.

But the truth is this: When emotional safety is missing, refusal is not punishment. It is wisdom. It is protection. It is sovereignty.

And any system—religious or therapeutic—that calls it something else is reinforcing the very abuse it claims to treat.

THE SPIRITUAL ABUSE OF FORGIVENESS CULTURE

Forgiveness, in its pure form, is a sacred release. But under patriarchal conditioning, it becomes something else: a coercive demand. A shortcut. A way to bypass accountability.

Forgiveness culture tells women especially—but not exclusively—that the real moral task isn't healing, repair, or protection. It's appeasement. It's silence. It's protecting the ego comfort of those who harm.

The Systemic Imbalance

Forgiveness culture flips the focus:

Not on whether the person who caused harm has acknowledged what they did . . .

Not on whether they've shown genuine remorse . . .

Not on whether they've done the work to repair the damage or changed their behavior . . .

Instead, the focus turns to the person who was harmed:

Have they forgiven?

Have they let it go?

Why are they still holding on?

The emotional and spiritual labor is offloaded onto the victim, leaving the one who was harmed expected to do the work of repair.

A Culture That Protects the Immature

Forgiveness culture mirrors the emotional logic of patriarchy we've already mentioned: *You must relate to me. I do not relate to you.*

This reinforces the demand that we protect the emotionally immature from discomfort, consequences, and the requirement to grow. If the harmed person says, "That apology wasn't real," they are punished—called petty, bitter, unforgiving. The message is clear: Don't name the harm. Don't speak of the lack of repair. Smile. Move on.

DARVO: The Patriarchal Playbook

Dr. Jennifer Freyd coined the acronym DARVO to describe a specific pattern of abuse:[142]

Deny the harm

Attack the person who names it

Reverse Victim and Offender

This is patriarchy's emotional magic trick: a total moral inversion, wherein the person who harmed becomes the "real" victim, and the one who was harmed is accused of "acting like a victim."

While being told they're cruel for naming the truth, they're punished for refusing to forgive—or for noticing that forgiveness hasn't been earned.

DARVO is more than a defense—it's a form of double abuse.

Not only does it deny and distort the original harm, but it also multiplies the punishment of the harmed person, doubling down on harm and recruiting the surrounding culture to enforce a gauntlet of social shaming, moral inversion, and institutional betrayal.

Moreover, in becoming cultural infrastructure, it trains entire communities to:

- Recenter the comfort of the one who caused harm
- Punish those who react to harm
- Reframe the memory of harm as an inconvenience
- Demand forgetting in the name of reconciliation

When Memory Becomes the Crime

In forgiveness culture, even naming what happened is taboo. Victims are shamed for "bringing up the past"—even when that past is denied, unhealed, or ongoing. The word *victim* itself becomes suspect, as if naming harm is more dangerous than causing it.

This culture reserves its sharpest punishment not for the violation, but for the reaction to the violation, demanding that we erase memory, smooth the edges, and protect the fragile ego of the one who did the harm.

In short, forgiveness culture isn't about peace. It's about preserving the comfort of the emotionally immature and enforcing the same inversion we explored in DARVO and the inverted moral pyramid:

- Betrayal becomes expected
- Accountability becomes taboo
- And the one who asks for repair is cast as the problem

Forgiveness then becomes a standing entitlement, a blanket pardon. A statute of limitations that guarantees non-prosecution for anything outside the present moment—and even a preemptive promise of immunity for future "mistakes," creating immunity from consequences and from growth.

The Final Twist: Erasing the Demand for Maturity

Forgiveness, as used in any immature system, becomes a tool of selective amnesia, where "forgive and forget" is not about peace—but rather about disappearing the evidence. Why? Because when the evidence remains, the pressure shifts to the victim—and minimization in personal relationships becomes mockery at scale:

- ❖ "You're always so angry" becomes accusations of man-hating, misandry, or being a feminazi.

- ❖ "You're too sensitive" becomes a cultural narrative that women are too emotional to be taken seriously.

- ❖ "You're imagining things" becomes a widespread claim that men are the *real* victims—of courts, of women, of false accusations, of "cancel culture."

This is DARVO turned cultural. A mass gaslight, wherein the crime is not the harm itself—it's daring to remember the harm, to describe it, to expect repair or reformed behavior.

In other words, forgiveness culture demands betrayal blindness from everyone, asking us to abandon our perception, erase our memory, and sanitize our expectations.

And behind it all is the same demand from a system built on emotional immaturity: *You must relate to me. I do not relate to you.*

And the final destination of that demand is erasure.

SECTION VI: ERASURE — THE ULTIMATE DOMINATION

> *BLUF: Examines the systemic silencing of women in history, religion, science, and culture as the final act of coercive control. When domination is complete, the dominated are made to disappear.*

Coercive control doesn't always use violence to dominate. Sometimes, it just makes you disappear. Not through murder or exile—but through silence and invisibility. Through never being counted, never being named, never being believed to exist at all.

Erasure is the final form of control.

When domination is total, the one being dominated vanishes from the narrative. Her labor is used. Her genius is stolen. Her body is consumed. Her name is gone. Even the word we use for the past—history—reminds us of whose story it has been. *His Story.*

Across cultures, systems, and centuries, women have been erased from the most basic institutions of human memory and value.

In History: Women's achievements, political acts, survival innovations, and leadership have been minimized or rewritten under male names. Their activism has been credited to their husbands, their movements dismissed as emotional "waves."

In Science: Women's inventions and discoveries were claimed by men, discredited, or published under pseudonyms. Their bodies were excluded from medical studies. with their pain still ignored as "anxiety."

In Religion: Female spiritual leaders were declared heretics. The feminine divine was demonized or erased. In some theologies, women's bodies are seen as temptation, their voices as corruption.

In Law and Government: Women were legally property. They could not vote, speak in court, escape rape in marriage, or press charges without male witnesses.

In Literature and Art: Women had to adopt male pen names. Their stories were often dismissed as domestic, hysterical, or sentimental and were edited to make them palatable for men.

In Economics and the Workplace: Women's labor has been uncounted, unpaid, or underpaid. Their ideas have been interrupted, their credibility questioned, and their authority undermined in rooms they had to fight to enter.

In Leadership: Even now, women who lead must perform superhuman competence to be taken half as seriously. One mistake confirms every bias. One success is "an exception."

In Psychology: Freud called women's trauma "hysteria." Theories defined maturity through male development and female anger became "borderline," female resistance "disorder." Even now, women's boundaries are pathologized, their intuition dismissed, and their pain repackaged as instability.

And in some societies, erasure is even more extreme.

In Afghanistan under Taliban rule, girls are banned from school past sixth grade. Women are forbidden from most jobs, and even from traveling without a male guardian.

In Saudi Arabia until recently, women couldn't drive or travel freely.

In cultures that require full-body veiling, women may view the world only through a mesh screen—reduced to anonymity, stripped of visibility of face and form.

These are not customs or cultural treasures. They are technologies of disappearance.

This is not just misogyny. This is strategic erasure as a tool of domination.

It's not that women haven't achieved, invented, discovered, or led. It's that they've been erased, or their work absorbed by a system that treats them as extensions of men.

The brilliance of women has not been missing. It's been intentionally unrecorded, redistributed, disbelieved, or erased.

This is not benign neglect. This is domination by deletion. The final act of control is to vanish you. And it is the final frontier of coercive control: when the dominated no longer even appear in the record, so that those who come after cannot see what is possible, what has been done, or who they really come from.

SECTION VII: THE CITIZENSHIP DIVIDEND — PATRIARCHY'S SILENT STIPEND

> *BLUF: Introduces the metaphor of the Patriarchal Permanent Fund— unearned emotional, sexual, and social rewards distributed to men simply for being men, not dependent upon their contributions or maturity.*

Here's the heart of the conundrum: in patriarchy, many men don't need to earn leadership, intimacy, or care. They are granted automatic citizenship in the emotional, sexual, and logistical ecosystem of others—not because of what they give, but simply because they are men.

This is the silent stipend of patriarchy: the expectation of unearned benefits drawn from others' labor, bodies, care, and attention.

Like Alaska's Permanent Fund dividend—where residents receive a payout from oil wealth not because they work in the oil industry or serve the state, but simply because they reside there—patriarchal systems also deliver a Permanent Fund dividend: a reward not for labor, but for identity.

ENTITLEMENTS, SYSTEMICALLY DISTRIBUTED

Even without merit, many men are:

Looked up to as authority figures—despite no leadership experience

Automatically regarded as competent—while women must prove theirs repeatedly

Assumed to be the expert—even when a woman originated and developed the idea

Treated as natural decision-makers—even when others are doing the research and advocacy

Honored in public memory—while women are written out of the record

Allowed to speak for God—while women's moral and spiritual authority is questioned

And regardless of behavior, many men still expect:

- Praise for not being "as bad as others"
- Credit for "helping" with work women are expected to do invisibly
- Admiration for "providing" even if it comes with resentment or strings attached
- Expectation of sexual access—or impunity for harm
- Loyalty to a preferred self-image—regardless of its accuracy

The "right" to emotional labor, child care, household labor, respect, sex, deference, and loyalty is not earned—it's inherited. And in patriarchal systems, it's treated not as a gift, but a given—and this historically and systemically entrenched coercive control is the source of the distributed loot of the Patriarchal Permanent Fund.

SECTION VIII: COERCIVE CONTROL AT SCALE

BLUF: Demonstrates how the eight behaviors of coercive control—originally used on prisoners of war—are scaled into institutions. Draws parallels between interpersonal abuse and systemic domination.

Coercive control doesn't just live in households, and it's not limited to private spaces or "bad relationships." Rather, it's the blueprint of patriarchal society.

The same tactics used by controlling partners, cult leaders, and narcissistic families show up in boardrooms, courtrooms, churches, media, and politics. Control moves from person to institution, from behavior to policy, from whisper to law.

In other words, it scales.

What a narcissist does in a living room, a cult does in a compound, and patriarchy does with entire populations.

- The abusive father who demands obedience mirrors the authoritarian government that suppresses dissent.

- The partner who tracks your every move echoes the employer who surveils those who organize, resist, or ask for fairness and penalizes autonomy.

- The religious leader who demands purity and submission reflects the legal system that grants men reproductive control over women's bodies.

- The family system that scapegoats one child echoes the media that demonizes assertive women, whistleblowers, or survivors who speak out.

These are not separate problems. They are the same operating system, running on different machines.

Coercive control doesn't just remove autonomy—it rewrites identity. It doesn't just harm people—it recruits them into the machinery of domination. And once internalized, the system barely needs external enforcement. People begin to police themselves—and each other.

That's the genius of it. And that's the tragedy of it.

It is how personal abuse becomes cultural architecture.

How manipulation becomes theology.

How dominance becomes economy.

How silence becomes virtue.

How erasure becomes legacy.

We are not merely living in a world that occasionally mirrors abusers. We are living in a world built on the same logic that abusers use.

Coercive control is not just a personal tactic. It is the operating system of patriarchy itself. The same eight behavioral strategies that define coercive control in interpersonal abuse are deployed systemically in patriarchal institutions: governments, religions, media, law, and family.

Let's take a closer look.

1. *Isolation*

Interpersonal: "Your friends are a bad influence."

Systemic: Restricting women's movement, controlling access to education or technology, criminalizing female autonomy (e.g., driving, travel, abortion, divorce). Separated from power, money, public space, and from one another.

2. *Monopolization of Perception*

Interpersonal: Gaslighting or rewriting events.

Systemic: History—literally his-story.

Religious, academic, and media narratives center male perception as objective and trustworthy while painting women as irrational, emotional, or dangerous. Women are told they need men to speak, vote, and interpret reality for them.

Media marginalizes female experience as fringe or unrelatable—even though women comprise half the world.

3. *Induced Debility and Exhaustion*

Interpersonal: Sleep disruption manufactured chaos.

Systemic: The grinding weight of unpaid or low-paid labor, emotional caretaking, survival under violence and harassment, and constant double binds.

4. *Threats*

Interpersonal: "You'll lose everything."

Systemic: "You'll be a bad mother." "You'll burn in hell." "No one will want you." "You'll die alone with your cats."

The consequences of defiance are ever-present in threats of loss of human rights, custody loss, spiritual damnation, poverty, social shunning, or professional sabotage.

5. *Occasional Indulgences*

Interpersonal: A gift after a fight.

Systemic: A single woman promoted in a company.

One law passed, a praise-filled ad campaign. These are held up as signs of progress—while the system itself remains unchanged.

6. *Demonstrating Omnipotence*

Interpersonal: Constant surveillance or control.

Systemic: Policing women's bodies, clothing, tone, and speech.

Harsh punishments for disobedience—from social shaming to state violence: murder, imprisonment, stoning, exile.

The glass ceiling and old boys' networks preserve male monopolization of leadership and wealth under the false guise of meritocracy.

At its extreme, omnipotence shows up in prominent men enjoying full immunity for egregious and well-known crimes—a cultural message that says: "I can do anything I want. And you can do nothing about it."

7. *Degradation*

Interpersonal: Mockery, shaming, minimization.

Systemic:

- Public slut-shaming

- Religious rituals of female confession and "purity"

- Online abuse campaigns

- "Mommy wars" and judgment around caregiving choices

- Constant erasure of women's accomplishments

- Making women beg—for justice, for safety, for basic recognition of harm

- Mocking women for having needs, for being angry, for asking to be taken seriously

Degradation isn't always subtle. It's often ritual humiliation disguised as culture.

8. Enforcing Trivial Demands

Interpersonal: "Say it nicer." "Smile more." Tone policing.

Systemic: Modesty codes. Tone policing. Virginity tests. Arbitrary dress codes.

These serve no real purpose except to enforce conformity, control, and subservience. Smile, apologize. Be likeable. Raise your hand. Speak softly. Be twice as good for half the credit. These are not niceties, they are compliance drills.

The net result?
Exhaustion and psychological captivity disguised as tradition.
A system where women are trained to soothe, serve, and stay—even when they are not safe, seen, or supported.

INFANTILIZATION AS CONTROL

Coercive control flourishes when men are systematically permitted to claim both infantilization and authority at the same time—treated not as emotionally competent adults, but as dependents whose comfort must be constantly protected.

In a mature adult system:

Care is mutual

Responsibility is shared

Power is accountable

But in patriarchy:

Men are awarded grown-up roles while allowed to act like children.

Women are framed as children in society while simultaneously expected to always be the adult in the room—and to serve as emotional regulators for grown men, assume accountability for male behavior, act as crisis managers of the home and family, and assume the bulk of parenting duties.

Enabling infantilization isn't compassion and it's not charming. It's a strategic refusal to grow—one that transfers the burden of maturity to others.

THE LAZY ARCHITECT BUILDS THE PRISON

Coercion doesn't always shout. Sometimes it sighs. It forgets. It shrugs. It waits for you to do the labor it refuses to do.

And when that passive entitlement is interrupted—when women stop complying—the system doesn't crumble right away. It hardens.

Cruelty is reframed as order.

Punishment is reframed as peace.

Control is reframed as love.

The laziest people build the most elaborate prisons—not to keep others out, but to keep themselves from having to grow up.

So, what happens when emotional immaturity is no longer indulged? When the comforts of care and compliance are withdrawn? We begin to see what was there all along:

A dependency that isn't just passive, but hostile.

Hostile dependency isn't what happens when someone stops getting what they want. It's what happens when someone *needs* others—but resents needing them. It's the core contradiction of patriarchy:

Desiring the fruits of relationship while refusing its responsibilities.

This is not a collapse. It's not a regression. It's a revelation.

In the next chapter, we'll explore how emotional laziness turns to emotional warfare—how rage replaces effort, and how the shame of dependence is projected outward through punishment, deflection, and blame.

16

The Mask, the Mirror, and Shame Dynamics

BLUF: THIS CHAPTER EXPLORES HOW SHAME, IMAGE MANAGEMENT, AND MANIPULATION SUSTAIN PATRIARCHAL SYSTEMS. IT TRACES THE ROOTS OF INTERNALIZED SHAME AND SHOWS WHY HONEST REFLECTION BECOMES DANGEROUS IN SYSTEMS BUILT ON ILLUSION. FROM SHAPESHIFTING AND MASKS TO DOUBLE BINDS AND HOSTILE DEPENDENCY, IT REVEALS HOW PATRIARCHY TRAPS PEOPLE IN NO-WIN DYNAMICS—OFFLOADING SHAME ONTO OTHERS, ESPECIALLY WOMEN, AND PUNISHING NOT FAILURE, BUT REFLECTION.

THE MYTHIC THRESHOLD

In myths and fairy tales, the mask often represents illusion—an attempt to conceal true identity or hide one's shadow. Masks can be worn to deceive others, protect the self, or perform roles demanded by culture. But they also signal a split: a disconnection between the outer performance and the inner truth.

The mirror, by contrast, is the great revealer. It reflects not only appearances but the unseen—conscience, character, and consequence. From Snow

White's mirror to Perseus's shield, mirrors hold power. They strip away illusion, expose vanity and deception, and often serve as the threshold between fantasy and truth. In some tales, they offer insight, in others, unbearable confrontation.

Together, the mask and the mirror create a powerful tension. One hides. One reveals. One is chosen. One is forced.

This chapter enters that symbolic space—not to escape reality, but to illuminate it.

In emotionally immature systems, the mask is not just a disguise, it becomes a survival strategy, hiding dependency beneath superiority, shame beneath control, and fear beneath anger. But the mirror is always waiting, sometimes held up by others, sometimes revealed by consequence. This chapter explores what happens when the mask slips, when the mirror is refused, and when intimacy is used not to connect but to coerce. Through shame dynamics, hostile dependency, and double binds, we examine how relational distortion becomes a way of life and what it costs everyone involved.

In myth and fairy tale, the mask often hides more than a face; it hides a hunger, a fear, a secret pact with shadow. The mask is not merely a disguise; it is a survival strategy. It allows the villain to move undetected, the enchantress to gain trust, the wounded to appear powerful. But the mirror—that ancient revealer—cannot be fooled. The mirror sees through performance. It reflects not just appearance but essence.

This is why, in so many tales, the mirror is feared. The Queen in Snow White asks it for affirmation but cannot tolerate its truth. Narcissus drowns in his reflection, mistaking surface for soul. And villains often rage when someone glimpses behind their mask—not because they are caught, but because they are seen.

In emotionally immature systems, this same pattern holds. The mask hides dependency beneath dominance, shame beneath contempt, and fragility beneath control. But when intimacy, conflict, or consequence holds up the mirror, revealing the gap between performance and reality, the reaction is rarely gratitude. It is often rage, withdrawal, or punishment.

When the mask is mistaken for the self, and when emotional connection is distorted into a weapon, we enter the theater of appearance vs. reality. Where seeing clearly results in punishing others, whether one sees oneself in the mirror and doesn't like the reflection, or someone else sees behind the mask.

In short, seeing comes with a price.

SECTION I: SHAME AND THE INNER JUDGE — THE ARCHITECTURE OF ACCOUNTABILITY AND GROWTH

> *BLUF: Explores the origins and functions of shame—distinguishing healthy from toxic shame—and introduces the Inner Judge as a key developmental structure. It shows how emotionally mature environments cultivate this internal compass through modeling, boundaries, and repair, ultimately enabling individuals to process shame, take responsibility, and grow without collapse.*

Before we lie, we pretend. And before we pretend, we often feel shame—not always from wrongdoing, but from not knowing, not belonging, not measuring up. Shame arises not only from harm we've caused but from comparison, exposure, inadequacy. The feeling of falling short in the eyes of others—or our own.

But the way we process that shame depends on one critical inner structure: the Inner Judge.

HEALTHY SHAME VS. UNHEALTHY SHAME

Healthy shame arises when we disappoint ourselves—when we fall short of our own values or expectations. Maybe we failed to prepare. Maybe we didn't do the work. Maybe we ignored a warning sign. Maybe we acted selfishly or stayed silent in the face of harm.

Healthy shame is a moral emotion, one that signals we've strayed from integrity and need to realign. It doesn't collapse us; it invites us to repair, to grow, to try again.

Unhealthy shame, by contrast, arises when we cannot bear to see ourselves clearly. It's the shame that comes when we don't yet possess the developmental tools to self-reflect, take responsibility, or hold complexity.

Instead of processing shame through inner discernment, we experience it as personal annihilation. We deny, deflect, blame, and project.[143] Not because we're dishonest—but because the Judge never made it to the bench.

HOW THE INNER JUDGE DEVELOPS (AND SOMETIMES DOESN'T)

In early childhood, parents, teachers, and caregivers function as external judges and guides, providing boundaries, structure, consequences, and feedback about behaviors and their effects. If a child is surrounded by emotionally mature adults—wise boundary holders who offer both safety and clarity—they begin to understand cause and effect in ways that support growth rather than shame.

In the best-case scenario, children learn that natural consequences are not personal punishments but rather predictable outcomes. If I throw my toy, I might lose it for the day. If I hit my friend, I might need to apologize and take a break from playing. These are not signs that they are bad; they are signs that actions have effects.

Good caregivers protect children from big consequences—like running into traffic or losing a friend forever—and instead, offer smaller, teachable moments: a day without screen time, a reflective conversation, or an insistence that they return the toy they took and make amends. Over time, children begin to associate correction not with humiliation, but with learning.

In these environments, children don't only learn rules but how to anticipate outcomes. With emotional maturity, they begin to regulate themselves. With cognitive development and executive functioning, they begin to weigh options, calculate risks, consider others, and—most importantly—pause before acting. They begin to modify behavior not because someone is watching, but because they are becoming someone who watches themselves. This is the early architecture of the Inner Judge.

In healthy environments, children begin to build this Judge through the slow accumulation of lived experience:

Modeling – witnessing adults take responsibility for their own mistakes

Guidance – being taught the Laws of Life: fairness, honesty, kindness, reciprocity, and accountability

Practice – learning to initiate, persevere, self-regulate, and repair

Boundaries – experiencing age-appropriate consequences that teach what belongs to me and what belongs to others, what is my responsibility and what is theirs

This process is rarely linear. It unfolds through trial, error, correction, and repair. For example, a child might lie and get caught. "No, I didn't eat the cookie," while chocolate smears their face. They might blame their sibling for taking the toy that's clearly in their own hand. These aren't signs of bad character. They are developmentally normal defenses, an effort to escape shame or punishment before the ego is strong enough to metabolize truth.

But with consistent support—not humiliation—children learn to tell the truth, to sit with discomfort, and to take responsibility. They begin to feel remorse rather than simply fear consequences. And slowly, they internalize what it means to have a moral center—an inner compass that can weigh, reflect, decide, and correct.

That compass is the Inner Judge.

WHAT THE INNER JUDGE IS

The Inner Judge is not just a rule-enforcer. It is a teacher. It grows alongside us as we mature, helping us notice patterns, consequences, and truths that don't rely on someone else catching us. It becomes the voice inside that says, that wasn't right—what can I do to make it better? Or: That didn't reflect who I want to be—how can I realign?

A healthy inner Judge is:

* Compassionate, not cruel

* Discerning, not reactive

* Oriented toward accountability and growth, not punishment

It doesn't collapse us in shame. It gives us the structure to work with shame—to use it as information, not identity. It asks: What happened? What was the impact? What repair is needed? What will I do differently next time?

And because it prioritizes *what* is right over *who* is right, it invites maturity.

The Judge grows with us—and helps us become someone sovereign, grounded, and trustworthy—not because the law is enforced from outside, but because we carry it within.

Without this Judge, there can be no sovereignty.

No peace.

And no sustained growth.

WHY SHAME MUST BE FELT TO BE OUTGROWN

To grow, we must develop the capacity to feel shame without collapse and to distinguish being wrong from being bad; to process mistakes, ignorance, boundary violations, and consequences; and to let shame signal where repair is needed—then act accordingly.

Because when we embrace accountability—when we welcome growth instead of resisting it—shame shows up far less often.[144] The inner Judge doesn't need to shame the remorseful individual—it simply shows the way to making amends and restoring integrity.

The Inner Judge protects our honor and dignity before our ego. And in protecting our integrity, it strengthens our ego and our healthy self-regard, helping us stand taller in the world, navigate storms, and avoid unnecessary chaos and pointless damage. It further allows us to hear hard truths without melting or attacking, and it reminds us that remorse is not weakness.

Remorse and repair are the province of the strong.

The Inner Judge is wisdom in motion.

SECTION II: THE MIRROR — REFLECTION, EXPOSURE, AND THE CHILD'S FIRST REACTIONS TO BEING SEEN

> *BLUF: Explores how children first encounter shame through being seen by others, and how early reflections—both accurate and distorted—shape their sense of self. Examines three common immature reactions to exposure (collapse, deflection, and defiance) and how, without support, these become long-term strategies for avoiding accountability.*

Before the mirror reflects us to the world, it reflects us to ourselves. And for children, that moment can be terrifying.

When we are young, the mirror is held by others—often by caregivers, teachers, or peers—who reflect what they see in us. Sometimes the reflection is gentle and true:

"You're kind."

"You tried hard."

"That hurt someone—can you make it right?"

But sometimes the reflection is warped, sharp, or humiliating:

"What's wrong with you?"

"Why can't you ever get it right?"

"Why do you always have to be so much?"

These first experiences of being seen—accurately or inaccurately—leave a deep imprint. They teach us what is acceptable to show, and what must be hidden. They teach us which parts of ourselves earn connection, and which evoke disapproval, ridicule, or withdrawal. And because a young child cannot yet separate self from behavior, shame from worth, or projection from truth, even small corrections can feel like total rejection.

In short, the mirror—so necessary for self-awareness—can feel like a weapon. Or a threat.

THREE PRIMARY REACTIONS TO BEING SEEN

When a child is caught in a lie, exposed in failure, or simply observed too closely, three common shame responses emerge:

1. *Collapse*

The child melts into tears, hides under a table, or says, "I'm sorry! I'm sorry!" even when no apology is asked for. This isn't always true remorse—it's overwhelm. The shame feels too big. The nervous system short-circuits. "I'm bad" replaces "I made a mistake."

2. *Deflection*

The child redirects or rationalizes:

"It wasn't me."
"He started it."
"You didn't say I couldn't!"

This isn't calculated manipulation. It's a desperate, immature attempt to dodge shame. The ego isn't yet strong enough to metabolize accountability.

3. *Defiance*

The child lashes out:

"So what?"
"You're not the boss of me."
"I hate you!"

Here, shame is so unbearable that it's repelled with anger and control. The child regains power by rejecting the one who reflected the truth. These aren't moral failings—they're developmentally normal defenses. But if these reflexes aren't named and guided toward integration, they calcify.

Collapse becomes chronic helplessness. Deflection becomes lifelong blame-shifting. Defiance becomes rigid armored dominance.

And the child—now an adult—builds a life around avoiding the mirror.

THE LAST-RESORT RULE: SHAME REACTIONS IN ADULTHOOD

There's a saying in legal circles sometimes called *The Last Resort Rule*:

"If you have the facts, pound the facts.
If you have the law, pound the law.
If you have neither—pound the table."

Children, with limited reasoning skills, often reach their last resort quickly. They can't argue facts. They can't appeal to law. So, they pound the table—with tantrums, tears, or fury.

But emotionally immature adults also reach for their last resort—often instantly. And because they possess adult vocabulary, psychological insight, and social awareness, their "table-pounding" looks more polished. But it is just as primitive.

SECTION III: ADULT SHAME DEFENSES IN EMOTIONALLY IMMATURE PEOPLE

> *BLUF: This section identifies the three primary shame defenses used by emotionally immature adults—collapse, deflection, and defiance—and illustrates how each one operates in real time to defend and evade responsibility*

1. *Collapse—Victimhood as Evasion*

Looks like:

* Shattering into helplessness

* Role-shifting into the victim—even if they were the aggressor

* Recruiting sympathy ("I'm just anxious," "You don't understand how hard it is for me")

* Triangulating others ("Even [third party] agrees you're being unfair")

❖ Emotional flooding or anxiety as a shield

❖ Refusing repair by staying stuck in overwhelm

They pound the table with **sympathy for themselves**—weaponizing empathy to displace responsibility.

Impact on others:

The person asking for repair is suddenly cast as the bully—pressured to comfort the one who caused harm, forced to abandon their own truth to manage another's emotional fragility.

2. *Deflection—Word Salad and Disorientation*

Looks like:

❖ Rationalization, "whataboutism," or circular logic

❖ Minimizing the issue ("You're making a big deal out of nothing")

❖ "I didn't know," "You never told me," "You misunderstood"

❖ Memory-holing: letting time pass, then acting like the issue never happened

❖ Charmwashing: sudden gestures of niceness to reset without resolution

❖ Disorienting flurries of pseudo-logic or "both sides" arguments

❖ Pivoting repeatedly to avoid emotional contact with the core issue

They pound the table with **cognitive confusion**—using intellect to destabilize reality.

Impact on others:

The person asking for clarity feels gaslit, overwhelmed, and exhausted —forced to defend observable reality while the other dances away from accountability.

3.   Defiance—Counterattack as Defense

Looks like:

- ❖ "You're attacking me" (even if the feedback was calm and kind)
- ❖ Tone-policing ("Why are you so aggressive?")
- ❖ Stonewalling, selective amnesia, passive resistance
- ❖ Delay tactics, sabotaging follow-through, false promises
- ❖ Triangulation or threats of abandonment
- ❖ "You're too sensitive." "You're not the boss of me." "You always nag."

They pound the table with **dominance**—reframing truth-telling as abuse and control.

Impact on others:

The person requesting change is treated as a threat—met not with dialogue but with dismissal, fear tactics, and intimidation.

When enough emotionally immature people hold power, these defenses become norms. Collapse becomes male fragility. Deflection becomes institutional gaslighting. Defiance becomes authoritarianism. What we couldn't metabolize privately becomes policy.

SECTION IV: HOW COLLAPSE, DEFLECTION, AND DEFIANCE SCALE TO PATRIARCHY

BLUF: Explores how the childhood shame reactions of collapse, deflection, and defiance evolve into adult strategies for avoiding accountability. Shows how these defenses—when left unexamined— become tools of manipulation, distortion, and dominance. Highlights how emotionally immature individuals weaponize victimhood, intellect, and aggression to evade reflection and responsibility.

Each of these shame responses—**collapse, deflection,** and **defiance**—can be seen not just in individuals, but scaled up into the logic, behaviors, and enforcement mechanisms of patriarchal systems. These aren't just private defense mechanisms—they become public architecture.

COLLAPSE → FRAGILITY AS A POWER MOVE

Individual:

The person melts down when confronted with truth, turning accountability into a personal injury.

Patriarchy:

- Male fragility is institutionalized—truth-telling is reframed as an "attack on men" or "reverse sexism" or charges of misandry.
- Emotional labor is demanded from women to comfort or soothe those who hold power.
- Systems collapse into performative victimhood whenever their dominance is challenged—e.g., "Men are under attack!" narratives when feminist critiques emerge.

Result:

The system demands caretaking, pity, and exemption from consequence—weaponizing weakness to avoid reform.

Fragility in women is weaponized and used to justify exclusion, infantilization, or blame.

Fragility in men is split: outward tenderness is mocked, but ego-fragility is protected.

The male ego must not be challenged. It is treated as sacred ground—even when it causes harm.

DEFLECTION → DISTRACTION, BLAME-SHIFTING, AND NARRATIVE CONTROL

Individual:

The person changes the subject, intellectualizes, or turns blame onto the accuser.

Patriarchy:

- *Whataboutism* in public discourse ("But what about men's problems?")
- Blame-shifting to women ("She shouldn't have dressed like that," "She provoked him")
- Endless distraction tactics (focusing on tone, timing, or delivery rather than content)
- Historical revisionism, denial of statistics, or reframing of oppression as benevolence (e.g., "traditional family values")

Result:

The system preserves itself by fostering confusion, distortion, and misdirection—gaslighting the culture.

DEFIANCE → AUTHORITARIANISM, COERCION, AND PUNISHMENT

Individual:

The person lashes out, becomes punitive, or doubles down in control.

Patriarchy:

- Laws and policies that punish dissent (e.g., anti-abortion legislation, anti-LGBTQ+ laws)
- Militarized policing of resistance—from protest crackdowns to domestic power plays

- Religious or political rhetoric asserting divine right or unquestionable moral authority
- Aggressive counter-blaming of the oppressed: "You're destroying tradition," "You're tearing families apart."

The system ensures obedience through fear, force, and moral condemnation—punishing those who see or speak.

SKEPTIC'S LENS

But couldn't someone argue that these are just features of any dominant system under critique and not unique to patriarchy?

Yes, and that's precisely the point. Patriarchy functions as a dominance system rooted in emotional immaturity, much like narcissistic family systems or authoritarian cults. What makes patriarchy distinct is how its defenses are gendered, institutionalized, and spiritualized:

Collapse is feminized—but male fragility is protected.
Deflection becomes doctrine.
Defiance becomes law.

The pattern isn't just present, it's enshrined.

THE SHAPE-SHIFTING DEFENSE

Most emotionally immature adults or systems don't stick to one pattern, they pivot. From collapse to defiance. From logic to tears. From victim to bully.

They expect perpetual mercy, regardless of impact, interpret consequences as cruelty, and demand to be treated like innocent children and then rage when asked to grow.

And if they apologize, it's often a token:

"I'm sorry *you* feel that way."

"I'm sorry, but . . ."

Their tactics may include:

- ❖ Justification and blame-shifting: counteraccusations and revisionism
- ❖ Stonewalling: pretending the rupture never happened
- ❖ Charmwashing: friendliness instead of repair
- ❖ Outsourcing judgment: seeking external validation rather than internal growth
- ❖ Scapegoating: punishing the one who saw clearly

This is not healing. It's trying to outrun shame and accountability but results in stagnation. It results in a refusal to grow and a punishment of anyone who dares to evolve. And behind it all, beneath the rage and the resets, waits the thing they fear most: the mirror.

Self-reflection. The reflections of others. So they reach for protection.

SECTION V: WHEN THE MIRROR IS REFUSED — THE FUNCTION OF THE MASK

> *BLUF: Explores how emotional immaturity leads to mask-wearing as a defense against shame and self-confrontation. Differentiates between sacred shapeshifting and manipulative performance. Introduces common mask archetypes and shows how these masks evolve from protective strategies into false identities.*

The child who could not bear the mirror does not vanish. They grow older and develop adult language, adult routines, adult responsibilities. But if the core shame wasn't metabolized—if it was collapsed into self-loathing, denied through blame, or guarded with defiance—the emotional reflexes remain.

They just become more sophisticated.

We don't call them tantrums anymore—we call them cold shoulders, sharp words, subtle digs, or righteous indignation.

We don't say "I didn't do it"—we say, "You're too sensitive," or "That's not what happened," or "You're misinterpreting."

We don't scream "I hate you!"—instead, we withdraw affection, offer surface-level charm, or quietly punish.

We refuse the mirror—and then we do everything we can to avoid passing by one that might show our reflection.

What better way to do that in ordinary life than by wearing a mask?

THE MASK AS STRATEGY

The mask is not inherently malicious. It begins as protection. It helps us function and keeps us from being shamed, rejected, humiliated, or cast out. It allows us to show the parts of ourselves that are likely to be rewarded— and hide the parts that still carry unprocessed shame.

But over time, the mask becomes more than a strategy. It becomes a substitute for identity. We forget it's a mask, thereby confusing performance with personhood and role with reality. We then build entire relationships, careers, and communities around a version of ourselves that is digestible, admired, and safe.

In mythology, masks often appear as shapeshifting, glamour, or enchantment—tools of transformation, illusion, and seduction. They are magical—but dangerous, allowing the wearer to hide, survive, or trick. But they also sever the wearer from their true form. The longer the mask is worn, the harder it is to remove.

WHAT THE MASK PROTECTS

As you may surmise, the mask does not protect our true self—it protects our *wounded self.* Specifically:

- The part of us that still feels small, bad, or not enough

- The part of us that learned vulnerability leads to humiliation or loss

- The part of us that fears the mirror not because of what it shows —but because of what it *confirms*

When the mirror shows a contradiction—between mask and reality, between performance and impact—the shame rushes in. And without an inner Judge to metabolize it, we regress and experience adult intellects driven by childlike defenses.

COMMON MASKS: WHAT WE WEAR TO SURVIVE

In emotionally immature or unsafe environments, the mask becomes our passport—our way of belonging, protecting ourselves, and managing others' reactions. Some masks are culturally sanctioned. Others are forged in childhood. Many are mistaken for personality. But each has a purpose. Each tells a story. None, however, tells the whole truth.

Here are some of the most common masks worn in emotionally immature systems.

The Good One

Purpose: To earn safety, approval, or worthiness by being compliant, helpful, and self-sacrificing.

Origin: Often emerges in chaotic or critical environments where love feels conditional.

Shadow: Resentment, invisibility, repression of authentic needs.

The Child

Purpose: To provoke or elicit care or love by being helpless, "young," charming, or special.

Origin: Formed in systems where vulnerability is rewarded with attention, and direct needs are unsafe to express.

Shadow: Manipulation, emotional regression, strategic helplessness, covert control.

The Wounded One/Victim

Purpose: To secure connection, care, or exemption from responsibility by appearing broken, fragile, or perpetually healing.

Origin: Often develops in environments where sickness or injury—emotional or physical—is the only reliable route to receiving care.

Shadow: Weaponized victimhood, self-sabotage, chronic crisis, refusal to grow.

The Performer

Purpose: To gain admiration or belonging through charm, achievement, or success.

Origin: Environments where image, productivity, or exceptionalism are rewarded over real connection.

Shadow: Loneliness, imposter syndrome, burnout.

The Tough One

Purpose: To protect oneself by being invulnerable, stoic, or aggressive.

Origin: Settings where sensitivity is mocked, punished, or exploited.

Shadow: Emotional isolation, rigidity, repressed grief.

The Caretaker

Purpose: To maintain connection and reduce conflict by tending to others' emotions, needs, and chaos.

Origin: Often arises when a child becomes parentified or emotionally responsible for caregivers.

Shadow: Codependency, chronic depletion, lack of boundaries.

The Rebel

Purpose: To avoid shame or powerlessness by being oppositional, unpredictable, or defiant.

Origin: Environments of control or moral rigidity.

Shadow: Alienation, self-sabotage, unhealed rage.

The Invisible One

Purpose: To avoid conflict or harm by disappearing, staying small, or flying under the radar.

Origin: Homes where presence drew punishment or indifference.

Shadow: Disconnection from self, chronic anxiety, difficulty being seen or chosen.

The Expert

Purpose: To feel safe and valuable by always knowing the answer or staying in control intellectually.

Origin: Environments where emotion was unsafe but intellect was rewarded.

Shadow: Emotional bypassing, superiority, difficulty receiving.

These masks serve a function—and they are not inherently bad. But they are camouflage, and over time, they can become prisons. What began as survival becomes identity and we forget: the mask is not the self. Naming it is the first act of reclamation.

Unmasking requires tenderness, not blame. We take the mask off slowly and only when it's safe to do so.

Unfortunately, these individual defenses calcify into cultural scripts. The shame we couldn't face is buried beneath the roles we are expected to play. In patriarchy, masks become sanctioned identities—roles that carry both privilege and punishment, depending on your placement.

SECTION VI: WHEN ROLES BECOME MASKS — HOW PATRIARCHY PERFORMS ITSELF

> *BLUF: Shows how patriarchy assigns roles as masks—scripts that obscure truth, excuse harm, and preserve dominance. These roles manage perception, not reality, turning systems into performances that protect power and avoid accountability.*

The individual who cannot bear the mirror often adopts a mask, yes. But systems do the same thing—and patriarchy, at scale, does not wear a single mask; it assigns them. It hands out roles. And these roles function exactly like psychological masks: they obscure vulnerability, preserve dominance, and manage perception. They are not just identities. They are scripts—designed to stabilize the system, not to reflect truth. And because they are scripted, they flatten the complexity of everyone involved. In other words, real people disappear behind the performance.

Patriarchal Roles as Masks

Mask/Role	Function	Who Typically Wears It
The Father	Source of authority, provider, unquestionable moral voice	Men in leadership/family roles
The Strongman	Enforcer of obedience, protector via coercion	Authoritarian men, politicians
The Know-It-All	Discredits emotional or intuitive insight	Men with intellectual dominance
The Child (Women)	Portrays women as helpless, in need of guidance	Cultural script for female dependence
The Scapegoat (Women)	Carries blame, shame, and moral responsibility	Women in families/systems

Mask/Role	Function	Who Typically Wears It
The Martyr / Happy Servant	Earns love and approval through self-erasure	Women in caregiving roles
The Exile / Monster	Designates abusers as anomalies, not products of the system	Abusers, rapists—used to preserve the "Good Guy" myth
The Innocent / Not-All-Men	Refuses responsibility, demands exemption from critique	"Good guys," passive allies
The Provider (Golden Child)	Deserves loyalty, sex, and service due to material contribution	Men who "do their duty" economically
The Holy Man / Prophet	Speaks for God, interprets morality, erases dissent	Religious male leaders
The Cool Girl / Pick-Me	Upholds the system in exchange for male favor	Women aligned with patriarchal proximity to power
The Broken Bird / Wounded Genius	Excuses harm through trauma or brilliance	Abusive or neglectful men, "tortured artist" types

These roles are not neutral. They encode emotional expectations and relational positioning, telling us who deserves compassion, who must stay silent, and who will be believed. They also serve as a form of social glamour—dressing up power as virtue, dependence as purity, cruelty as divine order.

Skeptic's Lens

"But aren't some of these just real roles? Aren't people actually fathers, providers, or spiritual leaders?"

Yes—and this isn't an attack on the reality of those roles. It's a clarification of how *roles become masks* when they are used to:

Avoid accountability
Hide fragility or shame
Excuse harmful behavior
Extract loyalty without reciprocity

A true father earns trust through presence and care—not by hiding behind a role that demands deference or obedience. A real provider doesn't demand servitude in return. A genuine spiritual teacher doesn't claim divine immunity from critique. It's not the role—it's the emotional function of the role that matters.

When collapse, deflection, and defiance become cultural norms—and roles become glamoured masks to protect a system from truth—we are no longer in a healthy society. We are in a system performing itself to avoid the mirror. But just like the emotionally immature child, that system has another option:

It could take off the mask.
It could face the mirror.
It could grow up . . . if it wanted to.

These systemic defenses don't just operate through denial or dominance. They evolve into entire *personas*—roles so polished and culturally embedded that we no longer see the mask at all. And this is where patriarchy becomes especially cunning: in its ability to shape-shift.

SECTION VII: THE ULTIMATE SHAPE-SHIFT — PATRIARCHAL DOUBLE BINDS

BLUF: Contrasts sacred shapeshifting with manipulative masks. Introduces the double bind as patriarchy's most powerful form of deceptive communication.

In mythology and Indigenous traditions, shapeshifting is a sacred skill—a conscious act of transformation. Shamans and mystics don masks to experience another reality and to reveal truth from another angle. The mask becomes a tool of access—not to manipulate, but to embody a truth, to cross thresholds, to integrate paradox, to evolve.

But shapeshifting has a darker side. Long known to thieves, predators, and lazy con artists, masks are a tool for a different kind of access—to slip by undetected, to fool defenses, to violate, exploit, and avoid getting caught.

Patriarchy shapeshifts, too. And like any emotionally immature system, it uses the mask not for insight, but for manipulation. In place of true transformation, the mask is used to pretend—to perform goodness, to pass as trustworthy, to conceal a hidden agenda. The mask isn't worn to evolve—it's worn to reshape others, so they can be used, controlled, or extracted from. So, they can embody what the dark shaman wants.

In the previous section, we named some of the common masks in patriarchy. But its most cunning disguise isn't brute dominance—it's the double bind.

WHAT IS A DOUBLE BIND?

A double bind is a psychological trap that creates the illusion of choice while punishing every option.[145] In other words, each path invalidates the other. There is no right answer. No clean exit. Every choice leads to failure.

The starkest example comes from the film *Sophie's Choice.* In one of its most devastating scenes, a Nazi officer tells Sophie she must choose which one of her two children will be sent to die—because if she refuses to choose, both will be killed. This is the emotional logic of a double bind: compliance is destruction. Refusal is destruction. There is no safe exit. Only shame, grief, and helplessness.

But not all double binds are about explicit choices. Some are more insidious.

In emotionally immature systems—especially patriarchal ones—the most powerful double binds are linguistic, not delivered as orders, but as mixed messages, conflicting expectations, or public performances that contradict private demands. What makes them especially entrapping is that the person receiving the double bind is forbidden from naming the contradiction—even though their body and soul are reacting to it.

These are communication double binds, and they function like masks. One message is spoken aloud—for the world to hear. That's the mask. But another message is enforced behind the scenes—unspoken, invisible, and real.

The public message: men are strong, independent leaders.

The private message: men must be soothed, protected, admired, and never emotionally challenged.

This is the emotional sleight of hand that traps women in impossible roles: Serve me. Soothe me. Manage life. But also admire me. Pretend I'm the real leader. And it traps men, too, in a mirrored bind: I must appear strong and autonomous—but I am dependent on others to hold up the reality I perform.

Double binds are not simply contradictions. They are systems of emotional captivity.

Unlike hypocrisy, which may be accidental or inconsistent, double binds are strategic and engineered. And in patriarchal systems, they are repeated so often, with such cultural authority, that the contradiction becomes internalized. You begin to doubt your own perception. You begin to shape-shift yourself—just to survive the no-win rules.

Patriarchy is riddled with double binds for the Other. Here are some examples:

Double Bind	Contradictory Demands	Result
Be small, but carry everything	Women are expected to stay in the background *and* manage all the emotional labor, caregiving, and relational upkeep	Overfunctioning without recognition
Be sexy, but pure	Female desirability is demanded but punished	Chronic self-monitoring, shame, and double standards

Speak up, but don't make anyone uncomfortable	Assertiveness is expected in theory but punished in practice ("Why didn't you say anything?" or "Why didn't you report the assault?")	Silencing and self-doubt
Be strong, but never need anything	Men are taught that asking for help is weak	Shame around dependence, hidden fragility
Take care of him, but don't emasculate him	Women must manage men's emotions while pretending he's the leader	Invisible labor, distorted power dynamics
You're responsible, but not allowed to decide	Women are blamed for outcomes but blocked and tackled when seeking roles of power and financial independence	Burnout and guilt
Do everything, but be grateful he stays	Overfunctioning women are told they're lucky to have a partner at all	Chronic depletion and eroded self-worth

There is a growing chorus of men—Mark Greene, Jackson Katz, Terry Real, and others—bravely naming the truth the manosphere refuses to admit: that patriarchy's blueprint for manhood is riddled with internal contradictions that harm men profoundly.[146]

Boys are told to be leaders—but given no emotional education.

They're told to be providers—but mocked if their partner earns more.

They're handed status—but not the skills to sustain it.

They're praised as "knowers"—but shamed for not knowing, which discourages the vulnerability essential for learning.

They're cast as protectors—but only trained to dominate.

When these roles prove hollow or impossible to maintain, men aren't offered understanding or support by the system. They're offered shame.

And that brings us to an essential truth about double binds:

They're not always imposed by malevolent outside forces. Sometimes, they are self-constructed.

When we deny others agency, we set traps that eventually catch us too. And when we deny our own agency—our responsibility, our power—we guarantee a trap. That's the logic of self-imposed double binds.

The person who treats consequences as punishment—rather than the outcome of their own choices—abandons their agency for short-term relief from blame. But now they've written themselves into a corner: if they're the victim, they lack the power to change things. If being held accountable feels like an attack, then growth becomes impossible.

Double binds are vicious circles. They generate escalating pressure—psychologically, emotionally, relationally, where the only true escape is not to "win" the bind, but to see it clearly. To cut through the illusion. To name the contradiction and walk away from the counterfeit payoffs. But if we don't? If we can't let go of the mask, the performance, the special treatment, the unearned roles?

That pressure must go somewhere. And that's where we enter the next layer of contradiction: Hostile Dependency.

SECTION VIII. HOSTILE DEPENDENCY — PATRIARCHY'S MOST TABOO DOUBLE BIND

> *BLUF: Behind the myth of male independence lies a forbidden truth: the system depends on women, even as it calls them weak. But when care threatens a fragile ego, it breeds hostility. This section exposes the double bind at the heart of patriarchal manhood—"I need you, but I hate that I do"—and shows how unspoken shame fuels both private contempt and public systems of control.*

THE BEATING OF THE HEART

In Edgar Allan Poe's *The Tell-Tale Heart*, a man commits murder and buries the body beneath the floorboards. He thinks the crime is concealed, but as time passes, he begins to hear a sound—faint at first, then pounding. It is the heartbeat of the man he killed—or so he believes. No one else hears it. But the guilt, shame, and unreconciled truth presses outward until he erupts, "It is the beating of his hideous heart!" revealing his crime by his own confession.

That story is not just horror—it's psychology. It reveals what happens when a forbidden truth festers. The lie may be hidden from others, but the psyche keeps score. And it begins to demand coherence.

The truth presses outward—not to destroy, but to restore.

Not for vengeance, but for integration.

THE PRESSURE COOKER OF FORBIDDEN TRUTH

Carrying a forbidden truth doesn't feel neutral. It feels volcanic. It pressurizes your inner world. And the most dangerous truths aren't always those that threaten others. They're the ones that threaten our own self-image.

Truth—especially truth rooted in shame, injustice, or contradiction—functions like steam in a sealed container.

It doesn't vanish. It builds and seeks a way out. You might try to:

Reframe it
Numb it
Minimize it
Spiritualize it
Pretend it doesn't matter

But the psyche demands coherence because what is split will seek integration, and what is suppressed will look for a witness. But when the system doesn't allow that truth to be spoken, it finds other ways out:

Projection. Rage. Contempt. Sabotage. Covert cruelty.

PATRIARCHY'S MOST FORBIDDEN TRUTH

The most taboo truth of all in patriarchal systems is not just male dependency—it's who the real adult is. Patriarchy builds its mythology on the premise that men are the grown-ups:

The providers
The protectors
The rational leaders

And that women are the dependent ones:

The children
The receivers
The ones who must be guided, soothed, or restrained

But here is the truth: The system that assigns women to the role of dependent child is often entirely dependent on those women to keep functioning. And the men performing "adulthood" within it are often emotionally regressed:

Unwilling to tolerate discomfort
Unwilling to take ownership
Unwilling to self-reflect, grow, or change

As a result, they are often emotionally and logistically dependent on the very women they call weak and not a fit for leadership.

THE CLASSIC DOUBLE BIND OF IMMATURE ADULTHOOD

This is the root of hostile dependency—a double bind that forms inside the emotionally immature self:

"I want to be seen and respected as an adult, but I don't want to do the emotional labor of becoming one."

What results is a contradictory and confounding stance:

"I want the privileges of adulthood, but not the responsibilities."

"I want to be seen as competent, but I don't want to develop competence."

"I want to be regarded as wise, but I don't want to labor for clarity."

"I want to be seen as strong, but I collapse, avoid, or explode when confronted."

"I want to be the authority, but I reject accountability."
"I want the admiration of being the grown-up, but I still demand the indulgence of a child."

This contradiction creates an unbearable pressure—because eventually, someone holds up the mirror.

THE REFLECTION BECOMES TOO SHARP

When women step into the public world—into competence, into autonomy—when they stop colluding with the myth that men are innately more suited to lead, provide, or protect, the illusion begins to dissolve.

And the performance is revealed for what it is: a story.

When that happens, some men respond not with introspection—but with hostility. Because deep down, they already knew.

Knew they were performing.

Knew they weren't providing but taking.

Knew they weren't protecting, but preying.

We see this clearly in the words of men who use violence and coercive control. In multiple interviews, they name exactly what they're getting out of their behavior:

- Control
- Sexual access
- Compliance
- Ego protection
- Emotional soothing
- Avoidance of accountability

These men know they are the extractors. They know they're not holding up their side of the relational—or moral—contract. And many say this with a kind of duper's delight: pleased with their ability to exploit their partner.

But that knowledge—that they are not strong men, not providers, not protectors—violates the myth of patriarchal manhood. And the pressure of that shameful contradiction must go somewhere.

That's where hostility comes in: not just to control, but to punish the one who reflects the truth.

THE PSYCHOLOGY OF HOSTILE DEPENDENCY

Hostile dependency is not exclusive to patriarchy. It appears in families, workplaces, friendships, same-gender partnerships, and nations.

The emotionally immature person cannot tolerate the gap between their fantasy of themselves as independent and mature and the lived reality of dependency and the entitlement to be exempt from the consequences of their choices and behaviors. And so, the shame gets projected onto the one they rely on and who will carry the responsibility.

Not for the responsible one failing to provide—but for being needed.

This is the psychological logic behind the phrase:

"They bite the hand that feeds them."

But in patriarchal systems, it becomes an especially volatile and taboo force—because the system glorifies what it secretly resents: the Other who makes life livable.

For emotionally immature individuals or systems, this contradiction metastasizes. In short, hostile dependency is what happens when the reality of circumstance and need shames the ego.[147] Not because the care is unearned or unwelcome—but because receiving it threatens a fragile self-image.

"If I let myself know I need you, then I am weak."

"If I need you, then I'm not the man I claim to be."

So, the person giving the care becomes the target. Not for what they've done, but for what they reveal.

Psychologically, hostile dependency arises from:

Entitlement and Narcissism

The belief that care is owed, not mutual. Any limit feels like betrayal.

Shame and Resentment

Receiving help triggers inferiority. That shame gets redirected as blame.

Attachment Wounds and Mistrust

Care feels dangerous. It evokes fear of being manipulated or controlled.

Contempt for One's Own Need

Vulnerability is unbearable, so the caregiver is punished for witnessing it.

Power Struggles and Regression

The cared-for person rebels—not against care itself, but against the imbalance it exposes.

Projection of Inner Conflict

The caregiver becomes a stand-in for past wounds—an authority figure to be punished, not received.

Put simply: Hostile dependency is not about the helper. It's about the unbearable mirror they hold up, the shame of not living up to the image, the terror of being seen as a receiver in a system that pathologizes need.

WHEN CARE BECOMES AN INSULT

Even in less extreme situations—where there is no overt violence—this dynamic plays out.

Men who believe in equality may still:

Expect to be cared for without offering reciprocity
Avoid accountability while enjoying the perks of partnership
Resent partners who point out the imbalance

And all of this exists under the illusion of "mutuality."

But relationships are perceptive ecosystems. We *know* when they are unequal—even if we pretend not to. And when reality and image diverge, the psyche keeps score.

And patriarchy? It assigns need to women but calls their labor "natural" and their requests "burdensome." So, when the truth comes too close—that the woman is not dependent, but the man is, that she is the adult, and he is playing one—hostility erupts.

Sometimes it shows up as cruelty. Sometimes it leaks sideways as resentment, withdrawal, mockery, or passive sabotage.

But the source is the same: a lie the psyche can no longer carry.

Hostile dependency doesn't just damage individual relationships. When repeated across households, communities, and generations, it becomes the emotional blueprint for systemic control. The logic of "you owe me care and admiration—but I will punish you for giving it, *and* for not giving it" becomes cultural law.

HOW HOSTILE DEPENDENCY SCALES INTO A COLLECTIVE PATTERN

Hostile dependency doesn't always escalate. But when it does, it follows a familiar arc:

- Seething resentment and envy
- Passive aggression and covert sabotage
- Demands for inflated praise or compensation—insisting their physical, emotional, or intellectual labor be overvalued beyond fairness
- Withdrawal, stonewalling, emotional punishment
- Entitlement rage
- Control disguised as concern
- Smear campaigns, manipulation, coercion
- Cultural narratives telling women to "do more" to keep a man
- Religious or political efforts to "put women back in their place"
- Workplace hostility, sexual harassment, gender violence
- Excusing, ignoring, or pardoning men who prey on women—especially those who are famous, powerful, or well-connected

Eventually, it becomes structural misogyny—not a system to support men's growth, but a system to prevent both men and women's escape.

THE MIRROR NEVER LIES

In the fairy tale *Snow White*, the Queen looks into the enchanted mirror. She expects praise, reassurance, to be told she is the most beautiful of all.

But the mirror tells the truth.

And she hates it. She doesn't grow. She doesn't reflect. Instead, she tries to kill the one who reflects what she no longer wants to see.

Snow White has done nothing wrong. She is simply the mirror's answer. And so, the Queen sets out not to change her reflection—but to destroy.

This is the emotional defense of patriarchy.

There's no actual enemy, just a mirror and a reflection. But the reflection threatens the spell, showing the gap between performance and reality.

And in emotionally immature systems, truth itself becomes the threat. Because the inner Judge never forms, institutions externalize blame and protect status. As a result, truth-tellers are punished. Growth is resented.

Refusing the mirror doesn't erase the truth. It delays the reckoning—and compounds the cost. Every time reflection is avoided, a consequence is deferred but not erased. And growth that's refused doesn't just disappear, it accumulates interest. Missed thresholds don't vanish, they stack up. And one day, the distance between image and reality becomes unbearable.

In short, the emotionally immature person doesn't just stagnate, they fall behind.

Others grow and walk away. Relationships end. Trust dissolves.

Interest in connection or partnership dries up.

And the result?

Sadly, not self-awareness, but increasing resentment.

Not change, but punishment of those who did change.

Not growth, but a war against those who dared to grow.

A system that claims truth—yet cannot bear reflection.

A system that claims strength—but despises it in the other.

A culture that claims virtue—yet cannot bear truth.

A system that claims authority—but centers on immaturity.

A hierarchy that rewards masks—and crucifies the seers.

That system and its people become brittle, defensive, and cruel.

Because the mirror doesn't just reflect truth. It calls us to grow—or to harden.

Which leads us into The Dark Tetrad.

17

Patriarchy, Misogyny, and the Dark Tetrad

BLUF: THIS CHAPTER EXPLORES THE ESCALATION FROM COERCIVE CONTROL TO OVERT CRUELTY. IT DEFINES THE DARK TETRAD—NARCISSISM, MACHIAVELLIANISM, PSYCHOPATHY, AND SADISM—AS BOTH PERSONALITY TRAITS AND CULTURAL ARCHITECTURE. THE CHAPTER ANALYZES PATRIARCHY AS A NARCISSISTIC MEGASTRUCTURE, AND POSITIONS MISOGYNY AS THE ENFORCEMENT MECHANISM OF THE SYSTEM. THROUGH THIS LENS, SEX BECOMES A TECHNOLOGY OF DOMINATION, AND CRUELTY BECOMES ENTERTAINMENT. YET EVEN IN THIS DARKNESS, MIMICRY IS POSSIBLE IN BOTH DIRECTIONS—AND THE POWER OF CLARITY, REFUSAL, AND REBUILDING REMAINS.

Once the mirror is rejected and the mask clings tight, a darker transformation begins. The defenses that once shielded shame now seek control. The child who could not bear reflection grows into a ruler who cannot tolerate resistance. And so emotional immaturity curdles into cruelty—not in all, but in enough to shape the system.

What follows is not a flaw in patriarchy. It is its final form:

Narcissism, Machiavellianism, Psychopathy, and Sadism—not merely as personality traits, but as cultural architecture, where the mask is no longer just defensive, it becomes predatory.

SECTION 1: NARCISSISM ON A CONTINUUM

> *BLUF: Frames narcissism not as a binary but as a spectrum—ranging from emotional immaturity to systemic violence. Introduces pathological immaturity as a root cause of patriarchal harm, and connects narcissism with violence, betrayal blindness, and societal denial.*

Narcissism is not binary but rather lives on a spectrum, from garden-variety emotional immaturity with narcissistic traits to full-blown personality disorders.[148] At one end of that continuum is the person who craves praise, can't manage criticism, and subtly manipulates others to stay in control. We might call this the "everyday narcissist"—the boss who needs to be the smartest person in the room, the father who pouts when his newborn gets attention, the partner who gives only to receive. Annoying, but largely harmless, simply less narcissist and more emotionally immature.

These behaviors are common in patriarchal systems because patriarchy rewards them. Why? Because it frames emotional immaturity as strength and equates dominance with leadership. It tells men that their fragility is someone else's fault—and someone else's responsibility to soothe.

However, as we move along the continuum from common immaturity to diagnosable narcissism, traits begin to solidify.

Entitlement deepens.

Empathy recedes.

Conscience vanishes.

And sadism—the enjoyment of watching others suffer—can emerge.

At this end of the narcissism spectrum, we enter malignant narcissism. This used to be called sociopathy or psychopathy but is now classified under antisocial personality disorder, wherein control becomes the primary mode of connection. Others become props, not people. Their need to be admired overrides your need to be safe. Their entitlements override your human rights. Their discomfort justifies your silence.

A reminder here: we're not diagnosing individuals—this is about traits that patriarchy selects for and scales.

PATHOLOGICAL IMMATURITY AS VIOLENCE IN PATRIARCHY

While there is no shortage of research documenting the shocking levels of violence against women worldwide, this book has not centered on statistics. Not because they don't matter—they do. But because statistics are the outcomes. This book is after the root system.

And at the root of patriarchal violence is not simply hatred or ignorance.

It is pathological immaturity—often in the form of narcissism.

Narcissism, especially when fused with patriarchal power, doesn't just produce emotional manipulation or coercive control. It escalates.

Studies like the one led by Brad Bushman at Ohio State University have shown that narcissistic individuals are significantly more prone to violence—ranging from verbal abuse to physical assault.[149]

When expressed through patriarchal systems, narcissism often manifests as physical, sexual, emotional, and economic violence—used to assert and maintain dominance.

In these systems, violence becomes more than a tactic.

It becomes a method of emotional regulation—and for some, a form of sadistic satisfaction.

This is not hypothetical. It's operational.

The narcissistic behaviors patriarchy rewards—entitlement, control, disdain for boundaries—aren't just psychological. They leave bruises. They shatter lives. They justify cruelty in the name of order, or romance, or righteousness. But because this harm is often unseen by those who don't directly experience it, it becomes easy to dismiss—easy to deny.

This is where betrayal blindness, which we explored in Chapter Twelve, returns. As a brief reminder, psychologist Dr. Jennifer Freyd coined the term to explain why people refuse to see or acknowledge violence—even when it's happening nearby.[150] Unfortunately, if we are not the ones being harmed, we often assume the harm doesn't exist—or that it's being exaggerated. We tell ourselves the story we need to stay comfortable.

But this collective blindness allows violent systems to flourish unchallenged and enables narcissistic patriarchy to persist by rendering its worst abuses invisible—or excusable.

And at the extreme end of this spectrum, we reach what psychologists call Cluster B personality disorders—most notably, Narcissistic Personality Disorder.

But what happens when narcissism isn't just a disorder—but a strategy? What happens when it merges with manipulation, emotional deadness, and a taste for cruelty? When violence becomes not a breakdown—but a design?

That's when we cross into Dark Tetrad territory.

But before we go there, it's important to name this:

Yes—patriarchal behavior is disordered. But most people participating in it are not sociopaths. They're not calculating abusers. They're simply doing what they were taught and mimicking what they've seen work. They're surviving within a system that rewards emotional avoidance and dominance.

Some, however, do know what they're doing. And some go even darker. When they do, patriarchal culture rarely intervenes—unless it becomes public. And even then, the response is often silence, spin, or scapegoating.

The whistleblowers are punished while the predators are protected.

And the system laughs.

SECTION II: THE DARK TETRAD – WHEN SADISM JOINS NARCISSISM

> *BLUF: Defines the four traits of the Dark Tetrad and shows how they scale into institutional power. This is where domination becomes delight, and where emotional immaturity fuses with cruelty to form a systemic pathology.*

There comes a point on the narcissism spectrum where emotional immaturity turns into something more calculated—and more cruel. When narcissism merges with strategic manipulation, lack of empathy, and a taste for humiliation, we arrive at what psychologists call the Dark Tetrad.

The Dark Tetrad is made up of four interlocking traits:[151]

Narcissism: Grandiosity, entitlement, a fragile ego masked by arrogance, and an insatiable need for admiration. It demands praise and punishes indifference.

Machiavellianism: Cold, strategic manipulation. Lies are tools. People are pawns. The end always justifies the means.

Psychopathy: Lack of empathy, remorse, or emotional depth. Prone to impulsivity and risk, the psychopath feels no guilt for harm done.

Sadism: The most disturbing of all—sadists experience pleasure from inflicting pain. They don't just dominate; they delight in the distress of others.

These traits are associated with what the DSM classifies under Cluster B and antisocial personality disorders, especially in their more extreme forms. But they also show up—quietly, publicly, institutionally—anywhere power is unaccountable. The home. The church. The boardroom. The political stage.

They are not always obvious. They may wear a suit. Quote scripture. Speak in full sentences. But underneath the polish, these traits define how some people ascend to dominance and stay there: not through excellence, but through calculated cruelty.

The Dark Tetrad is not simply a psychological term. It is also a cultural architecture. It is what happens when control is no longer about order, but about harm. When systems fail in protecting the vulnerable, they feed off them.

These aren't just personality traits. They are operating systems—codes of cruelty that scale from individuals to institutions. This is how pathocracies are built: not on policies, but on personalities made into power.[152]

ARCHETYPE OF THE DARK TETRAD — THE STRONGMAN

At the top of every dominance hierarchy—whether in a family, a cult, a corporation, or a nation—sits a figure known by many names, but always the same essence: **The Strongman.**

Sometimes he is literal:

A dictator.

A domestic tyrant.

A spiritual leader who rules by fear and calls it faith.

Other times he is mythic:

A warrior god.

A founding father.

A conquering hero who kills with conviction and demands loyalty in return.

The Strongman is not just a person. He is the cultural embodiment of the *Dark Tetrad.*

He wears malignant narcissism as charisma. He uses manipulation as strategy. He governs without empathy.

And he takes pleasure in domination—not just to win, but to see others lose. He rebrands cruelty as leadership, turns fear into loyalty, and models power not as responsibility, but as impunity.

Even when the Strongman dies, the archetype survives. He becomes not a cautionary tale but rather an icon, etched into monuments, canonized in scripture, echoed in slogans. His legacy seeps into cultural memory—and into the performance of masculinity itself.

Boys are taught to admire him.

Leaders are taught to mimic him.

And dissenters are punished for challenging the image he left behind.

The Strongman is not just a man. He is a blueprint—for every man—for what power is allowed to look like . . .

. . . and for what humanity must be sacrificed to hold it.

SECTION III: THE PSYCHOPATHIC MEGASTRUCTURE

BLUF: Patriarchy is not just narcissistic—it is psychopathic. This section exposes how patriarchal systems mirror the psychological architecture of psychopathy: marked by callousness, deceit, domination, emotional detachment, and exploitation.

Built on the same blueprint as narcissistic families and cults, patriarchy becomes a megastructure of relational abuse—where the traits of psychopathy aren't pathologized, they're rewarded.

Through this lens, patriarchy is revealed not as a flawed but fixable tradition—but instead as a clinical-level disorder masquerading as culture.

Patriarchy functions as **distributed narcissism**—a global and inherited system built on the same psychological blueprint that governs narcissistic families, high-control cults, and authoritarian regimes. It may not have a singular face, but it does have a singular structure.

In narcissistic families and cults, the disordered individual at the center rarely works alone. They surround themselves with enablers and recruits—some of whom are low-orno-conscience individuals who share the same hunger for power and impunity, while others are trauma-bonded followers, seduced by the illusion of protection, belonging, or divine purpose. Together, they form a self-reinforcing web of control.

As you might imagine, these systems rely on scapegoats to absorb shame, golden children to reflect glory, and lieutenants to conduct harm. In patriarchal cultures, this looks like loyalists who defend abusers, punish truth-tellers, and uphold the status quo. Harm becomes not just a byproduct—but a group project that supports abuse by proxy, violence by committee.

Patriarchy operates just like this at a collective level, where it is not merely narcissistic but a **pathocracy**: a system ruled by the emotionally disordered and morally unwell.[153]

In a pathocracy, narcissistic, antisocial, and sadistic traits are rewarded—not reined in.

As trauma therapist Christine Forner bluntly puts it:

"Patriarchy is psychopathic. It is a way of attempting to get through life by harming other people, by stressing other people out, by not taking accountability, by being strictly an individual, by not being emotional."[154]

Psychopathy is a clinical construct with observable traits—and patriarchal systems exhibit many of them at scale.

CORE TRAITS OF PSYCHOPATHY

(adapted from the Hare Psychopathy Checklist–Revised)[155]

- Callousness; lack of empathy
- Egocentricity
- Grandiose sense of self-worth
- Superficial charm
- Impulsivity and irresponsibility
- Lying, deceit, and manipulation
- Shallow emotional range
- Lack of remorse or guilt
- Exploitation of others for personal gain
- Refusal to take responsibility
- Need for control and dominance
- Multiple types of offense/criminal versatility
- Conning; lack of sincerity
- Parasitic lifestyle
- Poor behavioral control; short temper
- Promiscuous sexual behavior
- Irresponsibility in shared obligations

To call patriarchy a large-scale system of psychopathy is not hyperbole. It is not metaphor. As you can see, these are diagnostic traits—scaled.

If you think back through the earlier chapters, you will recognize how many traits from the Hare Psychopathy Checklist are not limited to individuals. They appear systemically, woven through the very architecture of patriarchy.

Coercive control and relational laziness

→ Reflect impulsivity, dominance, and a refusal to take responsibility

Mythologies that gaslight so profoundly they invert reality

→ Echo pathological lying, deceit, and a shallow emotional range

Scapegoating and hostile dependency

→ Rooted in exploitation of others, refusal to take responsibility, and emotional manipulation

Systemic lying, deceit, and manipulation

→ Direct match with conning, insincerity, and lack of remorse

Egocentricity, callous disregard, and relational entitlement

→ Align with grandiose sense of self-worth, self-centeredness, and lack of empathy

Weaponized irresponsibility and emotional parasitism

→ Parallel the parasitic lifestyle, poor behavioral control, and failure to honor obligations

The expectation of sex without mutuality—and sadistic pleasure in cruelty

→ Reflect promiscuous sexual behavior and sadism (which, while not on the Hare list, is deeply adjacent)

The entertainment value of watching women suffer

→ Correlates with emotional shallowness, lack of remorse, and thrill-seeking cruelty

Revenge against anyone who dares to name the abuse

→ Connects to impulsivity, lack of empathy, and aggression triggered by ego threat

Multiple types of offense

→ This includes all the above—and more. Coercive control, workplace discrimination, legal abuse, financial abuse, sexual domination, institutional gaslighting, reputational harm, restrictions on education, mobility, and bodily autonomy, and spiritual abuse. The violence is not limited to one domain—it's a system of extraction deployed across many.

We haven't even detailed the data on violence against women, but patriarchal systems clearly meet the definition of **"criminal versatility"**:

Domestic violence
Rape and coercive sex
Stalking
Femicide
Sexual harassment
Genital mutilation
Acid attacks

And this is only a partial list. Sadly, it reveals the cruelty, the exploitation—and the criminality—of a system operating without conscience, one that enacts harm and then pardons itself.

Patriarchy doesn't merely resemble a disordered mind; it functions like one. In policy, in practice, at scale.

What's pathological in a person becomes structural in a system. In other words, it is organized relational abuse at scale.

What a narcissist does in a living room, a cult does in a compound—and patriarchy does with entire populations. And the more narcissistic a culture becomes, the more violent it becomes—physically, sexually, economically, spiritually.

SECTION IV: MISOGYNY AS THE ENFORCER OF THE PATHOCRACY

> *BLUF: Distinguishes sexism as ideology and misogyny as punishment. Uses Kate Manne's concepts of "misogyny" and "himpathy" to show how resistance is punished and domination is rewarded. Misogyny is framed as a weapon and a grooming tool for cruelty.*

Sexism is the script. Misogyny is the punishment for not following it.[156]

As philosopher Kate Manne explains in *Down Girl: The Logic of Misogyny*, sexism is the belief system that justifies traditional gender roles.[157] It frames them as natural, God-ordained, or biologically inevitable: Men lead. Women nurture. Men protect. Women serve. Sexism tells a story about why things are the way they are—and why they shouldn't change.

Misogyny, on the other hand, is not an ideology. It's a system of social control, the reactive force that polices women who dare to step out of line. It's the backlash.

When a woman stops smiling. When she says no. When she demands equality. When she walks away, stops apologizing, calls out abuse, asks to be treated as fully human—misogyny is the cultural immune response that seeks to bring her back into line, or to destroy her for refusing.

In personal relationships, it shows up as punishment and coercion, in workplaces as being passed over, talked over, retaliated against. It shows up in the law as disbelief, discrediting, and dismissal, and in religion as moral condemnation and spiritual exile.

Manne also coined the term "Himpathy," describing the cultural impulse to protect men—especially those accused of harm—by putting their feelings, reputations, and careers at the center of everything, even at the expense of justice. The result turns abusers into tragic heroes and their victims into unreliable narrators.[158] What follows is that we ask, "What will this do to his future?" instead of "What did this do to her life?"

This is not random. This is not a glitch. It is the enforcement arm of patriarchy, ensuring the system centers "him" and remains intact by shaming, silencing, and scapegoating those who resist it.

Misogyny functions like a heat-seeking missile, zeroing in on women who deviate from their assigned roles—not because they are weak or failing, but because they are refusing.

Refusing to mother grown men.

Refusing to manage everyone's feelings.

Refusing to disappear.

Refusing to submit.

In a patriarchal pathocracy, misogyny is the loyal guard dog at the gate of change. It barks. It bites. And too often, it wins.

But misogyny is more than just the guard dog—it's also a reward system. It offers the followers of patriarchy a taste of dominance, a chance to participate in the spectacle of cruelty. For some, it is an opportunity to indulge sadism in public, under the guise of morality or tradition. For others, it's a sanctioned outlet for humiliation, rage, or sexual frustration.

In this way, misogyny becomes a kind of social grooming for cruelty, by developing the musculature of domination, eroding the conscience, and training the collective psyche to value subjugation over connection, punishment over understanding, hierarchy over humanity.

And as cruelty becomes normalized, conscience becomes suspect. Those who speak of care, equality, or tenderness are mocked as weak. In time, the society doesn't just stagnate emotionally—it regresses. It becomes more crass, more punitive, more indifferent to suffering.

The enforcement of patriarchy becomes its entertainment. And the erosion of empathy becomes a shared identity.

SECTION V: SEXUALITY IN THE PATHOCRACY

> *BLUF: Explores how sexuality is weaponized in patriarchal cultures. From emotional regulation to sadistic desecration, sex becomes a form of extraction and a reflection of emotional immaturity. Distinguishes between pornography and erotica as mirrors of cultural psyche.*

In emotionally immature systems, sexuality becomes distorted. It no longer reflects intimacy or mutuality and instead becomes a tool of regulation, dominance, and punishment.

We can trace two core patterns in the patriarchal pathocracy.

Sex as Emotional Regulation Entitlement

This is common among coercive controllers. Here, sex is used to soothe male anxiety, tension, and shame. The partner becomes a pacifier, a vessel to absorb dysregulation. There may be no overt cruelty—but there is no real intimacy either. The body of the partner is used, not met.

Sex as Scapegoating / Emotional Dumping Ground

This is where Dark Tetrad personalities live. Rage, shame, contempt, and humiliation are offloaded onto another human being through sex. There is no "with" in this act—only "to" and "for." Rape becomes a psychological sewer: an emotional dumping ground masked as dominance.

At this level of consciousness, empathy is gone. And with the loss of empathy, all that remains is usury, cruelty, and sadism.

There is no mutuality. No sacredness. No shared experience. Only one person extracting. The other surviving.

We see this reflected in the heavy use of pornography in patriarchal cultures—especially pornography that glorifies domination, degradation, and submission. These are not fantasies of connection. They are performances of cruelty.[159] Over and over, they reinforce a model of sexuality rooted in conquest, not communion. Erotica invites presence—mutual breath, mutual gaze, mutual becoming. Pornography scripts roles and control.

True sexuality is never just the exposure of bodies—it is the nakedness of soul.[160] The bedroom reveals the psyche. If someone is self-centered, it shows. If someone is disconnected, it shows. If someone is cruel, it shows. This may be why sexuality is so heavily policed, shamed, and hidden: it exposes the truth of our emotional and moral maturity.

At this level, women are treated not as people but as animals for use— to be bred, consumed, discarded. We see this in the logic of forced birth, in the erasure of female pleasure, and in the way wartime rape is normalized as a soldier's "reward."

Here, depravity is not the exception. It is ritualized. Taboos exist not to be respected, but to be broken. Child molestation, incest, and rape become thrilling violations to those whose souls have long since detached from empathy. And where there is no empathy, sex becomes not connection—but desecration.

SECTION VI: MIMICRY OR MATURITY — THE CULTURAL CROSSROADS

> *BLUF: Disarms the belief that patriarchy is biologically destined. Shows how behaviors are modeled, mimicked, and rewarded. Encourages a new form of modeling rooted in empathy, clarity, and refusal. Frames emotional maturity as a radical alternative to mimicry of abuse.*

Patriarchy is not embedded in male DNA. It is not rooted in testosterone. It is not a biological destiny. It is learned behavior.

Most men are not predators. Most men are not sadists. But many men —and women—have been taught to admire those who are.

When we confront the cruelty of patriarchy, men often respond by personalizing the critique:

Accusation of misandry: "You hate men." This is a projection tactic that derails the conversation and centers male fragility.

Biological excuse: "That's just how men are." This is not biology—it's a story, a surrender of agency and responsibility disguised as fact.

But there is a third way—and it's the only path forward with dignity. What's more, it demonstrates that we are not condemned to repeat what we were shown. We can choose to become something else.

In psychology, Bandura's Social Learning Theory explains how children learn: not through what we tell them, but through what they see.[161] They model behaviors that get attention, which achieve results, and avoid punishment. If cruelty is rewarded, it is copied. If domination is admired, it becomes the template. If women are degraded, children will learn to degrade or to accept degradation as normal.

We are not dealing with an epidemic of individuals born disordered. We are dealing with a culture that mimics its abusers, one that lifts bullies, protects tyrants, and teaches boys that to be loved, they must be feared.

But mimicry can go both ways. We can also model care. Boundaries. Courage. Empathy.

Like children from violent homes, we can mimic the abuser, or we can build something new. We can be like the children who grow up in abusive homes and say, "I will not become what hurt me. I will not build what I barely survived."

When we mimic cruelty, we arrest our development. When we choose clarity, care, and refusal, we mature.

In short, we are not fated to repeat the structures we inherited. Awareness is the turning point.

But first, this:

I acknowledge that we've been uncovering over the last several chapters are overwhelming. It's a lot to hold, seeing how callous and cruel some people—and systems—can be. And I know how disheartening and frightening it is to live in a world where those without conscience so often rise to the top.

It can make us feel powerless.

But I hope you will also remember something vital: these people wear masks for a reason—to deceive, to avoid accountability. The mask is a tell—a signal of what they fear, and what they fear is being seen for who and what they really are.

And even more than that—they fear losing their entitlements, the unearned rewards the mask gains them access to, the loot they've stolen through deception and coercion, respect they haven't demonstrated, connection they haven't reciprocated, labor they haven't matched, access they haven't earned.

That is their Kryptonite.

Your seeing has more power than their mask.

You are not crazy. You are waking up.

And there are others waking with you.

You are seeing the personalities that rise when we fail to grow up, the systems they build when we stay asleep. But once we see the patterns, once we name the structure, we are no longer under its spell. Clarity becomes the first act of refusal.

Now, let me be clear: clarity alone does not rebuild.

But it *does* break the spell.

And that break is the beginning of everything.

In the next chapter, we'll look at how emotional immaturity is not exclusive to men. Women—even as they suffer under patriarchy—are often recruited into it and some enthusiastically support it, precisely because the system depends on willing participants. Some are rewarded for defending the system while others are broken in until submission feels like safety.

THE RETURN TO SELF: AWAKENING FROM THE SCRIPT

You cannot fight a system while still believing its story. Part II revealed what emotional immaturity builds when scaled into culture: narcissistic families, authoritarian religions, coercive structures of control. Systems that drain life and dress up domination as love. But walking away from those systems is only the first act of liberation. What comes next is disorientation. Because when we refuse to participate in the lie, we are left with questions the system never wanted us to ask: Who am I without a role? What do I believe without a script? How do I find my way without a leader? This is the terrain of Part III. It is not about rebellion. It is about reorientation. It is not about certainty. It is about clarity. This is where emotional maturity becomes a compass. Not because it gives us all the answers —but because it helps us navigate the truth. And this time, we do not need a map handed down from power. We begin to draw our own.

18

When Women Uphold the System That Harms Them

BLUF: THIS CHAPTER EXPLORES HOW WOMEN, WHILE OPPRESSED BY PATRIARCHAL SYSTEMS, ARE ALSO OFTEN RECRUITED INTO UPHOLDING THEM. IT UNPACKS THE SURVIVAL STRATEGIES, SOCIAL CONDITIONING, AND EMOTIONAL DYNAMICS THAT LEAD WOMEN TO INTERNALIZE AND ENFORCE PATRIARCHAL NORMS. THROUGH SIX CORE MOTIVATIONS AND FIVE COMMON ARCHETYPAL ROLES, THE CHAPTER REVEALS THE COSTS OF COLLUSION— PERSONALLY AND COLLECTIVELY. IT ALSO CHARTS A LIBERATORY PATH: AWAKENING, RECKONING, REDEFINITION, RETURN, AND SOLIDARITY.

As I said at the end of Chapter 15, patriarchy is not upheld by men alone. While they are often the primary beneficiaries of patriarchal systems, many women also participate in sustaining them. This isn't because women are inherently oppressive—but because survival, belonging, and recognition have often required proximity to power, even when that power harms them.

To say that some women collude with patriarchy is not to shame them, but rather to name a survival strategy—one forged in scarcity, fear, and deeply internalized conditioning.[162]

SECTION I: WHY WOMEN COLLUDE WITH PATRIARCHY

> *BLUF: Outlines six core reasons women align with patriarchal norms: for social rewards, internalized beliefs, borrowed power, familial loyalty, emotional avoidance, and permission to remain immature. These behaviors are framed not as moral failings but as survival strategies shaped by context and conditioning.*

1. Social Rewards for Compliance

From an early age, girls are taught that good behavior is rewarded and resistance is punished. They are praised for being pleasing, accommodating, self-sacrificing, and agreeable. Women who mirror patriarchal values—especially those who uphold traditional gender roles—are often celebrated as virtuous, wise, or maternal, which may lead to being granted proximity to power, financial protection, or cultural reverence.

In contrast, women who challenge these roles are often ridiculed, punished, or erased. Feminists are called angry. Leaders are labeled controlling. Survivors are dismissed as dramatic or divisive. In many environments, it is simply safer to conform.

In short, collusion can be a strategy of self-preservation.

2. Internalized Misogyny

Unfortunately, many women unconsciously absorb the belief systems that devalue women. This isn't self-hatred—it's the outcome of being raised in a culture that equates femininity with inferiority, irrationality, or danger.[163] And when those beliefs go unexamined, women may project their shame or fear onto other women:

- ❖ The woman who judges another for being "too ambitious" may have learned that success is unsafe.
- ❖ The woman who insists that modesty is moral may be protecting herself from sexual scrutiny.

❖ The mother who enforces traditional gender roles may believe she's keeping her daughters safe from rejection, violence, or social exclusion.

In these cases, judgment becomes a way of managing internal dissonance.

3. *False Empowerment Through Proximity to Power*

Some women find a sense of safety or significance by aligning themselves with dominant men or patriarchal values. They may reject feminist ideals or distance themselves from "other women" to be seen as exceptional, rational, or trustworthy in male-dominated spaces.

This is often a form of borrowed power—conditional upon obedience, silence, or performance.[164]

❖ "Cool girls" who distance themselves from women to gain male approval.

❖ Religious women who uphold strict gender hierarchies in exchange for status in the community.

❖ Corporate women who enforce patriarchal values to rise through the ranks.

This strategy may provide short-term rewards—but often comes at the cost of connection, authenticity, or collective liberation.

4. *Generational Loyalty and Fear of Exile*

In tightly controlled families, cultures, or religious systems, challenging patriarchal norms can feel like betraying one's lineage or spiritual identity.[165] Many women remain loyal to the structures that harmed them because leaving would mean losing everything—family, community, security, identity, or salvation.

In these cases, collusion isn't just about comfort. It's about survival.

Some stay inside the system, hoping to change it from within. Others internalize the rules so deeply that they become enforcers—punishing those who deviate, not out of cruelty, but out of fear.

5. *Avoidance of Emotional and Existential Disruption*

To admit that a system is harmful can be destabilizing—especially when one has invested a lifetime in adapting to it. Some women defend patriarchy because the alternative would require grieving, reckoning, and radical transformation.

It's easier, sometimes, to blame the victim than to question the entire structure. It's easier to shame the outspoken woman than to face one's own silenced truth. It's easier to cling to a familiar injustice than to risk the unknown of freedom.

6. *Permission to Remain Emotionally Immature*

Patriarchy doesn't just promote and excuse emotional immaturity in men —it often invites and incentivizes it in women.

In a system that glorifies obedience and dependence, some women find relief in the roles that ask them *not* to grow. Within patriarchy, emotional immaturity can be framed as virtue: innocence, modesty, humility, or deference. And in exchange for conforming, many women are spared the crucibles that lead to growth:

- They may never have to develop financial independence.
- They may never have to risk public failure or hold a leadership position that draws attack.
- They may never have to confront the stress, conflict, or competition of the workplace.
- They may never have to individuate, wrestle with their calling, or carve out a voice in a world that resists women's visibility.

This isn't to say their lives are easy—far from it. But in choosing the approved feminine path, they are protected from certain forms of exposure. And that protection can feel like safety, even when it is also a cage.

In patriarchal systems, immaturity is often rewarded if it takes the form of submission.[166] And the cost of developing true agency—financial, intellectual, emotional, or spiritual—is often so high that some women choose not to pay it.

SECTION II: THE ROLES WOMEN OCCUPY IN PATRIARCHAL SYSTEMS

> *BLUF: Introduces five archetypal roles—The Enforcer, The Martyr, The Gatekeeper, The Token, and The Silent Ally. Each role offers short-term safety, praise, or power, but upholds the system and exacts a personal toll. These roles are presented as masks worn for survival, not as permanent identities.*

When survival depends on conformity, women develop roles that allow them to navigate patriarchal systems with as little punishment—and as much reward—as possible.

These roles are not always chosen.[167] They're inherited, spiritualized, rewarded, or quietly expected. But no matter how polished or praised, they serve the system, not the soul. This is not failure. It is a choice shaped by pressure, conditioning, fear, and often very real danger. But it is also a place where transformation becomes possible—because when women begin to recognize the trade-offs, they can also begin to reclaim what was sacrificed.

These roles are shaped not only by gender, but also by race, class, sexuality, and culture. The costs and rewards of collusion are not distributed evenly, but these archetypal roles are all strategies—crafted in response to danger, scarcity, or pressure—and over time, they can harden into identities.

1. *The Enforcer*

This is the woman who polices other women. She shames those who break the rules, stray from tradition, or ask for more. She may call it "protecting virtue," "upholding values," or "keeping the peace"—but often, it's about managing her own fear by punishing the freedoms of others.

- ❖ She tells young girls to dress modestly to avoid male attention— rather than challenging male entitlement.

❖ She critiques other women for being "too much" when they speak out, lead boldly, or refuse to comply.

❖ She becomes the mouthpiece of patriarchy, doing its work so the men don't have to.

2. *The Martyr*

She is praised for her sacrifice. She gives and gives and then gives some more. Her worth is measured by how much she disappears—how little she needs, how tirelessly she serves, how quietly she suffers.

This role is especially celebrated in religious or familial systems. But beneath the surface is often a woman who has never been allowed to have a self.

❖ She defers to her husband in all things, believing it is holy to be small.

❖ She resents other women's boundaries but doesn't know how to form her own.

❖ She teaches daughters to disappear, calling it love.

3. *The Gatekeeper*

This woman has earned limited power within a patriarchal structure—and she guards it fiercely. She may be the only woman at the table, the exceptional one, the trusted insider. But to maintain her status, she must reinforce the rules that keep others out.

❖ She dismisses accusations of sexism in the workplace to avoid rocking the boat.

❖ She criticizes women who are "too sensitive" or "don't play the game right."

❖ She aligns with power, not solidarity.

Gatekeepers don't always intend harm. But their survival is tied to the system's approval—and so they often uphold what they once longed to resist.

4. *The Token*

The token woman is elevated just enough to suggest progress—but not enough to change the system. Her presence is used to defend against critique: "We can't be sexist—look at her!"

Tokens are often selected for their ability to perform acceptance, gratitude, or exceptionalism. They are expected to succeed without challenging the structure that holds them.

- She may be celebrated in public and unsupported in private.

- She is visible, but not free.

- She is pressured to be palatable—not powerful.

The token role can be a double-bind: accept invisibility, or risk expulsion.

5. *The Silent Ally*

This woman doesn't agree with the system—but she doesn't speak up either. She may be aware of the harm. She may even grieve it. But she has calculated that the cost of resistance is too high.

Silence becomes her strategy. Not because she lacks conviction—but because she lacks safety, support, or clarity on how to act.

- She says nothing when misogynistic jokes are made.

- She avoids conflict when women are being scapegoated or dismissed.

- She tells herself, "It's not my place," even when it is.

Silence is often the first thing a woman learns in patriarchy. Breaking the silence is one of the first acts of liberation.

Each of these roles has its logic. None of them automatically mean a woman is weak or malicious. They are shaped by context, culture, conditioning, and survival. But they are not the final word. They are roles—not identities.

And the moment a woman sees the role for what it is, she gains the power to choose something else.

SECTION III: THE COST OF COLLUSION

> *BLUF: Explores five major costs women incur by aligning with patriarchy: loss of self, isolation from other women, emotional exhaustion, complicity in harm, and deferred liberation. These costs are presented as consequences, not punishments—and as turning points for potential transformation.*

The roles women occupy in patriarchal systems are not without reward. They may bring protection, approval, belonging, or even power—of a certain kind. But they also come with profound costs, both personal and collective.

These costs are often invisible at first. They hide beneath praise. They're softened by tradition. They're disguised as virtue. But over time, they show up—in the body, in relationships, in the soul's quiet grief that something essential has been traded away.

1. *Loss of Self*

Each of the roles described—Enforcer, Martyr, Gatekeeper, Token, Silent Ally—requires the suppression of the full self. They demand silence where there should be voice. Deference where there could be agency. Performance where there should be presence.

To maintain these roles, women often disconnect from their own:

* Anger (because it threatens harmony)

* Desires (because they're "selfish")

* Truth (because it disrupts the script)

Over time, this fragmentation becomes internalized. A woman may wake up one day and realize she has built her entire life around a version of herself that isn't whole. She has mastered the role—but lost the reality.[168]

2. *Isolation and Rivalry*

Patriarchal roles are often designed to keep women apart. The Gatekeeper is pitted against the Outsider. The Token is separated from solidarity. The Enforcer is set up to shame those who deviate. This creates a culture of comparison, suspicion, and internalized misogyny wherein women learn to:

- Compete instead of connect.
- Police instead of support.
- Judge instead of empathize.

Sisterhood becomes suspect.[169] Solidarity becomes subversive. And women, instead of dismantling the system, become its unpaid foot soldiers—fighting one another while the system remains intact.

3. *Emotional Exhaustion*

Living inside a role is draining. It requires constant performance, vigilance, and emotional suppression. A woman may be praised for her selflessness, her patience, her elegance—but inside, she is exhausted.

- The Martyr is burning out.
- The Enforcer is brittle with repressed rage.
- The Silent Ally is anxious from years of biting her tongue.
- The Gatekeeper is lonely at the top of a ladder where she never wanted to be the only one on that rung.

What looks like stability on the outside is often depletion on the inside.

4. *Complicity in Harm*

This is the most painful cost—and the hardest to face. By occupying these roles, women may unintentionally perpetuate the very harm they once endured.[170] They may:

- ❖ Silence other women the way they were once silenced.

- ❖ Shun the outcast they once feared becoming.

- ❖ Punish the boldness they never had permission to express.

This is not because they are cruel—but because collusion often feels safer than truth-telling. And because systems train us to believe that if we stay aligned with power, we won't be targeted next.

But harm is still harm. And no role protects us forever.

5. *Deferred Liberation*

Perhaps the deepest cost is this: when a woman lives in service to patriarchy—whether willingly or unconsciously—her own becoming is postponed.

- ❖ The risks not taken.

- ❖ The voice not used.

- ❖ The call not followed.

- ❖ The life half-lived.

Every time a woman silences herself to preserve the system, her true self is deferred. And every system built on deferral becomes a graveyard for unlived lives.

These costs are not punishments. They are consequences. And the price of performance is never the same for every woman. Race, class, and culture shape not just the risks—but the stories we're told about what we owe.

And naming them is not about shame—it's about clarity.

Because clarity opens a door. And once we see the cost, we can decide if we want to keep paying it and if it's worth it.

SECTION IV: THE PATH OUT — AWAKENING, DISRUPTION, LIBERATION

> *BLUF: Describes the inner journey from role performance to self-reclamation. This includes the flicker of disruption, the grief-filled reckoning, the risk of redefinition, the return to self-trust, and the expansion into genuine solidarity with other women. Collusion is shown to be reversible—and awakening contagious.*

Disengaging from patriarchal roles isn't easy. It's not a single act of rebellion. Nor is it a dramatic confrontation. More often, it begins quietly: a moment of dissonance, a flicker of anger, a sudden grief. Something no longer fits. Something once tolerable becomes unbearable.

This is the start of awakening.

1. *The Flicker of Disruption*

Often, it begins with a whisper:

Why do I feel so tired?

Why do I dread being around them?

Why do I always second-guess myself when I'm right?

Why do I feel small in rooms where I should feel powerful?

At first, it's easy to dismiss. Patriarchal systems train women to doubt their perceptions. To call discomfort "too sensitive," to rename harm as "caring," to frame boundaries as "nagging," to label clarity as "arrogance."

But if the flicker isn't ignored, it grows. It becomes a truth that won't stay quiet. It becomes harder to keep performing.

2. *The Reckoning*

This is the moment the old role begins to feel like a costume. The woman who once felt proud of her sacrifice begins to feel hollow. The woman who once policed other women starts noticing her own projections. The woman who climbed the ladder starts asking who built it—and what it's leaning against.

This phase is often marked by grief:

Grief for the years spent performing.

Grief for the friendships sacrificed for proximity with power.

Grief for the truths swallowed.

Grief for the self-abandoned to survive.

The reckoning hurts. But it is also holy. Because every system that depends on women's silence begins to tremble the moment one woman tells the truth.[171]

3. *The Risk of Redefinition*

To stop colluding is to start risking:

Disapproval

Exile

The loss of comfort, status, or protection

It's the risk of becoming "too much," "too angry," "too ambitious," "too honest." But it's also the risk of becoming whole.

Redefinition means:

Saying no where you used to nod.

Speaking when you used to stay quiet.

Resting where you used to prove.

Walking away from roles that used to be your entire identity.

It means choosing integrity over approval.[172] Clarity over comfort. Liberation over performance.

4. The Return to Self

Every step out of collusion is a step back toward the self. It's not about becoming someone new—it's about reclaiming who you were before the roles were assigned. The self who was loud, brave, tender, intuitive, wild. The self who didn't perform. The self who didn't split. The self who belonged to herself.

This is where self-trust begins. Not in the brittle confidence of performance—but in the grounded knowing that comes from living in alignment with truth.

And it's here, in this return to self, that something even deeper becomes possible: the ability to marry others—not from need, role, or performance, but from presence. From wholeness. From mutual sovereignty.

This is the beginning of true partnership, true collaboration, true love.

Not a marriage of dependency—but a marriage of minds, bodies, and spirits that are no longer at war with themselves.

5. The Expansion of Solidarity

And finally disengaging from patriarchal roles makes space for something else: connection. Real connection. Not comparison, not competition, not performance—but shared humanity.

When a woman stops playing a role, she makes room for other women to do the same. She stops enforcing the system—and starts dismantling it. Her freedom is contagious. Her clarity invites others. Her life becomes a permission slip.[173]

Not everyone will like it. But those who are ready will recognize her.

Awakening is not betrayal. It's belonging—to yourself, and to a world that wants to grow. And it is never too late to stop performing and start returning.

SECTION V: THE QUIET REVOLUTION

> *BLUF: Names women's refusal to perform patriarchal roles as a revolutionary act. Every woman (and every man) who stops feeding the system becomes a signal flare for others. The chapter ends by reframing awakening not as betrayal, but as a sacred return to truth, to self, and to the lineage of women who choose freedom.*

THE AWAKENING OF ONE — THE LIBERATION OF MANY

When a woman stops colluding with patriarchy, the world doesn't end. But something false does:

The illusion that this is just how it must be.

The belief that silence is safer than truth.

The idea that her value depends on her obedience.

The system's spell begins to break—not because she fights it, but because she no longer feeds it. And though her awakening may begin in isolation, she is never truly alone. Because every woman who has ever stepped off the approved path has lit a small fire for the rest of us to see by.

She becomes part of a lineage—often unspoken, often unnamed—of women who dared to reclaim their minds, their bodies, their voices, their knowing.[174]

Not out of rebellion. But out of return.

Return to reality.

Return to responsibility.

Return to self.

And this return is not merely personal. It is political. Because the moment enough women stop performing roles for systems that harm them, the system itself begins to unravel.

This is the quiet revolution. Not the overthrow of power—but the refusal to play its games. Not the burning of the house—but the walking out of it. And the building of something honest in its place.

Because collusion is not our inheritance. Truth is.

And like all true awakenings, it comes with a cost.

19

The Cost of Patriarchy: Why Clarity Hurts Before It Heals

BLUF: THIS CHAPTER EXPLORES THE EMOTIONAL, RELATIONAL, AND SPIRITUAL TOLL OF AWAKENING FROM PATRIARCHAL CONDITIONING. IT REFRAMES CLARITY NOT AS COMFORT, BUT AS A COURAGEOUS DISRUPTION THAT BREAKS THE SPELL OF COLLUSION. IT OUTLINES THE GRIEF, DISILLUSIONMENT, AND LOSS THAT ACCOMPANY LIBERATION —WHILE ALSO HONORING THE SANITY, INTIMACY, AND GROUNDED SELFHOOD THAT CLARITY RESTORES. THIS IS NOT THE END OF THE JOURNEY, BUT THE THRESHOLD OF RETURN.

We were never meant to live this way. Not with half the world's voices silenced. Not with our instincts mistrusted. Not with our relationships distorted by roles instead of presence. And not with our power outsourced to those unwilling or unfit to lead with maturity.

This chapter is about that ache.

The ache of waking up. The ache of seeing clearly. The ache of liberation—not as a fantasy, but as a reality that costs something.

Because clarity does cost us. And it should. It costs us illusions, comfort, roles that once earned us praise but never gave us peace.

But it also gives us everything we were born to carry dignity, agency, intimacy, and truth.

SECTION 1: A UNITED FRONT OF THE SANE

> *BLUF: Repositions the conversation away from gender wars and toward emotional maturity. Argues that patriarchy harms everyone—men included—by distorting roles, restricting emotional range, and rewarding immaturity. Names a growing collective of people who refuse to perform sanity for an insane system, and who are choosing legacy over loyalty.*

This book is not about women versus men. It is not about victim and villain. It is about sanity versus distortion.

Patriarchy does not just harm women. It's violence and selfishness and amorality harms men too. It creates moral injury, replacing reality with role play. It turns full-spectrum human beings into caricatures—stoic breadwinners, submissive caretakers, angry protectors, obedient daughters. It feeds on simplicity. On absurdity. On immaturity.

And many men are tired of it too. Tired of being told their worth is measured in dominance. Or a paycheck. Or the size of their physique. Tired of being denied vulnerability, nuance, and tenderness. Tired of the pressure to always be strong, always be competent, always know the answer, always fix the problem.

There is a growing collective—men and women, black and white, queer and nonbinary folks—who are done. Who see through the roles. Who refuse to perform sanity for an insane system. Who are building something else.

And many of them aren't just walking away for their own sake. They're walking away for the sake of those who come next. Because once you see the cost of patriarchy—on your own psyche, your own relationships, your own freedom—you begin to see how it travels through generations. How it warps childhoods. How it calcifies roles. How it silences daughters, hardens sons, and turns tenderness into threat.

For many, personal liberation is only the first threshold. The deeper calling is this:

To leave behind a different legacy.

To raise children who are not rewarded for dominance or punished for sensitivity.

To model relationships built on mutuality instead of control.

To break the cycles of silencing, scapegoating, and emotional outsourcing that once felt normal.

To become the ancestors who hand down clarity—not confusion.

This isn't a burden, it's a privilege.

Not perfection, but a conscious refusal to continue what wounded you.

Not rebellion for rebellion's sake, but a sacred interruption of harm.

This is not men rescuing women. It is not women scolding men. It is people waking up, standing side by side, saying: Enough.

We will not be small to keep a brittle system intact. We will not betray reality to comfort immaturity. We will not keep handing the mic to those who have proven they do not know how to lead.

SECTION II: THE IMMATURITY OF ASKING THE UNFIT TO SAVE US

> *BLUF: Challenges the emotionally immature hope that the narcissistic, reactive, or entitled will one day transform the system they benefit from. Calls for the reclamation of agency from those unfit to lead, and frames walking away not as abandonment—but as wisdom.*

We keep waiting for the wrong people to change. We ask the narcissistic to become self-aware. The reactive to become steady. The entitled to dismantle the very system that made them king. We ask the people with the least incentive, the least regulation, the least conscience, and the least contact with reality to do what is right.

This is not just unwise. It is emotionally immature. Because emotional maturity means dealing with reality as it is. Not as we wish it to be.

It is time to stop expecting transformation from those who have shown no desire or capacity for it. It is time to reclaim the agency we keep handing to those who are committed to maintaining the dysfunction.

We are not waiting for kings to abdicate.[175] We are not waiting for narcissists to apologize. We are not waiting for dominators to grow a conscience.

We are walking away. We are building something else.

And yes—that will cost us.

SECTION III: THE EMOTIONAL COST OF LIBERATION

> *BLUF: Acknowledges the grief, rage, confusion, and isolation that often follow awakening. Names this as a natural part of healing, not a failure. Reminds readers that the collapse of illusion is not the end—but the beginning of self-belonging.*

To leave behind a system is not only an act of courage. It is an act of grief. The myths we were raised on will not go quietly. The roles we performed so well will claw at our hearts as we drop them. The people who loved us for who we pretended to be may not follow us into who we truly are.

This is the cost.

Grief for the years spent asleep. Rage for the ways we were used. Anxiety about who we are now. Confusion as old maps stop working. Loneliness from holding more truth than the people around us. Despair when we realize how deep the damage goes.

These feelings are not signs we are failing. They are signs we are healing.

No one tells you that freedom starts with heartbreak.[176] Not with fireworks. Not with triumph. But with a quiet undoing. That liberation is not always a rising. Sometimes, it's a falling apart.

Because we must feel what the system never let us feel. We must name what was never allowed to be named. We must lose what we were never meant to keep.

SECTION IV: THE COST/BENEFIT ANALYSIS OF CLARITY

> *BLUF: Affirms that while clarity is costly, it returns us to sanity, dignity, and truth. Reframes clarity as a threshold rather than a destination. Once we stop performing and start seeing, the system begins to lose its grip—and a deeper guidance begins to rise.*

And still—there is more.

Clarity doesn't only hurt. It liberates.

It gives us our lives back.

The cost is steep. But the benefit is sanity. The cost is grief. But the benefit is dignity. The cost is disillusionment. But the benefit is real love, real leadership, real belonging.

To see clearly is to step out of the play. To name the absurdity. To refuse to pretend.

The system wants us asleep. Clarity wakes us up. And while waking up may break your heart—it is often the first moment your heart truly belongs to you.

And what comes after the collapse?

Not action plans. Not five-step formulas. But the quiet, grounded power of emotional maturity itself—as a compass. As a refusal. As a return.

Because when we see clearly, we stop feeding the system. And that is where liberation begins.

Clarity is not a thought. It's a threshold.

You don't have to force change. You just have to see. Because when you truly see, something shifts.

Not in the world—at least not right away—but in you.

The noise quiets.

The striving stops.

And what's true begins to rise.

No more proving.

No more performing.

Just clarity—and the quiet courage to follow it.

That is enough.
It always has been.
Refusal is not the end.
It's the turning.
The moment the compass realigns—
and you begin to walk, at last,
toward what has always been calling you home.

The Real Revolution

*"You cannot solve a problem with
the same consciousness that created it."*
—*Albert Einstein*

Emotional maturity asks clearly for what it wants—and allows others to respond in freedom. So, I'm making a request of you, the reader.

Patriarchy—and every narcissistic system or individual—thrives on an *Us vs. Them* consciousness.

Even when we can see this clearly, it's easy to get pulled into the same trap.

And when we've been harmed, manipulated, or exploited, we have every right to be angry and to identify who or what harmed us.

As I wrote in my memoir, anger is a healthy immune response of the psyche. It clarifies. It exposes. It helps us name the truth of what happened—out loud, to ourselves, and to others. It fuels accountability and strengthens boundaries. It gives us the courage to act.

In short, anger is the moment we begin to reclaim our agency.

But anger is not the end game. It is a stage, not a destination. If we stop there, we become stuck in reaction rather than evolution.

So, this is my request:

Even in your justified anger, please don't weaponize this book.

Don't use it to label all men as immature.

Don't use it to silence women by pointing out how they can be immature too.

Don't use it as a tool to shame individuals.

Speak truth. Name harm. Get angry when you must.

Hold individuals and systems accountable.

Refuse the false choice of submission or domination.

But stay awake.

Stay responsible.

Stay human.

Even if your observations are true, this book is not for them.

It's for you.

It's not meant to become another cudgel in the endless battle of blame.

It's meant to help you step out of the frame entirely.

Because people do not just leave patriarchy for themselves.

They leave so their children don't have to inherit the same distortions.

They leave so the next generation doesn't have to unlearn as much just to feel free.

They leave so the pain stops with them.

That is a revolution too.

Quiet. Personal. Powerful.

Walk out of the house of domination—
and build something honest in its place.

Navigating from Clarity

Clarity is enough. But for those ready to lean into that clarity—this is a starting point, not a prescription.

Clarity is not just a concept. It's a form of labor—emotional, intellectual, even spiritual. Seeing clearly takes effort in a world built to confuse you and serve up fast-food, low-nutrition answers. It is work to tell yourself the truth in systems that have trained you to look away. If you were raised in a family, culture, or belief system where denial was survival, then simply noticing what's real—without collapse, panic, or explanation—is a revolutionary act.

In short, to metabolize the truth is not a small thing.

Especially in systems like patriarchy, where confusion is a tool of control and gaslighting is woven into the very fabric of normal, reclaiming your perception is one of the most subversive things you can do. That is emotional maturity in motion. Emotional maturity begins the moment we stop outsourcing our perception and reclaim responsibility for our inner compass—and for our reactions and choices.

Clarity, however, is not a static insight. It is a living process. It deepens only when we invest in it—when we choose to act from it. You don't need to overhaul your life. But clarity invites you to make even the smallest shift in how you relate to yourself, to others, and to the systems around you.

That action might look like setting a new boundary—or simply stopping the overexplaining of one. It might look like no longer translating someone else's vagueness. It might look like staying with your own discomfort instead of reflexively fixing someone else's.

So, if you've read this far and you're still hungry—not for more information, but for deeper clarity—what follows is a small collection of ways clarity begins to move. These are not prescriptions or checklists. They're invitations. Each one is a quiet refusal to return to confusion. None of them "solve" patriarchy, but each can help you liberate from it.

THE COURAGE TO SEE AND GROW

Clarity isn't about perfection. It's a journey of perception. As you begin to act from what you now see—even in subtle ways—you may also start to notice patterns within yourself that reflect the very systems you've been unmasking. This, too, is part of the process.

If you grew up in an emotionally immature family, religious community, or cultural system, it would be extraordinarily rare for you to emerge emotionally whole. How could you have developed skills that were never modeled for you? How could you have learned self-trust when confusion, distortion, blame, or denial were the norm?

The good news is this: once you begin to witness yourself clearly—without collapse, panic, or self-condemnation—you've already stepped into a more mature version of yourself.

Self-reflection without self-condemnation is a game-changer for personal growth. If you find yourself in the list below, don't spiral into shame. The ability to witness yourself without collapse is itself a sign of maturity—and your capacity to grow.

COMMON SIGNS OF EMOTIONAL IMMATURITY

These signs are not flaws. They are developmental leftovers—understandable strategies that once served a protective function but now inhibit clarity, connection, and sovereignty.

- Defensiveness when corrected or challenged
- Blaming others instead of taking ownership
- Difficulty tolerating discomfort, boredom, or delay
- Seeking validation or rescue instead of taking initiative
- Using charm, collapse, manipulation, or anger to get needs met or avoid responsibility
- Avoiding hard conversations or boundary-setting

- Resentment of others' reasonable needs or expectations
- Refusing to acknowledge, apologize, and repair relational harm
- Interpreting feedback or boundaries as attack, rejection, or abandonment
- Expecting others to "just know" your needs
- Entitlement—expecting benefits or support without mutuality or effort
- Inability to do teamwork or healthy collaboration
- Black-and-white thinking ("I'm either good or I'm worthless")
- Emotional reasoning ("I feel this way, so it must be true") feelings become facts
- Magical thinking ("If I wish hard enough, it will just happen")
- Projection—assuming others think/feel as you do
- Externalizing blame or pain rather than reflecting inward
- Victim mentality when challenged, questioned, or asked to grow
- Helplessness or incompetence patterns used to avoid responsibility or effort
- Fragile self-image—discomfort with being wrong, especially when problem-solving
- Taking refuge in vagueness, ambiguity, or avoidance
- Persistent expectation that others will center you or rescue you

If you recognize yourself in several of these patterns, it doesn't mean you're failing. It means you're beginning to see. And seeing clearly is the first act of freedom. And if you're wondering whether this applies to you— it probably means you're doing the work. (Spoiler: emotional immaturity doesn't love introspection.)

CLARITY IN MOTION: SMALL WAYS TO LIVE WHAT YOU NOW SEE

These small shifts below are not checklists. They are quiet refusals. Practices of discernment. Invitations to let clarity shape how you move.

1. **Stop overexplaining** to people who refuse to listen. Your clarity is not a courtroom argument. It does not require permission or performance. Save your breath for those who meet you with curiosity, not distortion.

2. **Let go of translating** other people's vagueness. If someone consistently fosters confusion, you don't have to become their decoder. Ask directly. And if you don't get a clear answer, accept the clarity of that.

3. **Refuse unpaid emotional labor** disguised as "healing." You are not a rehab center for people who hurt you. Maturity means supporting healing in mutual relationships—not subsidizing harm with your spirit.

4. **Stop trying to convert** the unwilling. You don't have to carry truth into spaces where it will only be twisted. Recognition is not always a precondition for release. Let go anyway.

5. **Enforce your boundaries** instead of explaining them. Boundaries are not debate topics. When you start living your no—or your yes—you stop inviting people to argue with your discernment.

6. **Allow discomfort to exist** without rescuing anyone from it. Clarity often disturbs the script. That's not cruelty—it's truth arriving. You don't need to cushion every moment of honesty to be loving.

7. **Make fewer excuses for systems** that rely on your confusion. You don't need to soften the edges of injustice to be fair. You can tell the truth about dysfunction without disclaimers.

RECOGNIZING IMMATURITY IN OTHERS

Despite your own growing clarity, you may find yourself enmeshed in relationships where emotional immaturity is not just present—it's being protected, justified, or even rewarded. These may be relationships with a partner, adult child, friend, boss, sibling, or community leader.

Sometimes the most dangerous immaturity isn't ours—it's the kind we enable.

In emotionally immature systems, charm, collapse, guilt, rage, or passivity are often used as tools to avoid emotional adulthood. And without realizing it, you may be carrying the relationship on your back— doing the emotional labor, the repair work, and the explaining. This is how emotionally extractive systems are sustained: not only by those who dominate, but by those who cushion, contain, and compensate.

SIGNS YOU'RE CARRYING TOO MUCH RESPONSIBILITY

- You feel more like a parent than a partner or peer
- You're constantly explaining, smoothing, or justifying
- You walk on eggshells to avoid setting them off
- You feel exhausted or bruised after every interaction
- You feel like you're being gaslit or emotionally spun
- They evade, ignore, or bulldoze over your boundaries
- You're haunted by guilt if you assert your needs
- You feel like you're in a performance—not a relationship
- You suspect they like things vague, so they don't have to commit
- You keep hoping they'll change once they see how much you love them
- You're always rescuing or protecting them from the consequences of their own choices
- They refuse to learn or grow, reduce their helplessness, or foster competence

It's not your job to drag another adult into growth. And some relationships may need to be exited—or seriously limited. But if that's not yet possible, here are two tools that may help.

TWO TOOLS FOR DISCERNMENT AND COMMUNICATION

Even when we see emotional immaturity clearly, knowing what to do about it can feel overwhelming. These two tools are designed to support clarity, boundaries, and self-protection—whether you're examining your own responses or navigating complex dynamics with others.

They are not scripts, formulas, or solutions. They are reflection aids. You may use them privately or in conversation—but always in service of discernment, not control.

Tool One: Reflective Clarifiers Toolkit

This tool is divided into two parts: Clarifiers to Ask Yourself, and Clarifiers to Ask Them. These prompts are not for debate or persuasion. They're meant to invite ownership, reduce reactivity, and cultivate emotional sobriety.

CLARIFIERS TO ASK YOURSELF

- What am I afraid to know by avoiding clarity in this dynamic?
- What do I fear will happen if I stop carrying this relationship?
- Am I hoping for change—or witnessing actual effort and growth?
- Am I seeking intimacy or avoiding abandonment?
- Do I feel more like a caretaker, counselor, or emotional manager than a peer?
- If I didn't explain or justify myself—what truth would remain?
- What have I been accepting as normal that hurts?
- If I believed I deserved maturity and reciprocity, what would I stop doing today?

CLARIFIERS TO ASK THEM

- **In what ways do you believe you're being punished?**

  → Use when someone interprets your boundary or withdrawal of overfunctioning as "punishment."

❖ **Is there a message you're communicating with silence?**

→ Use when you're being stonewalled but want to inquire without accusation.

❖ **Do you feel like something went unsaid here?**

→ Use when tension lingers but nothing is acknowledged directly.

❖ **Was there something in what I said that felt unsafe to you?**

→ Use when someone shuts down or becomes reactive without clear cause.

❖ **Is this a boundary for you—or something else?**

→ Use when someone disengages and you're unsure if it's avoidance or a limit.

❖ **Are you needing space, or is this a reaction?**

→ Use when someone withdraws after a difficult moment.

❖ **Do you want me to understand something you haven't said directly?**

→ Use when the person seems upset but hasn't communicated openly.

❖ **Does this feel like a pattern you've experienced before?**

→ Use when the intensity of their reaction seems rooted in the past.

❖ **What part of this feels the hardest to name right now?**

→ Use when they seem overwhelmed but unable to articulate it.

❖ **Is this about the present—or something it reminds you of?**

→ Use when small issues escalate in disproportionate ways.

Tool Two: Reflective Communication Toolkit

This toolkit offers language support for boundary-honoring, emotionally sober communication that can help de-escalate conflict, clarify expectations, and remain in emotional integrity when dealing with immaturity, defensiveness, or avoidance. Use them as scaffolding for calm, steady, communication.

1. GENTLE INQUIRY

I'm not looking to argue—I'm just trying to make sense of what shifted.

I'd rather ask directly than assume. Can I check something with you?

You don't have to answer now. But I'd like to ask something I've been sitting with.

I noticed something that confused me—are you open to a quick reflection?

2. SURPRISE OR SHIFT CLARIFIERS

I'm a little surprised by what I just heard—it feels different than what we said earlier. Are you open to clarifying, now or later?

I'm not trying to pin you down. I'm just trying to understand what I heard.

That sounded like a change in direction—was that your intent or just a passing thought?

This might be nothing, but I noticed a shift. Is it something you want to name?

3. TIME-SENSITIVE BOUNDARY REQUESTS

Would now be a good time to reflect on something—or should we come back to it later?

I don't want to overload you, so just let me know if now's not the right moment.

Would you rather I reflect this or let it go? I can do either, but I want to respect where you're at.

You don't have to talk now, but I want to be transparent about what I'm experiencing.

4. VULNERABILITY INVITATIONS

This is coming from care, not criticism. I want us to be able to navigate this better.

This might be uncomfortable to hear. I'm not asking for a fix—just a moment of honesty.

I want to say something without blame. Would now be a good time, or later?

I'm sharing this because I care about connection—not because I expect you to agree.

5. COMPETENCE-PRESSURE DEFUSERS

Neither of us has to be the expert—I'm just hoping we can figure this out together.

I don't expect you to have the answer—I'm asking so we can think it through, not so you'll fix it.

This isn't a test—I'm just asking what's coming up for you, not what's "right."

It's okay not to know. I just want us to look at it honestly so we can make a call together.

We don't need to get it perfect—we just need to stay in the conversation.

If this feels overwhelming, we can break it down and look at one piece at a time.

You don't have to carry this alone—and I don't either. Let's just see what we both notice.

6. PARTNERSHIP & HELP REQUEST QUALIFIERS

Would you be open to helping with something—not urgently, just sometime soon?

This would feel easier with two of us. Are you available to tag in—or should I find another option?

I'm not expecting a yes—just want to check if this is something you'd be willing to help with.

I'm asking for support, not perfection. I can adjust if it's not possible, but I wanted to ask first.

You don't have to solve this—but your presence or input would matter to me.

This is one of those times I'd love to feel like I'm not in this alone—can you check with yourself and let me know if that feels okay?

I know we both move at different paces. Would you be open to syncing up on this one thing?

IMPORTANT DISCLAIMER

This Afterword and its companion tools are intended for educational and reflective purposes only. I am not a licensed therapist, psychologist, physician, or mental health professional. These materials are not designed to diagnose, treat, or serve as a substitute for professional mental health care.

If you are in a relationship with someone who is abusive, controlling, violent, or you intuit they could become unsafe, these tools may not be appropriate or safe to use. Boundaries, truth-telling, and refusal—while essential to emotional maturity—can escalate danger in unsafe dynamics.

Please use your own best judgment. If you have any doubts or concerns about how these tools might apply to your specific situation, do not proceed alone. Contact a licensed therapist, domestic violence advocate, or trauma-informed professional who can guide you in a way that is safe, grounded, and attuned to your specific needs.

CLOSING: LET YOUR CLARITY LEAD

You don't need to do everything today, or anything today. You don't need to fix anyone. You don't need to explain your awakening or justify your clarity.

You only need to see what is true—and trust yourself not to look away.

Clarity is not a finish line. It is a compass.

Where it points may be different for each of us. But wherever it leads, let it take you home to yourself.

The Everyday Cost of Emotional Immaturity

Emotional immaturity doesn't just affect personal growth—it has far-reaching consequences in nearly every aspect of life. Here's a breakdown of how emotional immaturity negatively impacts different areas of life:

1. Relationships (Romantic & Friendships)

- ❖ Poor Communication: Reacting emotionally instead of expressing needs clearly, leading to constant misunderstandings.

- ❖ Lack of Accountability: Blaming a partner or friend instead of self-reflecting leads to unresolved conflicts.

- ❖ Fear of Vulnerability: Avoiding deep emotional connection makes relationships feel superficial or unstable.

- ❖ Impulsiveness: Acting on emotions without thinking leads to breakups, toxic cycles, or poor relationship choices.

- ❖ Clinging to Fairytale Expectations: Expecting love to "fix" personal struggles leads to disappointment.

2. Family Relationships

- ❖ Generational Trauma & Dysfunction: Emotionally immature parents pass unhealthy patterns to children.

- ❖ Inability to Set Boundaries: Avoiding hard conversations results in resentment and enmeshment.

- ❖ Favoritism & Power Struggles: Using emotional manipulation (guilt trips, silent treatment) damages trust.

- Avoiding Conflict Resolution: Holding grudges rather than addressing issues keeps family tension high.
- Emotional Suppression: Family members bottle up feelings instead of openly communicating.

3. Finances & Career

- Impulsive Spending: Prioritizing instant gratification over long-term financial security.
- Job Instability: Reacting emotionally to criticism or being reflexively anti-authority, leading to conflicts at work.
- Fear of Responsibility: Avoiding financial planning, budgeting, or long-term investments.
- Entitlement Thinking: Expecting financial rescue (from parents, partners, or employers) rather than taking ownership.
- Inability to Delay Gratification: Struggling to save money, invest, or work toward long-term goals.

4. Parenting

- Projecting Personal Issues onto Children: Expecting kids to meet unmet adult emotional needs.
- Inconsistent Discipline: Swinging between overindulgence and harsh punishment instead of steady guidance.
- Modeling Emotional Reactivity: Teaching children to manage problems through yelling, blaming, or avoidance.
- Unrealistic Expectations: Expecting children to be emotionally or mentally mature and behave perfectly.
- Failure to Teach Emotional Regulation: Not equipping kids with skills to process emotions in a healthy way.

5. Decision-Making & Problem-Solving

- ❖ Reacting Instead of Responding: Making choices based on emotions rather than logic and long-term thinking.

- ❖ Fear of Change & Growth: Clinging to comfort zones rather than adapting to life's challenges.

- ❖ All-or-Nothing Thinking: Seeing problems as impossible to fix instead of breaking them into manageable steps.

- ❖ Avoiding Difficult Decisions: Procrastinating or letting others decide, leading to a loss of personal agency.

- ❖ Seeking External Validation: Making decisions to please others rather than based on personal values.

6. Social & Community Engagement

- ❖ Tribalism & Extremism: Emotionally immature people struggle with nuance and gravitate toward rigid, black-and-white ideologies.

- ❖ Gossip & Drama-Seeking: Thriving on interpersonal conflict rather than meaningful connection.

- ❖ Lack of Accountability in Groups: Avoiding responsibility in teamwork, letting others pick up the slack.

- ❖ Emotional Fragility in Disagreements: Taking differing opinions as personal attacks rather than engaging in constructive dialogue.

- ❖ Resistance to Collaboration: Struggling to work with others due to power struggles and poor emotional regulation.

7. Health & Well-Being

- ❖ Self-Sabotage: Engaging in unhealthy habits (overeating, drinking, procrastination) to avoid emotions.

- Poor Stress Management: Emotionally immature people bottle up stress or explode rather than process it.

- Neglecting Self-Care: Not prioritizing sleep, nutrition, or exercise due to lack of self-discipline.

- Avoidance of Medical & Mental Health Care: Ignoring symptoms, refusing therapy, or fearing professional help.

- Blaming Others for Health Issues: Not taking personal responsibility for lifestyle choices.

BIDERMAN'S 8 TACTICS OF COERCIVE CONTROL SCALED TO PATRIARCHY

1. ISOLATION— Women are separated from money, education, and professional networks; told their place is in the home.

2. MONOPOLIZATION OF PERCEPTION—Women's presence is systematically excluded from history, law, religion, art, and economics.

3. INDUCED DEBILITATION AND EXHAUSTION—Women may face many pregnancies, endless caretaking, stress, and hypervigilance.

4. THREATS—Women are threatened with poverty, custody loss, ostracization, and violence.

5. OCCASIONAL INDULGENCES—Small rewards and displays of approval are used to reinforce compliance. Intermittent reinforcement

6. DEMONSTRATING OMNIPOTENCE AND OMNISCIENCE—The system sees and hears all and can punish, exile, or erase you for disobedience.

7. DEGRADATION—Women are undermined through treatment as inferior, and through slurs, harrassment, and humiliation.

8. ENFORCING TRIVIAL DEMANDS—Women are required to submit to petty, and often arbitrary, demands: what they wear and say, and where they go.

ENDNOTES

CHAPTER 1

[1] Gerda Lerner critiques the idea that patriarchy is biologically inevitable and argues instead that it is a historical construct rooted in social, economic, and religious developments. See Gerda Lerner, *The Creation of Patriarchy* (New York: Oxford University Press, 1986), 8–12.

[2] Heide Goettner-Abendroth documents the existence of cooperative, egalitarian matriarchal societies across cultures, challenging assumptions of male dominance as a universal evolutionary trait. See Heide Goettner-Abendroth, *Matriarchal Societies of the Past and the Rise of Patriarchy*, trans. Ute Klaus (Albany: SUNY Press, 2012), 22–31.

[3] Riane Eisler emphasizes that the persistence of patriarchal control depends on institutional reinforcement rather than natural hierarchy. See Riane Eisler, *The Chalice and the Blade: Our History, Our Future* (San Francisco: Harper & Row, 1987), 44–50.

[4] Projection, a defense mechanism identified by psychoanalytic theorists, involves attributing one's unacceptable impulses to others. Patriarchal fears of domination reversal often reflect their own operating logic. See Aaron T. Beck, *Cognitive Therapy and the Emotional Disorders* (New York: Penguin Books, 1976), 127–130.

[5] Goettner-Abendroth outlines matrilineal societies that practice gender balance, consensus-building, and spiritual reverence for the feminine. See Goettner-Abendroth, *Matriarchal Societies of the Past*, 40–49.

[6] In *Disrupting the Culture of Disconnection*, Christine Forner describes patriarchy as a global trauma system built on dissociation, emotional suppression, and inherited patterns of disconnection. She argues that widespread misogyny, violence, and emotional avoidance are the outcomes of systemic trauma and that patriarchy functions as a self-perpetuating dissociative structure. See Christine Forner, *Disrupting the Culture of Disconnection: A Guide for Therapists and Survivors of Complex Trauma* (Routledge, 2021), esp. chapters 3 and 4.

[7] Attachment theory originated with John Bowlby and Mary Ainsworth and has since evolved into a robust field that explores how early bonding patterns shape adult relationships. Although not all scholars agree on categorical labels, most recognize the broad patterns of secure, anxious, avoidant, and disorganized attachment. For an in-depth clinical application of adult attachment styles, see David J. Wallin, *Attachment in Psychotherapy* (New York: Guilford Press, 2007).

CHAPTER 2

[8] Lindsay C. Gibson identifies emotional immaturity as a pattern of shallow emotional processing, resistance to accountability, and poor relational functioning, rooted in developmental gaps rather than malice. See Lindsay C. Gibson, *Disentangling from Emotionally Immature People* (Oakland: New Harbinger Publications, 2023), 1–12.

[9] Elinor Greenberg explores how narcissistic and emotionally immature individuals view others in terms of utility, lacking sustained empathic regard. See Elinor Greenberg, *Borderline, Narcissistic, and Schizoid Adaptations* (New York: Routledge, 2016), 58–60.

[10] Aaron T. Beck explains how emotional reasoning—confusing feelings with facts—distorts perception and underpins many dysfunctional thought patterns. See Aaron T. Beck, *Cognitive Therapy and the Emotional Disorders* (New York: Penguin Books, 1976), 88–93.

[11] Jean Piaget described the pre-operational stage (ages 2–7) as characterized by egocentrism, magical thinking, and difficulty integrating multiple perspectives—traits echoed in emotionally immature behavior. See Jean Piaget, *The Psychology of the Child*, trans. Helen Weaver (New York: Basic Books, 1969), 22–33.

[12] Kate Manne critiques gender essentialism as a rhetorical tool used to justify and obscure systemic dominance. See Kate Manne, *Down Girl: The Logic of Misogyny* (New York: Oxford University Press, 2017), 27–31. This model of structural emotional immaturity draws from both clinical observations and systems theory. See also: Judith L. Herman, *Trauma and Recovery* (New York: Basic Books, 1992); Bessel van der Kolk, *The Body Keeps the Score* (New York: Viking, 2014); and Carl Jung's theory of the shadow and projection in *Modern Man in Search of a Soul* (New York: Harvest Books, 1933).

[13] Lindsay C. Gibson, *Adult Children of Emotionally Immature Parents*. The concept of emotional immaturity and its downstream relational effects is informed by Gibson's examination of emotionally immature caregiving and its impact on adult functioning. This appendix extends that framework beyond family-of-origin dynamics to explore the everyday costs of emotional immaturity in adult relationships and social structures. (Oakland, CA: New Harbinger Publications 2015)

CHAPTER 3

[14] Donald Winnicott emphasized that ego strength arises from "good enough" caregiving that provides mirroring, containment, and tolerable frustration. See D. W. Winnicott, *The Maturational Processes and the Facilitating Environment* (London: Hogarth Press, 1965),

[15] Donald Winnicott emphasized that ego strength arises from "good enough" caregiving that provides mirroring, containment, and tolerable frustration. See D. W. Winnicott, The Maturational Processes and the Facilitating Environment (London: Hogarth Press, 1965), 37–45.

[16] Erik Erikson proposed that autonomy and initiative, when supported in early childhood, build the foundation for identity and ego integration. See Erik H. Erikson, *Childhood and Society* (New York: W. W. Norton & Company, 1950), 240–265.

[17] Winnicott developed the concept of the "false self" to explain how children adapt to relational insecurity by constructing performative personas. See D. W. Winnicott, *Playing and Reality* (London: Tavistock, 1971), 140–152.

[18] Margaret Mahler outlined the process of separation-individuation as the psychological emergence of selfhood from early symbiosis with the caregiver. See Margaret S. Mahler, *The Psychological Birth of the Human Infant* (New York: Basic Books, 1975), 67–79.

[19] Heinz Kohut saw narcissism not as vanity, but as a developmental wound rooted in unmirrored emotional needs. See Heinz Kohut, *The Restoration of the Self* (New York: International Universities Press, 1977), 117–130.

[20] Wilfred Bion introduced the concept of "containment" to describe how caregivers help children process emotion by staying emotionally present and calm. See Wilfred R. Bion, *Learning from Experience* (London: Heinemann, 1962), 27–36.

[21] Daniel J. Siegel explains how interpersonal neurobiology shows emotional development as a function of relational experience. See Daniel J. Siegel, *The Developing Mind: How Relationships and the Brain Interact to Shape Who We Are* (New York: Guilford Press, 1999), 110–125.

[22] John Bowlby and Mary Ainsworth demonstrated how secure attachment provides the foundation for emotional regulation and ego development. See John Bowlby, *Attachment and Loss: Volume I. Attachment* (New York: Basic Books, 1969); Mary D. S. Ainsworth and John Bowlby, "An Ethological Approach to Personality Development," American Psychologist 46, no. 4 (1991): 333–341.

[23] Margaret Mahler emphasized that ego development depends on safe individuation and separation from caregivers. Without this, children may develop fused or fragmented identities. See Margaret S. Mahler, Fred Pine, and Anni Bergman, *The Psychological Birth of the Human Infant* (New York: Basic Books, 1975), 77–84.

[24] The phrase "manufactured consent" was popularized by Noam Chomsky and Edward S. Herman in *Manufacturing Consent* (1988), where it referred to how mass media shape public opinion within democratic systems. I use the term here in a developmental context to describe how consent is formed within relational systems—particularly how children learn what is safe to agree with and what is dangerous to question. I extend the

concept to examine how emotionally immature individuals and systems shape compliance in ways that later scale into patriarchal structures. Chomsky, Noam, and Edward S. Herman. *Manufacturing Consent: The Political Economy of the Mass Media.* Pantheon Books, 1988.

[25] Bessel van der Kolk shows how unintegrated trauma responses impair emotional regulation and relational functioning, often creating long-term fragmentation that extends into adulthood. See Bessel A. van der Kolk, *The Body Keeps the Score: Brain, Mind, and Body in the Healing of Trauma* (New York: Viking, 2014), 180–193.

[26] Walter Mischel's longitudinal study demonstrated how the ability to delay gratification in early childhood correlated with long-term emotional regulation and academic success. See Walter Mischel, *The Marshmallow Test: Mastering Self-Control* (New York: Little, Brown and Company, 2014), 45–57.

[27] Lukaszewski, Buss, and colleagues found that authoritarian belief systems are linked to early developmental experiences that foster anxiety, rigidity, and impaired self-regulation. See Alexander W. Lukaszewski, David M. Buss, et al., "The Origins and Structure of Authoritarianism," *Personality and Social Psychology Review 20*, no. 4 (2016): 371–397. https://doi.org/10.1177/1088868316662651.

[28] Erich Fromm argued that emotionally immature societies avoid freedom by submitting to authoritarianism in exchange for emotional security. See Erich Fromm, *Escape from Freedom* (New York: Farrar & Rinehart, 1941), 132–145.

CHAPTER 4

[29] Jean Piaget defined the stages of cognitive development in children, emphasizing the characteristics of egocentrism, animism, and concrete logic in the preoperational phase. See Jean Piaget, *The Psychology of the Child*, trans. Helen Weaver (New York: Basic Books, 1969), 24–37.

[30] Piaget's framework of childhood thinking—particularly black-and-white reasoning and egocentrism—has been widely applied to explore developmental gaps in adult behavior and leadership when those early patterns are not outgrown. See Piaget, *The Psychology of the Child*, 39–41.

[31] While this framework is original, it builds on the work of developmental theorists who show that psychological growth requires the integration of emotion, identity, and cognition. See Robert Kegan, *The Evolving Self: Problem and Process in Human Development* (Cambridge: Harvard University Press, 1982), and Daniel J. Siegel, The Developing Mind, 3rd ed. (New York: Guilford Press, 2020).

32 Kate Manne explores how misogynistic reasoning often relies on ego-preserving logic, projection, and "himpathy"—a distorted sympathy for male entitlement. See Kate Manne, *Down Girl: The Logic of Misogyny* (New York: Oxford University Press, 2017), 17–26.

33 Riane Eisler, Gerda Lerner, and Mary Beard have each argued that what we call tradition is often a codified form of emotional and psychological immaturity—rooted in domination, fear, and myth. See Riane Eisler, *The Chalice and the Blade* (San Francisco: Harper & Row, 1987), 94–107; Gerda Lerner, *The Creation of Patriarchy* (New York: Oxford University Press, 1986), 128–136; Mary Beard, *Women & Power: A Manifesto* (New York: Liveright Publishing, 2017), 34–40.

34 Carolyn Merchant explores how patriarchal culture has historically feminized and then subjugated nature through language and ideology, framing it as both nurturing and dangerous. See Carolyn Merchant, *The Death of Nature: Women, Ecology, and the Scientific Revolution* (San Francisco: Harper One, 1980), 1–23.

35 Riane Eisler and Mary Daly have documented how religious and mythological narratives animate male authority and frame the feminine as chaotic or subordinate, reinforcing gendered hierarchies. See Riane Eisler, *The Chalice and the Blade* (San Francisco: Harper & Row, 1987), 97–102; Mary Daly, *Beyond God the Father: Toward a Philosophy of Women's Liberation* (Boston: Beacon Press, 1973), 13–21.

36 Kate Manne critiques how women are symbolically vilified in patriarchal societies— cast as seductresses, monsters, or manipulators—to justify control. See Kate Manne, *Down Girl: The Logic of Misogyny* (New York: Oxford University Press, 2017), 59–68.

37 Naomi Wolf explains how infantilizing depictions of women—as delicate, ornamental, or passive—reinforce dependency and undermine autonomy. See Naomi Wolf, *The Beauty Myth: How Images of Beauty Are Used Against Women* (New York: Harper Perennial, 1991), 47–52.

38 bell hooks examines how patriarchal language elevates abstract values like honor and purity while using them to constrain female behavior and enforce obedience. See bell hooks, *Feminist Theory: From Margin to Center*, 2nd ed. (New York: Routledge, 2000), 93–98.

39 Lindsay C. Gibson explores how emotionally immature individuals frequently use magical thinking to avoid discomfort, insisting belief is reality. See Lindsay C. Gibson, *Disentangling from Emotionally Immature People* (Oakland: New Harbinger Publications, 2023), 51–57.

40 Aaron T. Beck identifies circular reasoning as a defense mechanism that protects the ego from contradiction by refusing to engage with counter-evidence. See Aaron T. Beck, *Cognitive Therapy and the Emotional Disorders* (New York: Penguin Books, 1976), 82–85.

41 Melanie Klein and Alice Miller both analyze projection as a psychological defense used to offload internal conflict onto others—especially in patriarchal and narcissistic systems. See Melanie Klein, *Envy and Gratitude and Other Works 1946–1963* (London: Vintage, 1997), 65–70; Alice Miller, *For Your Own Good* (New York: Farrar, Straus and Giroux, 1983), 67–74.

42 Phyllis Chesler documents how male entitlement is cloaked in tradition and institutional authority, particularly in the family system. See Phyllis Chesler, *Women and Madness*, 2nd ed. (New York: Palgrave Macmillan, 2005), 186–192.

43 bell hooks critiques the use of emotional mislabeling and narrative distortion as techniques for sustaining patriarchal power. See bell hooks, *Talking Back: Thinking Feminist, Thinking Black* (Boston: South End Press, 1989), 87–91.

44 George Orwell warns that controlling language and allowing contradictory logic are tools of authoritarianism used to erode clarity and suppress dissent. See George Orwell, *1984* (London: Secker & Warburg, 1949), 217–221.

45 *Gender essentialism* refers to the belief that men and women have fixed, innate natures —typically framed as biologically determined—that explain and justify their different roles. For discussions of gender essentialism across feminist theory and psychology, see, for example, Sandra Bem, *The Lenses of Gender: Transforming the Debate on Sexual Inequality* (New Haven: Yale University Press, 1993); Charlotte Witt, "What Is Gender Essentialism?" in *The Metaphysics of Gender* (Oxford: Oxford University Press, 2011); and Meredith Meyer and Susan A. Gelman, "Gender Essentialism in Children and Parents: Implications for the Development of Gender Stereotyping and Gender-Typed Preferences," *Sex Roles* 75, no. 9–10 (2016): 409–421.

CHAPTER 5

46 The developmental process of differentiation is foundational to identity formation and emotional maturity. This concept draws from Margaret Mahler's separation–individuation theory of early development (e.g., Mahler, Pine, & Bergman, *The Psychological Birth of the Human Infant*, 1975); Murray Bowen's concept of differentiation of self in family systems (Bowen, *Family Therapy in Clinical Practice*, 1978); and D. W. Winnicott's work on the true self and false self, mirroring, and emotional holding (for example, "Ego Distortion in Terms of True and False Self," 1960). It is also reflected in attachment theory (Bowlby, *A Secure Base*, 1988; Ainsworth et al., *Patterns of Attachment*, 1978), which emphasizes the role of a secure base in fostering healthy autonomy.

47 Erich Fromm, *The Fear of Freedom* (London: Routledge & Kegan Paul, 1942; originally published in the United States as *Escape from Freedom*, New York: Farrar & Rinehart, 1941), Foreword. Online text consulted: PDF, accessed 17 Nov 2025. https://

pescanik.net/wp-content/uploads/2016/11/erich-fromm-the-fear-of-freedom-escape-from-freedom.pdf (Contains Fromm's analysis of modern freedom and the psychological tendency to escape autonomy through submission, dependency, and the avoidance of responsibility.)

48 Joseph Campbell, *The Hero with a Thousand Faces* (Princeton, NJ: Princeton University Press, 1949; 3rd ed. 2008). Campbell outlines the "monomyth" structure commonly known as the Hero's Journey and explicitly acknowledges the influence of Jungian psychology. See also C. G. Jung, *Two Essays on Analytical Psychology*, trans. R. F. C. Hull, 2nd ed., Collected Works of C. G. Jung, vol. 7 (Princeton, NJ: Princeton University Press, 1966), for Jung's description of individuation as a lifelong developmental task.

49 "Felina," *Breaking Bad*, season 5, episode 16, written and directed by Vince Gilligan, first broadcast September 29, 2013, on AMC. Walter White's confession to Skyler includes the admission, "I did it for me. I liked it. I was good at it. And I was really... I was alive."

50 C. G. Jung, *Aion: Researches into the Phenomenology of the Self*, trans. R. F. C. Hull, Collected Works of C. G. Jung, vol. 9, part II (Princeton, NJ: Princeton University Press, 1978). Jung describes the puer-type as leading a "provisional life" out of fear of being trapped, with plans dissolving into fantasies rather than decisive action.

51 Marie-Louise von Franz, *The Problem of the Puer Aeternus* (Toronto: Inner City Books, 3rd ed., 2000). Based on von Franz's lectures on the puer archetype; includes her description of the puer as "not yet in real life" and dreading being bound to anything.

52 Caroline Myss, *Sacred Contracts: Awakening Your Divine Potential* (New York: Harmony Books, 2001). See her discussion of the Eternal Child/Puer eternus archetype, including its "consistent inability to be relied on" and tendency to be "floundering and ungrounded between the stages of life."

53 Ruth Ben-Ghiat explores the archetype of the strongman—authoritarian leaders who consolidate power through fear, spectacle, and emotional manipulation. See Ruth Ben-Ghiat, *Strongmen: Mussolini to the Present* (New York: W. W. Norton & Company, 2020), 9–15.

CHAPTER 7

54 Lindsay C. Gibson examines how emotionally immature coping strategies—such as obedience, manipulation, and control—become embedded in adult relationships and systems. See Lindsay C. Gibson, *Disentangling from Emotionally Immature People* (Oakland: New Harbinger Publications, 2023), 61–70.

[55]Erikson's model of psychosocial development positions identity formation and intimacy as core tasks of early adulthood. See Erik H. Erikson, *Childhood and Society*, 2nd ed. (New York: W. W. Norton & Company, 1963), 261–263.

[56]Erich Fromm, in *Escape from Freedom*, argued that the burden of self-responsibility in modern life leads many to relinquish autonomy in exchange for obedience to authoritarian structures. See Erich Fromm, *Escape from Freedom* (New York: Holt Paperbacks, 1941), 133–154.

[57]The insights on developmental arrest and the psychological difficulty of adulthood draw on foundational contributions from Erik Erikson, who defined adulthood as the integration of identity and intimacy; Donald Winnicott, who introduced the concept of the "good enough" parent and the importance of tolerable frustration in building inner structure; and Erich Fromm, who warned in *Escape from Freedom* that ungrounded liberty without emotional maturity leads not to empowerment, but to psychological terror and submission. Together, their work illuminates how systems of dominance often emerge as compensations for incomplete psychological development.

CHAPTER 8

[58] United States Holocaust Memorial Museum, "Women in the Third Reich," *Holocaust Encyclopedia* (Washington, DC: United States Holocaust Memorial Museum, n.d.). Online text consulted: web article, accessed 17 Nov 2025. https:// encyclopedia.ushmm.org/content/en/article/women-in-the-third-reich (Provides an overview of Nazi policies promoting *Kinder, Küche, Kirche*, financial incentives for marriage and childbirth, the Cross of Honour of the German Mother, and restrictions on women's education and professional roles.)

[59]Walt Disney Productions, *Pinocchio*, animated feature film, dir. Ben Sharpsteen et al. (Burbank, CA: Walt Disney Productions, 1940). Based on Carlo Collodi, *Le avventure di Pinocchio* (Florence: Felice Paggi, 1883). (The Blue Fairy's conditions that Pinocchio prove himself "brave, truthful, and unselfish," the episodes of Pleasure Island and the boys turning into donkeys, and the whale sequence come from the Disney adaptation, which popularized this version of the tale.)

[60] Jacob and Wilhelm Grimm, "The Fisherman and His Wife," in *Kinder- und Hausmärchen* (Berlin: Realschulbuchhandlung, 1812–15); Johann Wolfgang von Goethe, "Der Zauberlehrling" ["The Sorcerer's Apprentice"], in *Balladen* (Tübingen: Cotta, 1797); "Aladdin; or, the Wonderful Lamp," in *The Arabian Nights' Entertainments*, various editions; Ovid, *Metamorphoses*, trans. A. D. Melville (Oxford: Oxford University Press, 1986), Book XI (King Midas). (These stories all illustrate the classic motif that greed and the misuse of magic bring ruin to the one who seeks shortcuts.)

CHAPTER 9

61 Leon Festinger, *A Theory of Cognitive Dissonance* (Stanford, CA: Stanford University Press, 1957).

62 Peter Salerno, *Traumatic Cognitive Dissonance* (2025). The quotation in Section I beginning "Traumatic cognitive dissonance is one of the most debilitating trauma conditions…" and the description of associated symptoms are drawn from Salerno's discussion of traumatic cognitive dissonance and its clinical presentation.

63 Peter Salerno, *Traumatic Cognitive Dissonance* (2025). The characterization in Section IV of disordered personalities who "display an unwillingness to cooperate even at the most basic level in relationships, all while feigning earnest collaboration and cooperation" paraphrases Salerno's description of exploitative, empathy-impaired individuals and their relational stance.

64 Paul Ekman, *Telling Lies: Clues to Deceit in the Marketplace, Politics, and Marriage* (New York: W. W. Norton, 2009). Ekman uses the term "duping delight" to describe the pleasure some deceivers feel when successfully misleading others, a concept applied here to the emotional gratification some abusers experience when their destabilization tactics work.

CHAPTER 10

65 The concept of parentification—children being forced to emotionally or physically care for a parent or authority figure—is foundational in understanding how systems reverse maturity roles. See Lindsay C. Gibson, *Disentangling from Emotionally Immature People* (Oakland: New Harbinger, 2023), 62–66.

66 Lundy Bancroft describes how abusive individuals and systems maintain power by reversing accountability and distorting language to justify harm. These tactics are mirrored at both interpersonal and systemic levels. See Lundy Bancroft, *Why Does He Do That? Inside the Minds of Angry and Controlling Men* (New York: Berkley Books, 2002), 55–80.

67 Ross Rosenberg outlines how narcissistic systems rely on proxy enforcers—often referred to as "flying monkeys"—to carry out coercion and maintain control. See Ross Rosenberg, *The Human Magnet Syndrome: The Codependent Narcissist Trap*, 2nd ed. (Self-Love Recovery Institute Press, 2018), 117–123.

68 Margaret Thaler Singer and Janja Lalich outline how cult systems erode individual moral clarity and recruit members into self-policing mechanisms that protect the group's

power center. See Margaret Thaler Singer and Janja Lalich, *Cults in Our Midst: The Hidden Menace in Our Everyday Lives* (San Francisco: Jossey-Bass, 1995), 63–85.

[69] Lukaszewski and Buss identify how authoritarian structures exploit individual psychology to build group-level compliance, offering a framework for understanding cultural-level permission structures. See Alexander W. Lukaszewski, David M. Buss, et al., "The Origins and Structure of Authoritarianism," *Personality and Social Psychology Review 20*, no. 4 (2016): 371–397. https://doi.org/10.1177/1088868316662651.

[70] Alice Miller describes how individuals raised in emotionally oppressive environments often learn to suppress their own moral compass in exchange for survival, leading to adult complicity in abusive systems. See Alice Miller, *The Drama of the Gifted Child* (New York: Basic Books, 1997), 24–32.

[71] Janja Lalich and Madeleine Tobias explain how abusive systems use emotional manipulation, control over sexuality, and linguistic distortion as deliberate tools of compliance and extraction. See Janja Lalich and Madeleine Tobias, *Take Back Your Life: Recovering from Cults and Abusive Relationships* (Berkeley, CA: Bay Tree Publishing, 2006), 60–78.

[72] Erich Fromm, Judith Herman, and Alice Miller each emphasize, in different ways, that appeasing dysfunction emboldens it. See Herman, *Trauma and Recovery*, 102; Miller, For Your Own Good, 11; and Fromm, Escape from Freedom, 134.

[73] Bessel van der Kolk highlights how trauma-based systems gain power not only through overt harm but through emotional manipulation, language distortion, and betrayal. See Bessel van der Kolk, *The Body Keeps the Score: Brain, Mind, and Body in the Healing of Trauma* (New York: Viking, 2014), 221–230.

CHAPTER 11

[74] George Orwell explores the weaponization of language under authoritarian rule in *1984* and *Politics and the English Language*. See Orwell, *Politics and the English Language* (London: Horizon, 1946); *1984* (London: Secker & Warburg, 1949).

[75] Margaret Thaler Singer and Janja Lalich have both documented how high-control groups use manipulative language to extract emotional, financial, and psychological resources. See Singer, *Cults in Our Midst* (San Francisco: Jossey-Bass, 1995); Lalich and Tobias, *Take Back Your Life* (Berkeley: Bay Tree Publishing, 2006).

[76] Neil Postman discusses the erosion of meaning and truth through modern communication tactics in *Amusing Ourselves to Death* (New York: Penguin, 1985).

[77] S.I. Hayakawa explores how language structures perception and power dynamics in *Language in Thought and Action*, 5th ed. (San Diego: Harcourt, 1990).

[78] Robin Stern provides a comprehensive guide to gaslighting and its psychological effects in *The Gaslight Effect* (New York: Morgan Road Books, 2007).

[79] Jennifer J. Freyd introduced the term DARVO to describe manipulative reversal tactics commonly used by abusers and institutions. See Freyd, "Violations of Power, Adaptive Blindness, and Betrayal Trauma Theory," *Feminism & Psychology 13*, no. 1 (2003): 7–28.

[80] Lundy Bancroft details verbal domination and emotional manipulation strategies in *Why Does He Do That?* (New York: Berkley Books, 2002).

[81] Wendy Behary explores how narcissistic individuals often use sophisticated language to mask deep insecurity and emotional dysregulation. See Behary, *Disarming the Narcissist: Surviving and Thriving with the Self-Absorbed*, 3rd ed. (Oakland: New Harbinger, 2021), 42–45.

[82] Janja Lalich and Madeleine Tobias describe how emotionally manipulative leaders use spiritual, psychological, or intellectual language to maintain control. See Lalich and Tobias, *Take Back Your Life: Recovering from Cults and Abusive Relationships* (Berkeley: Bay Tree Publishing, 2006), 36–41.

[83] bell hooks discusses how language is used in patriarchal systems to police behavior and enforce obedience. See hooks, *Talking Back: Thinking Feminist, Thinking Black* (Boston: South End Press, 1989), 19–21.

[84] Judith Herman describes how abusers maintain power by cultivating public personas that directly contradict their private behavior. See Herman, *Trauma and Recovery* (New York: Basic Books, 1992), 110–112.

[85] Alice Miller emphasizes that healing from childhood harm begins by breaking the silence and naming the reality of one's experience. See Miller, *The Drama of the Gifted Child* (New York: Basic Books, 1997), xvii–xix.

[86] Neil Postman warned of how language and media can be manipulated to shape consciousness and enable control. See Postman, *Amusing Ourselves to Death: Public Discourse in the Age of Show Business* (New York: Penguin Books, 1985), 28–30.

CHAPTER 12

[87] bell hooks emphasizes that domination-based systems require the subjugation of others to maintain their illusion of superiority. See hooks, *Feminist Theory: From Margin to Center*, 2nd ed. (New York: Routledge, 2000), 87–89.

88 Data on the value of unpaid labor comes from Oxfam and the International Labour Organization. See Oxfam, *Time to Care: Unpaid and Underpaid Care Work and the Global Inequality Crisis* (Oxford: Oxfam International, 2020), 7–11.

89 Forbes, Eva Epker, "Women Handle 75%+ of All Unpaid Labor. Their Health Pays the Price," 31 Oct 2023. https://www.forbes.com/sites/evaepker/2023/10/31/women-handle-75-of-all-unpaid-labor-their-health-pays-the-price/.

90 Bureau of Economic Analysis (BEA), "Household Production Satellite Account," updated 29 Jan 2025. https://www.bea.gov/data/special-topics/household-production.

91 UN Women, "Redistribute unpaid work" (Facts & figures explainer). https://www.unwomen.org/en/news/in-focus/csw61/redistribute-unpaid-work.

92 Ann Crittenden outlines the long-term financial penalties of caregiving on mothers in *The Price of Motherhood: Why the Most Important Job in the World Is Still the Least Valued* (New York: Holt Paperbacks, 2001), 94–97.

93 Multiple scholars have documented the patriarchal double standard in which male competence is presumed while women are required to continually demonstrate and defend their competence. See Mary Ann Sieghart (*The Authority Gap*), Michelle P. King (*The Fix*), Joan C. Williams (on "prove-it-again" bias), and research by Madeline E. Heilman and Michelle C. Haynes on the systematic discounting of women's competence.

94 See UN Women, *Progress of the World's Women 2019–2020: Families in a Changing World* (New York: United Nations, 2019), 30–35.

95 Silvia Federici, *Wages Against Housework*. Bristol: Power of Women Collective and Falling Wall Press, 1975, pamphlet.

96 UN Women, "Call to action: Unite! Invest to prevent violence against women and girls," Statement, 22 Nov 2023. https://www.unwomen.org/en/news-stories/statement/2023/11/statement-call-to-action-unite-invest-to-prevent-violence-against-women-and-girls.

97 Adrienne Rich discusses how motherhood is shaped not only by biology but by institutions that control and politicize it. See Rich, *Of Woman Born: Motherhood as Experience and Institution* (New York: W.W. Norton, 1986), 13–15.

98 See Human Rights Watch, *Unequal and Unprotected: Women's Rights Under Iranian Law* (New York: HRW, 2017), and El Feki, *Sex and the Citadel: Intimate Life in a Changing Arab World* (New York: Vintage, 2014), 209–215.

99 Judith Herman explores how systems enable perpetrators to continue coercive control through legal means. See Herman, *Trauma and Recovery* (New York: Basic Books, 1997), 109–112.

100 Dorothy Roberts outlines how reproductive policies have historically been used to control marginalized women. See Roberts, *Killing the Black Body: Race, Reproduction, and the Meaning of Liberty* (New York: Vintage Books, 1999), 22–25.

101 See Pollitt, *Pro: Reclaiming Abortion Rights* (New York: Picador, 2015), 80–84, for a critique of moralistic framings that disguise reproductive coercion as ethical concern.

102 bell hooks critiques the economic reduction of men's value in patriarchal systems. See hooks, *The Will to Change: Men, Masculinity, and Love* (New York: Washington Square Press, 2004), 36–38.

103 Terry Real explores how patriarchal systems strip men of emotional wholeness and trap them in performance. See Real, *I Don't Want to Talk About It: Overcoming the Secret Legacy of Male Depression* (New York: Scribner, 1997), 95–98.

104 Phyllis Chesler documents how patriarchal family structures manipulate dependency and label control as love. See Chesler, *Women and Madness*, 2nd ed. (New York: Palgrave Macmillan, 2005), 204–210.

CHAPTER 13

105 René Girard explores the anthropological and psychological origins of scapegoating in early societies, arguing it serves as a foundational mechanism for managing collective violence and preserving social order. See Girard, *The Scapegoat* (Baltimore: The Johns Hopkins University Press, 1986), 3–8.

106 See Davies, *A Brief History of Death* (Malden, MA: Blackwell Publishing, 2005), 103–105, for an overview of sin-eater rituals in Celtic and Welsh cultures.

107 Alice Miller describes how immature family systems project shame and pain onto children who are forced to carry what adults cannot process. See Miller, *The Drama of the Gifted Child*, rev. ed. (New York: Basic Books, 2008), 67–71.

108 Judith Herman emphasizes how systems of power rely on denial and projection, rather than accountability, to preserve their image and function. See Herman, *Trauma and Recovery* (New York: Basic Books, 1997), 114–116.

109 bell hooks writes extensively on how patriarchy maintains itself by assigning moral and emotional labor to women. See hooks, *Feminist Theory: From Margin to Center*, 2nd ed. (Cambridge, MA: South End Press, 2000), 91–95.

110 Carol Gilligan critiques how patriarchal systems frame women's dissent and pain as pathology. See Gilligan, *In a Different Voice* (Cambridge, MA: Harvard University Press, 1982), 72–75.

[111] Phyllis Chesler explores how women who challenge patriarchy are demonized and ostracized. See Chesler, *Woman's Inhumanity to Woman* (New York: Plume, 2003), 134–139.

[112] Melanie Klein and Carl Jung both explored projection as a psychological defense. Klein saw it as a mechanism in early development, while Jung connected it to the shadow. For a modern systems view, see Alice Miller, *For Your Own Good* (New York: Farrar, Straus and Giroux, 1983), 68–72.

[113] bell hooks critiques the gendered moral expectations that require women to carry the emotional burdens of patriarchal systems. See hooks, *All About Love: New Visions* (New York: William Morrow, 2000), 129–134.

[114] Susan Faludi documents the media's repeated vilification of women who challenge traditional roles in *Backlash: The Undeclared War Against American Women* (New York: Crown, 1991), 70–78.

[115] Peggy Orenstein explores how daughters who resist or name family dysfunction are framed as disruptive. See Orenstein, *Girls & Sex* (New York: Harper, 2016), 183–186.

[116] Kimberlé Crenshaw's work on intersectionality highlights how race, class, and gender interact to deepen marginalization and scapegoating. See Crenshaw, "Mapping the Margins," *Stanford Law Review*, Vol. 43, No. 6 (1991), 1241–1299.

[117] René Girard ties moral panics and collective scapegoating to social instability and unresolved communal guilt. See Girard, *Violence and the Sacred* (Baltimore: Johns Hopkins University Press, 1977), 42–47.

[118] Judith Lewis Herman, *Trauma and Recovery: The Aftermath of Violence—from Domestic Abuse to Political Terror.* New York: Basic Books, 1992; updated ed. 1997.

[119] Giséle Pelicot's story and her insistence on a public trial were widely reported in France and referenced in the context of survivor-led justice. See Le Monde, "Giséle Pelicot: 'La honte doit changer de camp,'" April 2012.

CHAPTER 14

[120] Jennifer J. Freyd, *Blind to Betrayal: Why We Fool Ourselves We Aren't Being Fooled* (Hoboken: Wiley, 2013), 1–3.

[121] Freyd explains that betrayal blindness is not weakness, but an adaptive unconscious strategy designed to preserve necessary attachment in conditions of relational trauma. See Freyd, *Blind to Betrayal*, 17–22.

122 Judith Herman describes how social and systemic betrayal relies on the silence of both victims and bystanders. See Judith L. Herman, *Trauma and Recovery*, 2nd ed. (New York: Basic Books, 2015), 210–216.

123 bell hooks critiques the cultural conditioning that equates female virtue with self-sacrifice and silence. See bell hooks, *All About Love: New Visions* (New York: William Morrow, 2000), 125–130.

124 Rachel Louise Snyder underscores how normalized silence around violence perpetuates harm. See Rachel Louise Snyder, *No Visible Bruises: What We Don't Know About Domestic Violence Can Kill Us* (New York: Bloomsbury, 2019), 143–148.

125 Clarissa Pinkola Estés speaks of awakening as a descent before emergence—one that must include grief. See Clarissa Pinkola Estés, *Women Who Run with the Wolves* (New York: Ballantine Books, 1992), 324–330.

126 Clarissa Pinkola Estés describes these initiatory moments as "descents to the underworld," essential for reclaiming the wild self. See Clarissa Pinkola Estés, *Women Who Run With the Wolves: Myths and Stories of the Wild Woman Archetype* (New York: Ballantine Books, 1992), 372–375.

127 Michael Meade explores the idea of initiation as a liminal phase—an in-between zone where identity dissolves to be re-formed. See Michael Meade, *The Water of Life: Initiation and the Tempering of the Soul* (Seattle: Greenfire Press, 2006), 48–52.

128 Bill Plotkin emphasizes that true adulthood and soul encounter require a descent into the underworld of the psyche. See Bill Plotkin, *Soulcraft: Crossing into the Mysteries of Nature and Psyche* (Novato: New World Library, 2003), 69–74.

129 Joseph Campbell identifies threshold guardians as archetypal figures in the Hero's Journey who challenge the seeker to prove readiness. See Joseph Campbell, *The Hero with a Thousand Faces*, 3rd ed. (Novato: New World Library, 2008), 71–72.

CHAPTER 15

130 The term "relational laziness" has been used by trauma therapist Dr. Sherri Heller to describe patterns of passive entitlement, avoidance of emotional labor, and the expectation of intimacy without reciprocal effort. While earlier theorists have examined similar dynamics—such as emotional under-functioning, relational entitlement, and disengagement—Heller's framing emphasizes the chronic avoidance of relational responsibility as a form of immaturity. See Sherri Heller, "The Culture of Narcissism: A Look at Relational Laziness," *Medium*, June 2021.

[131] Evan Stark, who pioneered the concept of coercive control, defines it as a strategic pattern of domination designed to strip away a victim's freedom, autonomy, and dignity —often without physical violence. Stark emphasizes that coercive control operates with psychological precision, functioning more like hostage-taking or brainwashing than conventional domestic violence. See Evan Stark, *Coercive Control: How Men Entrap Women in Personal Life* (New York: Oxford University Press, 2007), 4.

[132] Dr. Emma Katz expands on Evan Stark's work by identifying three core features of coercive control: consistency, compliance, and conditioned surrender. She emphasizes that coercive control reshapes a victim's internal world—replacing self-trust and autonomy with the abuser's demands, expectations, and version of reality. Even without physical violence, this psychological domination creates a state of internal captivity. See Emma Katz, *Coercive Control in Children's and Mothers' Lives* (Oxford: Oxford University Press, 2022), 13–14.

[133] Sociologist and cult recovery expert Dr. Janja Lalich, who herself is a survivor of a high-demand group, draws strong parallels between coercive control and cultic systems. She emphasizes that the most powerful control structures operate not through overt violence, but through ideological capture—using emotional manipulation, false hope, and carefully orchestrated dependency to elicit obedience. See Janja Lalich, *Take Back Your Life: Recovering from Cults and Abusive Relationships*, 2nd ed. (Bay Tree Publishing, 2006), esp. introduction and chapters 1–3.

[134] Juan Carlos Areán and Fernando Mederos, "Abusive Men Describe the Benefits of Violence," *Voice Male Magazine*, Fall 2011. Based on facilitator notes from groups for men who batter, this article documents the candid admissions of abusive men about what coercive control and violence provide them—emotionally, materially, and socially.

[135] The Eight Elements of Coercive Control are adapted from sociologist Albert D. Biderman's "Chart of Coercion," first published in 1957 to explain the psychological tactics used to break down prisoners of war during the Korean War. These same techniques—such as isolation, degradation, and threats—have since been widely recognized as central strategies in domestic abuse, cults, and other systems of control. See Albert D. Biderman, "Communist Attempts to Elicit False Confessions from Air Force Prisoners of War," *The Bulletin of the New York Academy of Medicine 33*, no. 9 (1957): 616–625.

[136] Judith Herman notes that trauma survivors often experience exhaustion, confusion, and loss of agency due to sustained psychological coercion. See Judith L. Herman, *Trauma and Recovery*, 2nd ed. (New York: Basic Books, 2015), 93–95.

[137] While the term "intimacy labor" is less formally established than "emotional labor" or "intimate labor," it draws from the same lineage. Emotional labor, first coined by Arlie Russell Hochschild, describes the regulation of emotion in service of others—often in professional or domestic contexts. Scholars like Rhacel Salazar Parreñas and Eileen Boris

expanded the framework through the concept of "intimate labor," which explores the commodification of care, intimacy, and physical presence in both paid and unpaid relationships. This book uses the term "intimacy labor" to refer to the unseen work of building emotional closeness, attunement, and vulnerability in personal life. See Arlie Russell Hochschild, *The Managed Heart* (Berkeley: University of California Press, 1983).

[138] Following Hurricane Katrina, multiple reports surfaced of women being sexually assaulted in emergency shelters, including the Superdome. In interviews with some perpetrators, researchers and journalists found that the assaults were rationalized as "stress relief" during the chaos and breakdown of social structures. These incidents have since been studied as examples of gender-based violence in disaster contexts, where the collapse of law and visibility can enable predatory behavior. See Rebecca Solnit, *The Guardian*, "The Uses of Disaster," Sept 2005; also cited in Ann Cahill, *Rethinking Rape* (Cornell University Press, 2001); and Elaine Enarson, "Violence Against Women in Disasters," *Violence Against Women*, vol. 13, no. 7 (2007): 754–773.

[139] Riane Eisler describes how patriarchal systems sacralized domination through religious and cultural myths, often elevating male divinity and suppressing feminine spiritual authority. See Riane Eisler, *The Chalice and the Blade* (San Francisco: Harper & Row, 1987), 94–103.

[140] Sheila Wray Gregoire, Rebecca Gregoire Lindenbach, and Joanna Sawatsky, *The Great Sex Rescue: The Lies You've Been Taught and How to Recover What God Intended* (Grand Rapids: Baker Books, 2021), 15–36. Gregoire's research draws from over 20,000 Christian women's experiences and critiques harmful teachings around sex, submission, and duty in evangelical contexts.

[141] Feminist therapists and researchers have long observed that in some models of couples therapy—especially those shaped by patriarchal or conservative religious frameworks—women's sexual boundaries are pathologized rather than respected. Sexual refusal is often reframed as a failure of duty, emotional manipulation, or relational sabotage, rather than a valid expression of autonomy. This framing can pressure women to override their own discomfort or trauma, particularly when therapists side with the male partner's sense of sexual entitlement. See Sheila Wray Gregoire, Rebecca Lindenbach, and Joanna Sawatsky, *The Great Sex Rescue: The Lies You've Been Taught and How to Recover What God Intended* (Grand Rapids: Baker Books, 2021); also see Esther Perel, *Mating in Captivity* (Harper, 2006), Ch. 2; and Jennifer M. Freyd, "Institutional Betrayal and the Reproduction of Harm," *Journal of Trauma & Dissociation 14*, no. 4 (2013): 382–396.

[142] DARVO stands for Deny, Attack, Reverse Victim and Offender—a response pattern identified by Dr. Jennifer Freyd that describes how perpetrators of abuse often respond when confronted. While initially observed in individual cases, Freyd and others have noted how DARVO also manifests at cultural and institutional levels. See Jennifer J. Freyd, *Blind to Betrayal: Why We Fool Ourselves We Aren't Being Fooled* (Wiley, 2013); and Freyd, "Official DARVO Response to DARVO," *Psychology of Women Quarterly* 2017.

CHAPTER 16

[143] The distinction between healthy and unhealthy shame is central to the work of psychologists such as John Bradshaw, Brené Brown, and Sylvan Tomkins. Healthy shame is understood as a moral emotion that promotes growth, empathy, and integrity. In contrast, toxic or unresolved shame—especially when formed in early developmental contexts—can lead to deflection, blame, or projection, not as moral failure but as psychological defense. This framework has been expanded in trauma-informed work to emphasize the role of shame in identity formation, emotional maturity, and relational ethics. See John Bradshaw, *Healing the Shame That Binds You* (Health Communications, 1988); Brené Brown, *The Gifts of Imperfection* (Hazelden, 2010); and Sylvan Tomkins, *Affect Imagery Consciousness: The Complete Edition*, Vol. II (Springer, 2008).

[144] This idea builds on the concept that shame, when processed through self-awareness and accountability, becomes less necessary as a regulatory emotion. As Brené Brown and others have noted, the antidote to toxic shame is not avoidance, but resilience and repair. When growth is welcomed, shame no longer functions as a threat—it becomes a signal that is rarely needed. See Brené Brown, *Daring Greatly* (Gotham Books, 2012), Ch. 4.

[145] The concept of the double bind was first introduced by anthropologist Gregory Bateson and colleagues in the 1950s to describe a communication dynamic in which every possible response results in punishment, contradiction, or loss. Originally linked to family systems and theories of schizophrenia, the double bind has since been recognized as a powerful tool of coercion in abusive relationships, cults, and authoritarian systems. The film *Sophie's Choice* (dir. Alan J. Pakula, 1982), based on the novel by William Styron, dramatizes a literal double bind in one of its most haunting scenes. See Gregory Bateson et al., "Toward a Theory of Schizophrenia," *Behavioral Science 1*, no. 4 (1956): 251–264.

[146] Writers and advocates like Mark Greene, Jackson Katz, and Terry Real have publicly challenged traditional masculine norms and the emotional suppression required by patriarchal systems. Their work highlights how the "man box" narrative harms not only women, but men themselves—by severing them from vulnerability, connection, and accountability. See Mark Greene, *The Little #MeToo Book for Men* (Think Play Partners, 2018); Jackson Katz, *The Macho Paradox* (Sourcebooks, 2006); and Terry Real, *I Don't Want to Talk About It: Overcoming the Secret Legacy of Male Depression* (Scribner, 1997).

[147] The concept of hostile dependency describes a psychological dynamic in which a person is emotionally or practically reliant on another but experiences that reliance as shameful. Instead of acknowledging vulnerability, the dependent individual often externalizes that shame as blame, contempt, or sabotage toward the very person they need. Though the term has clinical roots in psychodynamic and family systems theory, it has more recently been recognized in cultural and relational analysis as a driver of abuse, coercion, and relational instability. See Robert W. Firestone, *The Fantasy Bond: Structure*

of Psychological Defenses (Routledge, 2010); and Theodore Lidz, *The Person: His and Her Development Throughout the Life Cycle* (Basic Books, 1976).

CHAPTER 17

[148] Contemporary psychologists widely agree that narcissism exists on a spectrum—from relatively common narcissistic traits (such as entitlement, attention-seeking, or emotional avoidance) to diagnosable narcissistic personality disorder. The term "everyday narcissist" is often used to describe individuals who exhibit self-centered or controlling behavior rooted in emotional immaturity rather than clinical pathology. See Craig Malkin, *Rethinking Narcissism: The Secret to Recognizing and Coping with Narcissists* (Harper Wave, 2015); Ramani Durvasula, *Don't You Know Who I Am?* (Post Hill Press, 2019).

[149] Research led by Dr. Brad Bushman has demonstrated a strong link between narcissism and aggression. In a meta-analysis covering over 400 studies and 123,000 participants, Bushman and colleagues found that narcissistic individuals are significantly more likely to engage in both verbal and physical aggression—especially when their egos are threatened. See Brad J. Bushman and Roy F. Baumeister, "Threatened Egos and Violence: The Narcissism-Aggression Link," *Journal of Personality and Social Psychology 75*, no. 1 (1998): 219–229; see also Sarah Konrath, Brad J. Bushman, and Richard W. Campbell, "Indirect Aggression in Narcissism: Meta-Analytic Review," *Perspectives on Psychological Science 1*, no. 1 (2006): 35–52.

[150] Betrayal blindness is a term developed by Dr. Jennifer Freyd to describe the phenomenon in which victims—or witnesses—remain unaware of or unable to acknowledge abuse, especially when the perpetrator is someone they depend on or trust. This unawareness functions as a survival mechanism, allowing individuals to maintain necessary relationships or belief systems in the face of danger or moral contradiction. See Jennifer J. Freyd, *Blind to Betrayal: Why We Fool Ourselves We Aren't Being Fooled* (Wiley, 2013); also see Freyd's foundational work, "Betrayal Trauma: Traumatic Amnesia as an Adaptive Response to Childhood Abuse," *Ethics & Behavior 4*, no. 4 (1994): 307–329.

[151] Paulhus and Williams first coined the term "Dark Triad" to describe narcissism, Machiavellianism, and psychopathy. Sadism was later added to create the "Dark Tetrad." See Delroy L. Paulhus and Kevin M. Williams, "The Dark Triad of Personality: Narcissism, Machiavellianism, and Psychopathy," *Journal of Research in Personality 36*, no. 6 (2002): 556–563. For sadism as the fourth trait, see Buckels, Jones, and Paulhus, "Behavioral Confirmation of Everyday Sadism," *Psychological Science 24*, no. 11 (2013): 2201–2209.

152 The term "pathocracy" describes a system governed by individuals with personality disorders, particularly those within the Cluster B spectrum. See Andrzej Łobaczewski, *Political Ponerology: A Science on the Nature of Evil Adjusted for Political Purposes*, 3rd ed. (New York: Red Pill Press, 2006).

153 The term "pathocracy" was coined by Polish psychologist Andrzej Łobaczewski to describe a system in which individuals with severe personality disorders—particularly psychopathy—ascend to positions of power and reshape institutions in their image. In such systems, emotional immaturity, cruelty, and moral inversion become normalized, and healthy individuals are marginalized or punished. See Andrzej Łobaczewski, *Political Ponerology: A Science on the Nature of Evil Adjusted for Political Purposes*, 3rd ed. (Red Pill Press, 2006).

154 In an interview on the Subject to Power podcast, trauma therapist Christine Forner described patriarchy as a dissociated, psychopathic system that avoids emotional responsibility and survives by outsourcing harm. Her framing aligns with her clinical work on dissociation, emotional immaturity, and structural trauma. See Christine Forner, *Subject to Power* podcast, episode "The Oldest Trauma," hosted by Lael Keen, December 5, 2022. Available at: https://subjecttopower.com/podcast/christine-forner-the-oldest-trauma/

155 The Hare Psychopathy Checklist–Revised (PCL-R), developed by Dr. Robert D. Hare, is a clinical tool used to assess psychopathic traits, particularly in forensic settings. While the full checklist includes specific scoring criteria, the traits listed here have been adapted and paraphrased for accessibility. See Robert D. Hare, *Without Conscience: The Disturbing World of the Psychopaths Among Us* (New York: Guilford Press, 1999); and Hare, *The Hare Psychopathy Checklist–Revised: Technical Manual*, 2nd ed. (Toronto: Multi-Health Systems, 2003).

156 Kate Manne defines misogyny not as individual hatred, but as a social system that punishes women for resisting traditional gender roles. See Kate Manne, *Down Girl: The Logic of Misogyny* (New York: Oxford University Press, 2018), 19–25.

157 Philosopher Kate Manne distinguishes between sexism and misogyny, describing sexism as the ideology that naturalizes traditional gender roles and renders them morally or biologically inevitable. In *Down Girl: The Logic of Misogyny*, she explains that sexism tells a story about why men should dominate and women should defer, often cloaked in religious, cultural, or scientific narratives. See Kate Manne, *Down Girl: The Logic of Misogyny* (New York: Oxford University Press, 2018), Ch. 2.

158 Himpathy refers to the disproportionate sympathy shown toward powerful men accused of misconduct, often at the expense of their victims. See Kate Manne, *Down Girl: The Logic of Misogyny* (New York: Oxford University Press, 2018), 197–205.

¹⁵⁹ Gail Dines critiques the rise of violent, degrading pornography and its impact on relational and cultural perceptions of sex in *Pornland: How Porn Has Hijacked Our Sexuality* (Boston: Beacon Press, 2010), 102–112.

¹⁶⁰ Psychologist Esther Perel explores how emotional maturity and eroticism are deeply interwoven, noting that real intimacy requires presence, vulnerability, and mutuality. See Esther Perel, *Mating in Captivity: Unlocking Erotic Intelligence* (New York: Harper, 2006), 89–94.

¹⁶¹ Albert Bandura's research demonstrated that children model behaviors they observe —especially when those behaviors are rewarded. See Albert Bandura, *Social Learning Theory* (Englewood Cliffs, NJ: Prentice-Hall, 1977).

CHAPTER 18

¹⁶² Psychologist Carol Gilligan emphasizes that women's apparent "compliance" in oppressive systems often reflects relational survival strategies rather than moral or political agreement. See Carol Gilligan, *In a Different Voice: Psychological Theory and Women's Development* (Cambridge: Harvard University Press, 1982), 68–75.

¹⁶³ Naomi Wolf explains how cultural narratives about femininity shape internalized beliefs, often leading women to police themselves and others. See Naomi Wolf, *The Beauty Myth: How Images of Beauty Are Used Against Women* (New York: Harper Perennial, 1991), 10–14.

¹⁶⁴ bell hooks critiques the illusion of empowerment through alignment with patriarchal authority, noting that such "power" is often conditional and requires the suppression of other women. See bell hooks, *Feminism Is for Everybody: Passionate Politics* (Cambridge: South End Press, 2000), 43–45.

¹⁶⁵ Psychologist Judith Herman discusses the emotional cost of leaving patriarchal or abusive systems, especially when identity and safety are rooted in belonging. See Judith L. Herman, *Trauma and Recovery*, 2nd ed. (New York: Basic Books, 2015), 113–118.

¹⁶⁶ Valerie Saiving and later feminist theologians argued that the traditional framing of female virtue (modesty, self-sacrifice, passivity) was often misrecognized as moral maturity rather than what it often is—emotionally sanctioned immaturity. See Valerie Saiving, "The Human Situation: A Feminine View," *The Journal of Religion* 40, no. 2 (1960): 100–112.

¹⁶⁷ Sociologist Erving Goffman described how roles are not only adopted but imposed, particularly in environments that reward conformity. See Erving Goffman, *The Presentation of Self in Everyday Life* (New York: Anchor Books, 1959), 56–63.

168 Psychologist Marion Woodman describes the loss of self that occurs when women over-identify with socially sanctioned roles, especially those that require emotional suppression and self-sacrifice. See Marion Woodman, *Addicted to Perfection: The Still Unravished Bride* (Toronto: Inner City Books, 1982), 36–41.

169 Gloria Steinem emphasizes that patriarchy fosters competition among women to divide and weaken collective resistance. See Gloria Steinem, *Outrageous Acts and Everyday Rebellions* (New York: Holt, Rinehart and Winston, 1983), 283–285.

170 bell hooks explains how internalized patriarchy often leads women to police and punish other women, despite their own histories of pain. See bell hooks, *The Will to Change: Men, Masculinity, and Love* (New York: Atria Books, 2004), 114–117.

171 Clarissa Pinkola Estés explores how storytelling and truth-telling act as subversive acts of liberation for women living under oppressive norms. See Clarissa Pinkola Estés, *Women Who Run With the Wolves* (New York: Ballantine Books, 1992), 28–33.

172 Brené Brown highlights the psychological toll of seeking approval and the power of choosing authenticity in the face of cultural conformity. See Brené Brown, *The Gifts of Imperfection* (Center City: Hazelden Publishing, 2010), 49–54.

173 Author and activist adrienne maree brown writes about the contagious nature of personal transformation and how it invites collective change. See adrienne maree brown, *Emergent Strategy: Shaping Change, Changing Worlds* (Chico: AK Press, 2017), 13–18.

174 Audre Lorde frames the act of reclaiming one's full self as a political act rooted in ancestral legacy and the ongoing pursuit of liberation. See Audre Lorde, *Sister Outsider: Essays and Speeches* (Berkeley: Crossing Press, 2007), 39–42.

CHAPTER 19

175 Trauma expert Judith Herman emphasizes that change rarely comes from those in power, but rather from those who have been harmed reclaiming their voice and agency. See Judith L. Herman, *Trauma and Recovery*, 2nd ed. (New York: Basic Books, 2015), 238–241.

176 Author Glennon Doyle writes about how liberation and clarity often begin with pain and breakdown, not joy or certainty. See Glennon Doyle, *Untamed* (New York: The Dial Press, 2020), 21–24.

A note on courage. Patriarchy often celebrates chest-thumping, performative, blood thirsty "courage"—hungry for applause, evasive of accountability. This book belongs to another kind: the quiet, accountable courage of badass souls—women and men alike—who, at real personal risk, move human dignity forward with no promise of reward. May we be worthy of your company.

To the researchers, historians, clinicians, journalists, advocates, pioneers, thought leaders, and whistleblowers who brought receipts, reversed male-centered narratives, and refused erasure—thank you for the work that makes clarity possible.

To the men who speak up not to look like "good guys," but because fairness matters—even when it costs: Jackson Katz, Mark Greene, David Challen, Evan Stark, Lundy Bancroft, Allan Berkowitz, Terry Crews, Tony Porter, Ted Bunch, and many others—you take the hits that come with refusing the loyalty pledge to patriarchy in favor of basic human decency.

To the women who spoke even when no one was listening, who moved all of humanity forward, this is a selected lineage across the millennia of those whose work made an impact on me (activists, scholars, and correctors of the record): Abigail Adams • Margaret Atwood • Simone de Beauvoir • Tarana Burke • Judith Butler • Shirley Chisholm • Ayaan Hirsi Ali • Angela Y. Davis • Riane Eisler • Mona Eltahawy • Betty Friedan • Ruth Bader Ginsburg • Hillary Clinton • bell hooks • Bella Abzug • Audre Lorde • Susan B. Anthony • Lucretia Mott • Anaïs Nin. • Emmeline and Sylvia Pankhurst • Marija Gimbutas • Eleanor Roosevelt • Huda Sha'arawi • Rebecca Solnit • Gloria Steinem • Sojourner Truth • Coretta Scott King• Malala Yousafzai • Ida B. Wells • Mary Wollstonecraft • Heide Goettner-Abendroth • Mary Beard • Cecile Richards • Riane Eisler • Jennifer J. Freyd • Carol Gilligan • Gerda Lerner • Janja Lalich • Emma Katz • Laura Richards • Elaine Pagels • Susan Faludi • Marilyn French • Robin Morgan • Deborah Tannen • Germaine Greer • Elizabeth Cady Stanton • Judith Herman . . . and the countless others—across countries, cultures, and millennia—whose names are absent here but present in this lineage.

Alongside every woman who insisted that reason and liberty include women, I honor the women in my own lineage who, while living inside a profoundly patriarchal culture, quietly rebelled—refusing to give up, moving the ball forward in ways both visible and invisible. They showed that resistance was possible even as they were asked to uphold the system. I carry your ember.

To the quiet supporters who made room for system questioning, who weren't afraid of hard conversations, and offered a soft place to land when "go along to get along" was the rule—thank you.

To my early readers—my son, Evan; my daughter, Morgan; and friends Mary B., Monica S., Lauren T., Kathy K., Liz B., , and Crista D.—whose steady support fueled the writing and whose insights led to sharper distinctions.

And to Stacey Aaronson—my editor, book designer, book champion, and good friend—whose collaboration makes the tedious work of editing, proofing, and refining a joy because I get to work with her. And whose design makes my books beautiful for the reader (which is so important to me) and whose insights and feedback none of my books could live without.

PATTY BEAR is a former military pilot and retired commercial airline captain who left a patriarchal religious tradition (Old Order Mennonite) to chart her own course toward wisdom, sovereignty, and soul-led leadership.

She brings a rare depth of insight into what it means to navigate high-stakes systems—whether in the cockpit, the family, or the culture at large. Her work explores the intersections of psychology, personal growth, power dynamics, and the subtle architecture of control. She blends the scholar's rigor, the survivor's knowing, and the teacher's precision—without ever claiming to be a guru. She shows people how to find their own compass.

She is the author of *House of the Sun: A Visionary Guide for Parenting in a Complex World*; *From Plain to Plane: My Mennonite Childhood, a National Scandal, and an Unconventional Soar to Freedom*; *Captain Patty's Wisdom Hacks: 20 Tools for Clarity, Direction, and Self-Leadership*; and now *Unmasking Patriarchy: Gender Is the Cover Story—Not the Culprit*.

JOIN THE CONVERSATION—LEAVE AN HONEST REVIEW

If this book helped you see more clearly—or even challenged you—I'd be grateful for an honest review. Your perspective helps readers decide, signals bookstores and libraries to stock it, and keeps thoughtful discussion visible.

Not sure where to start?

Try one prompt:

- What clarity or question are you taking with you?

- What insight surprised or liberated you?

- How did the big-picture, systemic lens (rather than "gender wars") help you notice something new?

- How did this book address patriarchy differently from what you've seen elsewhere?

- What passage did you highlight—and why?

- Who would you hand this book to?

Post a review (pick one):

Amazon • Goodreads • Barnes & Noble • Bookshop • Apple Books • Kobo

Please share a favorite line on social media or recommend it to your book club. You can also ask your library or local bookstore to carry it.

Thank you for keeping the conversation human.